Series: *Language, Media & Education Studies*

Edited by: Marcel Danesi & Leonard G. Sbrocchi

Cover: Compugraphics by Pierre Bertrand

Classic Readings in Semiotics

For Introductory Courses

Edited by

Paul Perron & Marcel Danesi

New York   Ottawa   Toronto

National Library of Canada Cataloguing in Publication

Classic Readings in Semiotics For Introductory Courses / edited by Paul Perron & Marcel Danesi.

Includes bibliographical references.
ISBN 1-894508-47-5

1. Semiotics. I. Danesi, Marcel, 1946- II. Perron, Paul

P99.C548 2003   302.2   C2003-900195-4

For further information and for orders:

http://www.legaspublishing.com

LEGAS
P. O. Box 040328   3 Wood Aster Bay   2908 Dufferin Street
Brooklyn, New York Ottawa, Ontario   Toronto, Ontario
USA 11204   K2R 1B3   M6B 3S8

Printed and bound in Canada

Contents

Appendices

Preface

With this anthology of classic readings in semiotic theory and practice it is our intention to provide students with a supplementary resource designed to give them and the interested general reader a first-hand glimpse into a selection of those texts that have either laid the foundation of the semiotic theoretical edifice or else helped shape its contemporary form. We also hope that they will spur the reader on to pursue the study of semiotics in a more in-depth way. In effect, our hope is that by reading a little Peirce or a little Saussure students will welcome the challenge of reading a lot more Peirce, Saussure, and all the other thinkers who have contributed to making semiotics such a powerful intellectual tool for probing human meaning systems.

We have attempted to make the present volume pedagogically useful in the following ways:

- we have written a general characterization of the field of semiotics;
- we have provided our own notes to the authors of the passages; these are not synopses of the readings, since it is important in such a text to leave their interpretation and evaluation to instructors and students without any interference from our part;
- we have appended a lexicon of commonly-used terms in semiotics and suggestions for further reading.

Needless to say, in an anthology such as this one, the process of selection is bound to be dictated by subjective criteria. Indeed, the texts we have chosen here reflect the sequence and content of our own introductory courses in semiotics at the University of Toronto. They have the purpose, in those courses, of providing students with the opportunity of familiarizing themselves with excerpts from the literature that have been foundational in establishing the current framework of semiotic theory and analysis. When used in tandem with introductory textbook materials, we have found that students find them less daunting than otherwise and, thus, tend to get quite a bit out of them.

Nevertheless, despite the fact that the readings herein grouped together reflect a personal choice of the editors, they nonetheless will be viewed by most of those working in the field of semiotics today as foundational and, thus, as "classic" texts. They have been arranged in a such a way as to reflect, more or less, a chronological sequence to the development of sign theory and of semiotic analysis. However, this order is in no way intended to be binding in the way this book can be used. In fact, the instructor can choose any of the readings in any order or way he or she deems appropriate to his or her situation.

In sum, we hope that this volume will be of practical use to instructors and students of semiotics. We have not interpreted the readings beforehand for the reader. This would be inappropriate on two counts: (1) at best it would be interference on our part in allowing the reader to get whatever is relevant out of them for himself or herself, (2) at worst, it would be academic patronizing and, thus, go counter to the open-minded spirit of semiotic inquiry.

Paul Perron & Marcel Danesi
University of Toronto

Semiotics: A General Characterization

The quest for *meaning* to life is the central characteristic that has guided and shaped human history. It is the motivating source of such unique conceptions as myths, art, science, language, and all the other probes of meaning that define human life. The study of this quest, as it manifests itself in such conceptions, comes under the rubric of *semiotics*. Simply defined, it is the discipline that aims to identify, classify, and understand the capacity for creating and using signs for thinking and communicating. The world of human beings is a *de facto* world of signs, the thoughts they elicit, and their overall organization into systems of communal meaning that we call *cultures*.

What Is a Sign?

The human brain is endowed with a remarkable capacity—the capacity to produce, understand, and make use of forms that allow it to carry around images of the world wherever it goes. These forms are known as *signs*. A sign is anything—a word, a gesture, a drawing, etc.—that stands for something other than itself in some specific way. Take, for instance, the word *cat*. It is a vocal form made up of the sounds *c-a-t* that comprise it. For those who know English, that combination of sounds is not just a randomly-produced set of vibrations hitting the eardrum, but rather a form that evokes an image of "a carnivorous mammal (*Felis catus*) domesticated catcher of rats and mice."

In effect, a sign is a form X that we replace for something in the world, Y, real, actual, imaginary, or potential that is captured in the relation $X = Y$ and thus made available for future recall to the memory system. Studying the relation $X = Y$ is the essence of semiotic method.

Semiotic Method

The academic study of semiotics as an "autonomous" disciplinary enterprise has never been a widespread one in most countries. The reason for this, in our view, is the "interdisciplinary" nature of the field and the fact that it is more of a "theoretical tool" for probing representational and knowledge systems, than a "data-generating" enterprise. It is thus very difficult for semiotics to find a niche in the structure of the modern university. Nevertheless, its study today is growing and, in some areas of the world, even flourishing. Its current "relative popularity" probably traces its roots to the late 1950s, when the French semiotician Roland Barthes (1915–1980) showed the importance of studying media and pop culture in terms of how they recycle ancient meanings. Semiotic method, as Barthes argued, is fundamental because it focuses on unraveling hidden meanings in all kinds of contemporary representations.

As Barthes showed a large audience of readers, semiotic method is characterized by two main investigative procedures:

- the study of the historical (and thus highly connotative) origin of meaning systems ;
- unraveling the nature of signification in human activities, whether it manifests itself as a word, a novel, a TV program, or some other human artifact.

Semiotics is most often linked to linguistics, and indeed, both disciplines overlap considerably. The agenda in both is shaped by a search for the "system" behind human semiosis—the capacity to produce and understand signs. The difference between the two is that linguistics focuses on verbal sign systems, whereas semiotics emphasizes the need to study the semiosic capacity as a single entity, not as one consisting of independent verbal and nonverbal components.

The Study of the Sign

The modern-day form of both semiotic and linguistic methods traces its origins to the writings of the Swiss linguist Ferdinand de Saussure (1857–1913) and the American philosopher Charles S. Peirce (1839–1914). A large part of the increase in the popularity of this field in the late twentieth century was brought about by the publication in 1983 of a best-selling medieval detective novel, *The Name of the Rose*, written by one of the most distinguished practitioners of semiotics, Umberto Eco (1932–). Thomas A. Sebeok (1920–2001), too, was instrumental in showing the relevance of semiotics to those working in cognate disciplines, aptly comparing semiotics to a spider's web because it rarely fails to entrap scientists, educators, and humanists into its intricate loom of insights into human cognition and culture.

But interest in signs reaches back several millennia. The first definition of *sign* as a physical *symptom* comes from Hippocrates (460–377 BC), the founder of Western medical science, who established *semeiotics* (from *semeion* "mark, sign") as a branch of medicine. The physician Galen of Pergamum (139–199 AD) further entrenched semeiotics into medical practice more than a century after Hippocrates, a tradition that continues to this day in various European countries. The study of how "things stand for other things" became the prerogative of philosophers around the time of Plato (c. 428–c. 347 BC), who suggested that words were deceptive "things" because they did not "stand for" reality directly, but as idealized mental approximations of it. Plato's illustrious pupil Aristotle (384–322 BC) accepted his mentor's notion of "ideal forms," but he also argued that these crystallized from observing the actual things that exemplified or "contained" them in the world. Together with the Stoic philosophers, Aristotle took it upon himself to investigate the "stands for" phenomenon in human representation more closely, laying down a theory of the sign that has remained basic to this day. He defined the linguistic *sign* as consisting of three dimensions: (1) the physical part of the sign itself (e.g., the sounds that make up a word such as red); (2) the *referent* to which it calls attention (a certain category of color), (3) its evocation of a *meaning* (what the referent entails psychologically and socially). Aristotle emphasized that these three dimensions were simultaneous in the sign. And, as Aristotle correctly claimed, it is indeed impossible to think of a word such as *red* (a vocal sign made up of the sounds *r-e-d*), without thinking at the same time of the color category to which it pertains (the referent), and without experiencing the personal and social meaning(s) that such a referent entails. In philosophical theories of the sign ever since Aristotle, this simultaneity has, *ipso facto*, been modeled as a triangular relation.

The next major step forward in the study of signs was, as is well known, the one taken by St. Augustine (354–430 AD), the philosopher and religious thinker who was among the first to distinguish clearly between *natural* (nonarbitrary) and *conventional* (arbitrary) signs, and to espouse the view that there was an inbuilt *interpretive* component to the whole "stands for" process. A *natural sign* is one that is present in Nature (a color, a sound made by an animal,, etc.); a *conventional sign*, on the other hand, is one invented by human ingenuity to make sense of things. St. Augustine also suggested that there was an *interpretive* component to the understanding of things through signs. This was consistent with the *hermeneutic* tradition established by Clement of Alexandria (150?–215? AD), the Greek theologian and early Father of the Church. *Hermeneutics* is the study of how to interpret ancient texts, especially those of a religious or mythical nature. Clement established the method of ascertaining, as far as possible, the meaning that a Biblical writer intended on the basis of linguistic considerations and relevant sources. Clement also maintained that the interpreter should not ignore the fact that the original meaning of the text developed in the course of history, and that the act of interpretation was bound to be influenced by cultural factors.

St. Augustine's views lay largely forgotten until the eleventh century, when interest in the nature of human representation was rekindled by Arab scholars who translated the works of Plato, Aristotle, and other Greek thinkers. The result was the movement known as Scholasticism. Using Greek classical ideas as their intellectual framework, the Scholastics wanted to show that the truth of religious beliefs existed independently of the signs used to represent them. But within this movement there were some—the nominalists—who argued that "truth" was a matter of subjective opinion and that signs captured, at best, only illusory and highly variable human versions of truth. The French theologian Pierre Abélard (1079–c. 1142) proposed an interesting compromise to the debate, suggesting that the "truth" that a sign purportedly captured existed in a particular object as an observable property of the object itself, and outside it as an ideal concept within the mind. The "truth" of the matter, therefore, was somewhere in between.

It was the British philosopher John Locke (1632–1704) who introduced the formal study of signs into philosophy in his *Essay Concerning Human Understanding* (1690), anticipating that it would allow philosophers to understand the interconnection between representation and knowledge. But the task he laid out, of discovering the properties of the sign, remained virtually unnoticed until Saussure and Peirce took it upon themselves to provide a scientific framework that made it possible to envision even more than what Locke had hoped for—namely, an autonomous field of inquiry centered on the sign. The subsequent development of semiotics as a distinct scientific domain, with its own methodology, theoretical apparatus, and corpus of findings, is due to the efforts of such twentieth-century scholars as Charles Morris (1901-1979), Roman Jakobson (1896–1982), Roland Barthes (1915–1980), A. J. Greimas (1917–1992), Thomas A. Sebeok (1920-2001), and Umberto Eco (1932–), to mention but a few.

Modern-day linguistic science is the twin sister of semiotics, since both trace their parentage to Saussure's *Cours de linguistique générale* (1916). Saussure distinguished between *langue*, the knowledge that speakers of a language share about what is acceptable in that language, and *parole*, the individual's particular abilities and tendencies to use *langue* in certain situations. In 1957, the American linguist Noam Chomsky (1928–) adopted Saussure's basic distinction, referring to *langue* as *competence* and *parole* as *performance*. Chomsky also entrenched Saussure's belief that the aim of linguistics proper was the study of *langue* into mainstream linguistics. Chomsky defined his version of *langue* (*competence*) as the innate knowledge that people employ unconsciously to produce and understand grammatically well-formed sentences, most of which they have never heard before. He then proposed a system of analysis, which he called *transformational-generative grammar,* that he claimed would allow the linguist to identify and describe the general properties of this innate knowledge, sifting them out from those that apply only to particular languages. In acquiring a language, both general grammatical processes and language-specific rule-setting mechanisms are activated in the child; the former, called *universal principles,* are part of a species-specific language faculty—known as a *Universal Grammar* (UG)—that has genetic information built into it about what languages in general must be like; the latter, known as *parameters,* constrain the universal principles to produce the specific language grammar to which the child is exposed. Although Chomsky assigns some role to cultural and experiential factors, he has always maintained that the primary role of linguistics must be to understand the UG constituting the faculty of speech. Chomsky's intractability in maintaining this position, in spite of research that has cast serious doubts upon it, understandably made him a target of bitter criticism throughout the 1980s and 1990s.

Since their emergence in the previous century as autonomous scientific disciplines semiotics and linguistics have been caught in a tug of war between two radically different views of human mental functioning, *environmentalism* and *innatism.* From the former point of view, humans are seen as being born with their minds a *tabula rasa,* assuming their nature in response to the stimuli they encounter in their social environments. From the latter perspective, humans are also seen as malleable organisms, but they are not viewed as being born with an empty slate. Rather, in the terminology of neuroscience, they are seen as being "hard-wired" from birth to learn and behave in certain biologically-programmed ways. The acquisition of language, for instance, is said to occur through the operation of an innate *language acquisition device* (LAD) which is governed by the rules of a *universal grammar* (UG). Humans have no more control over their LADs than they do over their breathing. Of course, they can set up obstacles to block the functioning of their LADs, just as they can prevent themselves from breathing: i.e., they can refuse to process input by shutting themselves off from what is being said around them.

The question that semiotics seeks to answer in this regard is how thought is imprinted in language, focusing on how human ideas, concepts, feelings and characteristic social behaviors are mirrored by the verbal categories that specific cultures employ to encode them. This suggests that grammatical properties cannot be studied in isolation, as the UG paradigm purports. To understand semiosis in the verbal domain, everything from verb tenses to adverb usage must be linked to the interconnected experiences of the world that are manifested in the use of a language by native speakers in cultural contexts.

The Nature vs. Culture controversy has been taken up constantly within the larger frame of semiotic analysis. We mention in particular the work and efforts of Thomas A. Sebeok (1920–2001) who adapted the pioneering work of biologist Jakob von Uexküll (1864–1944) and the Estonian cultural semiotician Jurij Lotman (1922–1993), taking semiotics back to its biological roots, given that the discipline grew, as mentioned, out of the work of the Ancient Greek physicians. Culture in the semiotic framework is viewed, by and large, as an extension of a creation of semiosis itself. This is, as mentioned, the innate ability to produce signs to stand for objects, events, feelings, actions, situations, and ideas perceived to have some meaning, purpose, or useful function. The sign may be imagined, in which case it is called by psychologists a *mental image*, or it may be something externalized, in which case it is called by semioticians and philosophers a *representation*. More specifically, a *sign* can be defined as a *form* that has been imagined or made externally (through some physical medium) to stand for an object, event, feeling, etc., known as a *referent*, or for a class of similar (or related) objects, events, feelings, etc., known as a *referential domain*.

Semiosis vs. Representation

Human representation, as it manifests itself in all kinds of forms, from narratives to scientific theories, is characterized by the deliberate use of signs to probe, classify, and hence *know* the world. The difference, but intrinsic interconnection, between semiosis and representation can be seen in early childhood behaviors. When an infant comes into contact with an object, his or her first reaction is to explore it with the *senses*, i.e. to handle it, taste it, smell it, listen to any sounds it makes, and visually observe its features. This exploratory phase of knowing is based on the innate *sensory* apparatus with which we are all born. It allows the child to explore an object in terms of how it feels, tastes, smells, etc. Now, as the infant grows, he or she starts to engage more and more in *semiosic* behavior that clearly transcends this sensory phase; i.e. he or she starts to point to the object and/or imitate the sounds it makes. This behavior is independent of cultural conditioning; it comes with having a body and a brain. It consists in the ability to imitate the sounds an object makes with the vocal cords and to indicate its presence with the index finger. At that point in the child's development, the object starts to assume a new semiosic form of existence; it has, in effect, been transferred to the physical strategy itself used by the child to imitate its sound features or indicate its presence. This strategy produces the most basic type of sign which, as Charles Morris suggested, allows the child from that point on to replace the sign for the object. As is well known, this replacement pattern is known psychologically as *displacement*. This is the ability of the human mind to conjure up the things to which signs refer even though they are not physically present for the senses to cognize or recognize. The displacement property of signs endows the developing infant to think about the world beyond the stimulus-response realm to which most other species are constrained, and thus to reflect upon it at any time and in any situation whatsoever. Now, as the child grows, he/she becomes increasingly more able to use signs to *represent* the world in a displaced manner. The word *represent* means, literally, "to present again," i.e. to present some referent again in the sign.

The instant children start to represent the world with signs, they make a vital psychosocial connection between their developing bodies and conscious thoughts to that world. To put it figuratively, signs constitute the "representational glue" that interconnects their body, their mind, and the world around them in a holistic fashion. Moreover, once the child discovers that signs are effective tools for thinking, planning, and negotiating meaning with others in certain situations, he or she gains access to the knowledge domain of his or her culture. At first, the child will compare his/her own attempts at representation against the signs he or she is exposed to in specific contexts. But through protracted usage, the signs acquired in such contexts will become cognitively dominant in the child, and eventually mediate and regulate her or his thoughts, actions, and behaviors.

Semiotics makes it explicit that there is an interconnectedness among the multifarious dimensions of semiosis and representation. It also allows us to establish a commonality among different representational systems. Because all such systems are composed of the same kinds of phenomena, semiotics provides a basis for showing an interrelation and interdependence among all areas of knowledge, from language to science and the arts. A digit in numerical representation, for instance, has the exact same structural features in representational terms that, say, a noun in language has—i.e. both are signs with specific forms, functions, and meanings. In practical terms, therefore, semiotics makes obvious the fact that both types of signs are structurally isomorphic in the ways in which they designate something, refer to the world, take on connotations, and so on. The difference between a digit and a noun is thus not to be located in structural patterns, but in the different functions of the representational systems to which they pertain. This is why, despite their different cognitive and social functions, both systems are understandable in exactly the same way. In essence, semiotics makes it clear why such seemingly diverse forms of representation as poetry and mathematics are not mutually exclusive—with adequate exposure to both, people will be able to extract meaning from either one of them in remarkably similar ways. Indeed, semiotics helps unravel the structural reasons why poetry and mathematics make their meanings, as different as they might appear to be, in comparable ways.

Structuralism

The term *structuralism* is used to characterize mainstream semiotic method. This is an appropriate term in that it brings out what semiotics aims to do—to flesh out the regular and predictable features of the $X = Y$ relation. It seeks to do so by asking three basic questions: (1) *What* does something mean? (2) *How* does it represent what it means? (3) *Why* does it mean what it means?

The premise that guides structuralist semiotics is that the recurring patterns that characterize sign systems are reflective of innate structures in the sensory, emotional, and intellectual composition of the human body and the human psyche. This would explain why the forms of expression that humans create and to which they respond instinctively the world over are so meaningful and so easily understandable across cultures. In his *Cours de linguistique générale* (1916), a textbook put together after his death by two of his university students, Saussure used the term *semiology* to designate the field he proposed for studying these structures. But while his term is still used somewhat today, the older term *semiotics* is the preferred one. Saussure emphasized that the systematic study of sign systems, such as language, should be divided into two branches—the *synchronic* and the *diachronic*. The former refers to the study of signs at a given point in time, normally the present, and the latter to the investigation of how signs change in form and meaning over time.

Signs are not forged in a totally random fashion; nor do they refer to things in a haphazard way. They beget their forms and meanings in *structured* ways. Consider the following words:

- pin *vs.* bin
- fun *vs.* pun
- duck *vs.* luck

What allows a speaker of English to determine the meaning of each one? It is, of course, the initial sound. This differentiation feature of signs is known as *paradigmatic* structure—i.e. the relation whereby some minimal feature in a sign is sufficient to keep it differentiated from all other signs of the same kind. Paradigmatic structure is found in all human meaning systems. In music, for instance, a major and minor chord of the same key are perceivable as distinct on account of a half tone difference in the middle note of the chord; the left and right shoes of a pair of shoes are identifiable in terms of the orientation of the shoe; and so on.

Now, note that the above words are legitimate signs, not only because they are differentiable in a specific way, but also because the combination of sounds with which they are constructed is consistent with English syllable structure. On the other hand, *tpin, tbin, tfun, tpun, tduck, tluck* would not be legitimate signs in English because they violate its syllable structure. Syllable structure is known technically as *syntagmatic* structure—i.e. the relation whereby signs are constructed in some definable sequence or combination. Syntagmatic structure too is found in all human systems. In music, for instance, a melody is recognizable as such only if the notes follow each other in a certain way (e.g. according to the rules of classical harmony); two shoes are considered to form a pair if they are of the same size, style, and color; and so on.

The Broader Picture

Strictly defined, semiotics is the study of the sign, i.e. of the $X = Y$ relation as it relates to some individual or social system. Since this very relation is noticeable in all human expressive and representational activities, it is little wonder that the basic ideas in the study of the sign have been extended to study everything humans make. One of these is *texts*. People make messages by constructing appropriate texts—conversations, letters, speeches, poems, myths, novels, television programs, paintings, scientific theories, musical compositions, etc. A *text* constitutes a specific "weaving together" of signs in order to express something. But in their overall composition, texts become "composite" signs themselves, and can be studied as unitary signs. A novel, for instance, is a verbal text constructed with language signs according to the rules of the language's orthographic and grammatical systems. But note that novels are not interpreted in terms of their constituent parts, but holistically as if they were single signs. This is why when we ask someone what a novel means, he or she couches the answer in the form $X = Y$ where X is the novel and Y the meaning he or she extracts from it: e.g. "The novel *Crime and Punishment* paints a grim portrait of the human psyche."

The signs that go into the make-up of texts belong to specific *codes*. Language, dress, music, and gesture are examples of codes. These can be defined as systems of signs that are held together by paradigmatic and syntagmatic relations. The Cartesian plane is a *code* because it has paradigmatic and syntagmatic properties. Now, this code can be used to make certain kinds of texts: e.g. maps with latitude and longitude lines, certain city designs (as downtown Manhattan), and so on. Language too is a code because it has paradigmatic (*pin* vs. *bin*) and syntagmatic (*plan* but not *pfan*) properties. Needless to say, it also can be used to make certain kinds of texts: e.g. conversations, novels, poems, etc. Codes, too, have become objects of semiotic analysis in the last fifty years.

Clearly, a text bears no meaning unless the receiver of the text knows the code(s) from which it was constructed and unless the text refers to, occurs in, or entails some specific *context*. The *context* is the environment—physical, psychological, and social—in which a sign or text is used or occurs. Consider a discarded and damaged beer can. If one were to come across this item on a sidewalk on a city street, one would no doubt view it as a piece of garbage or rubbish. But if you saw the very same object on a pedestal, displayed in an art gallery, "signed" by some artist, and given a title such as "Waste," then one would interpret its meaning in a vastly different way. One would, in fact, be inclined to interpret it as an artistic text, descrying a throw-away or materialistic society. Clearly, the package's physical context of occurrence and social frame of reference—its location on a sidewalk vs. its display in an art gallery—will determine how one will interpret it.

The study of context entails a study of *culture*, defined by anthropologists as the totality of socially transmitted behavior patterns, arts, beliefs, institutions, and all other products of human work and thought. These patterns, traits, and products are considered to be the expression of a particular period, class, community, or population. In strictly semiotic terms, *culture* can be defined as a complex system of different types of signs that cohere into codes which individuals and groups can utilize to construct texts in order to make meanings or exchange messages. The system can be called the *signifying order*. It is characterizable as a kind of *macro-code* that supplies the signs, the various codes, and the texts they make possible to the members of a society or group of societies.

It's All a Puzzle

In a sense, semiotic or linguistic analysis is comparable to solving a jigsaw puzzle. The goal of the puzzle-solver is to figure out how the pieces of the puzzle fit together to produce the hidden picture that they conceal as disconnected pieces. But solving the jigsaw puzzle tells the solver nothing about why he or she is fascinated by the puzzle in the first place, nor what relevance it may have to human life. Analogously, the semiotician or linguist seeks to figure out how the bits and pieces (signs, phonemes, morphemes, etc.) cohere into larger patterns. It is a snapshot of the "broader picture" that semiotics aims to achieve. The semiotic agenda is thus shaped by a search for the biological, psychic, and social roots of the human need for meaning, of the "story" behind human symbols and forms of expression.

Commentaries

1. *St. Augustine*

In our view, and that of many other semioticians, St. Augustine (354–430 AD) is to be considered the true "founder" of semiotics, for it was he to whom we owe an important change in the conception of the sign. As a matter of historical fact, it was Hippocrates (460–377 BC), the founder of Western medical science, who coined the term *semeiotics* as the study of *symptoms*—a *symptom* being, in effect, a *semeion* "mark, sign" that stands for something other than itself. The physician's primary task, Hippocrates claimed, was to unravel what a symptom stands for, namely to unravel the $X = Y$ relation in terms of knowledge about the body. For example, a dark bruise, a rash, or a sore throat might stand respectively for a broken finger, a skin allergy, a cold. The medical problem is, of course, to infer what that *something* is. The physician Galen of Pergamum (139–199 AD) further entrenched semeiotics into medical practice more than a century later, a tradition that continues to this day in various European countries: e.g. in some parts of Italy the study of symptoms within medicine is still called semeiotica.

The idea of *semeion* as a kind of "mental symptom" that could explain such things as words and symbols never really caught on in the ancient world, although there was great awareness of the power of words and symbols in themselves. Plato's (c. 428–c. 347) Doctrine of Forms, for instance, was essentially an unwitting study in signification. According to this Doctrine, reality exists in two realms, one inhabited by invisible ideas or forms, and the other by concrete familiar objects. The latter are imperfect copies of the ideas because they are always in a state of flux. Thus, for Plato true knowledge is the offspring of innate ideas or forms. In his *Republic*, he portrayed humanity as imprisoned in a cave where it mistook shadows on the wall for reality. Only the person with the opportunity to escape from the cave—the true philosopher—had the perspicacity to see the real world outside. The shadowy environment of the cave symbolizes the realm of physical appearances. This contrasts with the perfect world of ideas outside. Plato's forms can be best understood as geometrical figures or models. By the time of Aristotle (384–322 BC) and the Stoic philosophers (a Greek school of philosophy, founded by Zeno around 308 BC), the relation between forms (such as words) and ideas had become a topic of heated debate. Aristotle and the Stoics were among the first to take on the task of investigating the $X = Y$ relation of words in a comprehensive way, laying down a theory of meaning that has remained basic to this day. They defined the word as consisting of three dimensions: (1) the physical part itself (e.g. the sounds that make up the word cat); (2) the *referent* to which it calls attention (a certain category of mammal), (3) its evocation of a *meaning* (what the referent entails psychologically and socially).

The Latin translation of *semeion* as *signum* is probably what gave St. Augustine the idea that there is a distinction between the natural signs (*signa naturalia*), as studied by the Greek physicians, and conventional signs (*signa data*), as invented by humans to grasp the world. This distinction is, in our view, the defining moment in the history of semiotics. St. Augustine added the notion of an interpretive component to the conventional sign that was consistent with the hermeneutic tradition established by Clement of Alexandria (150?–215? AD), the Greek theologian and early Father of the Church. *Hermeneutics* is the study and interpretation of ancient texts, especially those of a religious or mythical nature. Clement established the method of ascertaining, as far as possible, the meaning that a Biblical writer intended on the basis of linguistic considerations, relevant sources, and historical background. Clement also maintained that the interpreter should not ignore the fact that the original meaning of the text developed in the course of history, and that the act of interpretation was bound to be influenced by cultural factors.

For St. Augustine natural signs include anything that, by itself, has no "intention" of signifying anything beyond themselves. This includes any natural phenomenon, such as smoke, which signifies "fire," and facial expressions which manifest unseen emotions. Words, on the other hand, are conventional signs that are constructed on purpose to communicate something other than themselves. In this opening passage, St. Augustine characterizes signs as forms that humans use to convey knowledge and understanding to each other.

St. Augustine also argues in the passage that nonverbal signs (nodding, gesturing, etc.) are really "visible words," thus interconnecting the verbal and nonverbal dimensions in a unitary way, even though the verbal one is the most productive one in human semiosis: "a multitude of innumerable signs by means of which men express their thoughts is made up of words." What St. Augustine is suggesting—perhaps for the first time ever—is that the meanings captured within one system of signs (the verbal) are found expressed in the other (the nonverbal) in parallel ways.

Most significantly, St. Augustine alludes, in this passage, to the interconnection between signs and though, between X's and Y's (in the $X = Y$) relation that is the sign. He asks, with great acumen: "But how is it that a word which is not yet formed in the vision of the thought? How will it be like the knowledge of which it is born, if it has not the form of that knowledge, and is only now called a word because it can have it?" He concludes that it is a "something in our mind," and that ultimately the two dimensions of meaning-making—the form X and what it stands for Y—are mysteriously linked since they have a kind of intrinsic *raison d'être*, so that "in what manner each thing is known, in that manner also it is thought."

Essentially, St. Augustine is claiming that forms and their content suggest each other, inextricably interlinked in the realm of human experience. Plato viewed representation and especially language as separate from experiential processes—a viewpoint that the French philosopher René Descartes (1596–1650) entrenched into Western philosophy by claiming that nonverbal forms of thought proceeded without logic, and so could not be studied scientifically. But, as St. Augustine argued, long before Descartes, even the most abstract forms of reasoning are tied to some intrinsically-felt connection to their content. Essentially, they call attention to the things, beings, events, feelings, etc. to which they refer, even if these are *displaced* in space and time, i.e. not physically present for the human being to observe.

2. *John Poinsot*

The Platonic view of the innateness of forms and on the power of logic to explain reality remained as cornerstones of Roman philosophy and, later, of the emerging Christian world. By the eleventh century, interest in the mind-body problem was kindled further by Arab scholars who translated the works of Plato, Aristotle, and other Greek thinkers. The result was the movement known as Scholasticism. Through dialectical reasoning, the Medieval Scholastics wanted to demonstrate the truth of existing religious beliefs. Their methods thus helped to entrench even further the Western tradition of rational logic. However, within this movement, there were some—the so-called "nominalists"—who maintained that truth was a matter of subjective opinion. The French theologian, Pierre Abélard (1079–c. 1142), proposed an interesting compromise between the two ideologies by suggesting that the Platonic forms existed in particular objects as "properties" and outside of them as "concepts" within the mind.

No doubt the greatest intellectual figure of the Medieval era was St. Thomas Aquinas (1225–1274), who combined Aristotelian logic with Augustinian theology into a comprehensive system of thought that came to be the acclaimed philosophy of Roman Catholicism. In his *Summa theologiae*, he constructed a theoretical structure that integrated Classical logic with religious experience. For Aquinas, the truths of science and philosophy were discovered by reasoning from the facts of experience, whereas the tenets of religion were beyond rational comprehension and, therefore, had to be accepted on faith.

Medieval perspectives on the mind culminate with the views of John Duns Scotus (c. 1266–1308) and William of Ockham (c. 1285–c. 1349). Both were adamant non-rationalists. Duns Scotus argued that Divine will was prior to Divine intellect and created, rather than followed, the laws of nature and morality. William of Ockham acerbically denounced Scholastic universalism, stressing that abstract entities were merely the result of words referring to other words, rather than to actual things. The subsequent period of the Renaissance encouraged a new, freer mood of debate. Out of this fertile intellectual terrain came the first major break with Platonic-Aristotelian rationalism. It was the English philosopher and statesman, Francis Bacon (1561–1626), who persuasively criticized Aristotelian logic on the grounds that it was futile for the discovery of physical laws. He called for a scientific method based on inductive observation and experimentation. Paradoxically, both Bacon's and Galileo's (1564–1642) emphasis on induction as a method of discovery led, by the late Renaissance, to the entrenchment of Aristotle's idea that a meaningful understanding of reality could be gained only by exact observation and logical thinking. By the seventeenth and eighteenth centuries this very same idea was extended to the study of mind. Philosophers like Thomas Hobbes (1588–1679), René Descartes (1596–1650), Benedict Spinoza (1632–1677), Gottfried Wilhelm Leibniz (1646–1716), and David Hume (1711–1776) assumed that the mind could, and should, be studied as objectively and as mechanistically as nature.

In his *Ars Logica* and *Tractatus de Signis*, John of St. Thomas, or John Poinsot (1589–1644), his given name, sees the study of signification (the production and use of signs) as the only means to constructing a true philosophy of the mind. His is the first attempt theoretically to justify St. Augustine's original proposal of signum as a general mode of being verified equally in the phenomena of Nature and Culture. He argued that the essence of signification lay in a triadic relation whereby one thing, X, represents something other than itself, Y, "to a cognitive power."

Poinsot divides this "cognitive power" into four categories. First, there is the *productive* form of cognition which is "the power itself which elicits an act of knowledge." Second, there is the *objective* form which literally inheres in any object "which stimulates or toward which a cognition tends, as when I see a stone or a man." Third, there is *formal* cognition, which "is the awareness itself whereby a power is rendered cognizant, as the sight itself of the stone or of the man." Fourth, there is *instrumental* cognition, which "is the means by which the object is represented to the power, as a picture of Caesar represents Caesar." The passage included here also deals with the Augustinian relation between natural and conventional signs, developing it further.

3. *Charles Sanders Peirce*

Following along the path laid out by John Poinsot, John Locke (1632–1704), the English philosopher who set out the principles of empiricism, introduced the formal study of signs into philosophy in his *Essay Concerning Human Understanding* (1690), anticipating that it would allow philosophers to understand the interconnection between representation and knowledge. But the task he laid out remained virtually unnoticed until the ideas of the American philosopher, logician, and mathematician Charles Sanders Peirce (1839–1914) became the basis for circumscribing an autonomous field of inquiry. Peirce was born in Cambridge, Massachusetts. He was educated at Harvard University, and lectured on logic and philosophy at Johns Hopkins and Harvard Universities. He conducted experiments to determine the density and shape of the earth and expanded the system of logic created by the British mathematician George Boole (1815–1864). But Peirce is best known for his philosophical system, later called *pragmatism*, which maintains that the significance of any theory or model lies in the practical effects of its application, and for his typology of signs. Peirce defined semiotics as the *doctrine* of signs, following in the tradition of Plato and others. The word *doctrine* is used, of course, in its basic meaning of "system of principles," not in any religious sense.

Peirce described three kinds of signs in human representational systems. He called these *qualisigns, sinsigns,* and *legisigns*. A *qualisign* is a sign that draws attention to, or singles out, some *quality* of its referent. In language, an adjective is a qualisign since it draws attention to the qualities (color, shape, size, etc.) of referents. In other codes, qualisigns include the colors used by painters, the harmonies and tones used by composers, etc. A *sinsign* is a sign that draws attention to, or singles out, a particular object in time-space: e.g. a pointing finger, the words *here* and *there*, etc. A *legisign* is a sign that designates something by convention: e.g. words referring to abstract concepts, mathematical symbols, etc.

Peirce then pointed out that there were three kinds of *objects* (or *referents*). A referent that has been represented through some form of replication, simulation, or resemblance is an *icon*: e.g. a photo resembles its referent visually, a word such as *bang* resembles its referent phonically, and so on. A referent that has been represented through some form of indication is an *index*: e.g. a pointing index finger is an indication of where an object is in space, smoke is an indication of a fire source, and so on. A referent that has been represented conventionally is a *symbol*: e.g. a *rose* is a symbol of love in some cultures, words such as *love* and *hope* refer by convention to various emotions or concepts, and so on.

Peirce suggested, moreover, that there were three types of *interpretants* (= what the sign-user or sign-interpreter intends with, or gets from, a specific kind of sign): a *rheme* is an interpretant of a qualisign (i.e. the kind of meaning that is extractable from a qualisign); a *dicisign* is an interpretant of a sinsign; and an *argument* is an interpretant of a legisign.

The passage included here is an elaboration, with illustrations, of this basic framework—a framework that now largely defines semiotic practice. Peirce called the sign a *representamen* (literally "something that does the representing"), suggesting that it entailed a form of knowing inhering in the physical strategy of representation itself (the use of sounds, hand movements, etc. for some representational purpose). Peirce termed the referent the *object*, suggesting that it entailed a form of knowing inhering in a recognition of a referent in the representamen, displaced from its (real-world) context of occurrence. He termed the meaning that one gets from a sign the *interpretant*, suggesting that it entailed a thirdness form of knowing, whereby the sign-user evaluates or responds to what the sign means socially, contextually, personally, etc.

Peirce refers to icons as *firstness* signs, because they are tied, *first*, to sense-based semiosis. In a sense they are substitutes for the stimuli they refer to themselves. Since icons must also be understood in cultural context, Peirce uses the term *hypoicon* to acknowledge this fact. Nevertheless, icons refer to objects by similarity, so that even in cultural contexts many of these can be figured out by those who are not necessarily a part of the culture. For Peirce *iconicity* is the primary form of semiosis or representation: i.e. it is innate and natural for all of us to resort to iconic signing first and then to proceed on to other forms subsequently. *Indexicality* is defined by Peirce as a *secondness* form of representation: i.e. one in which the sign directs attention to its referent by singling it out in time and/or space. Unlike icons, the sign is not a substitute for the stimuli. For instance, an arrow on a sheet of paper pointing out something in relation to a second referent is an example of an index. Perhaps the best known kinds of indexes are the pointing index finger and the indices used at the back of books. Finally, *symbols* reveal a *thirdness* form of representation, says Peirce, because in this case the sign, the sign-user, and the referent are linked to each other by the forces of historical and social convention.

Like Locke, Peirce attacked the prevailing belief of his times that knowledge was independent of experience. For Locke, all information about the physical world came through the senses and all thoughts could be traced to the sensory information on which they were based. After the Enlightenment, philosophy developed a split personality. Even today it is struggling to reconcile its objectivist and experientialist traits. Immanuel Kant (1724–1804) claimed to have solved Cartesian dualism by suggesting that the mind imposed form and order on all its experiences, and that this could be discovered *a priori* by reflection. He did not, however, see the intrinsic developmental link between these two cognitive modes, as did the Italian philosopher Giambattista Vico (1688–1744). Georg Wilhelm Friedrich Hegel (1770–1831) argued that reality was subject to mental processes, although there existed a rational logic that governed human actions. Karl Marx (1818–1883) developed Hegel's philosophy into the theory of dialectical materialism by which it was claimed that matter, not the mind, was the ultimate reality. For Marx history unfolded according to laws that were more concretely real than the mind. Friedrich Nietzsche (1844–1900) led the Romantic revolt against reason and logically-planned social organization by stressing natural instinct, self-assertion, and passion.

It was out of this climate that Peirce emerged to propose semiotics as a way of understanding this duality. John Dewey (1859–1952) developed the Peircean view into a comprehensive system of thought that emphasized the biological and social basis of knowledge, as well as the instrumental character of ideas. Edmund Husserl (1859–1938) went further than any of his predecessors in stressing the phenomenological basis of all cognition. For Husserl, only that which was present to consciousness was real. Phenomenology has, since Husserl, come to be a very powerful movement dedicated to describing the structures of experience as they present themselves to consciousness, without recourse to any theoretical or explanatory framework. Alfred North Whitehead (1861–1947) revived the Platonic theory of forms to show the failure of mechanistic science as a way of fully interpreting reality. Bertrand Russell (1872–1970) applied the methods of logic, mathematics, and physics to the investigation of mentality. Finally, Martin Heidegger (1889–1976) combined the phenomenological approach of Husserl with an emphasis on emotional experience into a modern form of Nietzschean nihilism.

4. *Ferdinand de Saussure*

The Swiss philologist Ferdinand de Saussure (1857–1913) was born in Geneva in 1857. He attended science classes for a year at the University of Geneva before turning to language studies at the University of Leipzig in 1876. As a student he published his only book, *Mémoire sur le système primitif des voyelles dans les langues indo-européennes* ('Memoir on the Original Vowel System in the Indo-European Languages', 1879), an important work on the vowel system of Proto-Indo-European, considered the parent language from which the Indo-European languages descended.

Saussure taught at the École des Hautes Études in Paris from 1881 to 1891 and then became a professor of Sanskrit and Comparative

Grammar at the University of Geneva. Although he never wrote another book, his teaching proved highly influential. After his death, two of his assistants collated their notes and the lecture notes of some of Saussure's students and other materials into the seminal work, *Cours de linguistique générale* (1916), that bears his name. The book reveals Saussure's ground-breaking approach to language that became the basis for establishing both semiotics and linguistics as autonomous scientific disciplines.

In the *Cours*, Saussure defined the sign as an entity made up: of something physical—sounds, letters, gestures, etc.—which he termed the *signifier*; and of the image or concept to which the signifier refers—which he called the *signified*. He called the relation that holds between the two *signification*. Saussure also claimed that these three dimensions were inseparable. Saussure used the term *semiology* to designate the field he proposed for studying signs. But while his term is still used somewhat today, the term semiotics is the preferred one.

Saussure considered signification to be an arbitrary process that human beings and/or societies establish at will. To make his point, he reasoned that there was no evident reason for using, say, *tree* or *arbre* (French) to designate 'an arboreal plant'. Indeed, any well-formed signifier could have been used in either language—a well-formed signifier is one that is consistent with the orthographic, phonological, or other type of structure characteristic of the code to which it appertains (*tree* is well-formed in English; *tbky* is not). Saussure did admit, however, that there were some instances whereby the signifier was fashioned in imitation of the signified. Onomatopoeic words (*drip, plop, whack*, etc.), he granted, did indeed attempt to reflect the sound properties that their referents are perceived to have. But Saussure maintained that this was a relatively isolated and infrequent phenomenon. Moreover, the highly variable nature of onomatopoeia across languages demonstrated to him that even this phenomenon was subject to arbitrary cultural perceptions. For instance, the word used to refer to the sounds made by a rooster is *cock-a-doodle-do* in English, but *chicchirichí* (pronounced "keek-keereekee") in Italian; the word employed to refer to the barking of a dog is *bow-wow* in English, but *ouaoua* (pronounced wawa) in French; etc. Saussure suggested that such onomatopoeic creations were only approximate and more or less conventional imitations of perceived sounds.

Many semioticians have begged to differ with this specific part of Saussurean theory. What Saussure seems to have ignored is that even those who do not speak English, Italian, or French will notice an *attempt* in all the above signifiers to imitate rooster or canine sounds—an attempt constrained by the respective sound systems of the two languages that are, in part, responsible for the different phonic outcomes.

Such attempts, in fact, probably went into the making of most words in a language, even though people no longer consciously experience them as physical simulations of their referents—because time and constant usage have made people forget the connection between signifier and signified.

5. *Susanne K. Langer*

The American educator and philosopher, Susanne Langer (1895–1985) introduced the distinction between the *discursive* signs used in conventional language and the nondiscursive ones (*presentational*) used in various art forms. Discursive forms have the property of detachment: e.g. one can focus on a word in a sentence or a phrase without impairing the overall understanding of the sentence or phrase. In contrast, presentational forms cannot be broken up into their elements without impairing the meaning: e.g. one cannot focus on a note or phrase in a melody without destroying the sense of the melody.

But the two modes of knowing can evoke each other. Think of: (1) the sound of thunder, (2) the feel of wet grass, (3) the smell of fish, (4) the taste of toothpaste, (5) the sensation of being uncomfortably cold, (6) the sensation of extreme happiness. Image (1) has an auditory modality, (2) a tactile one, (3) an olfactory one, (4) a gustatory one (5) a kinesic one, (6) an emotional one. These discursive forms, obviously, produce feelings, i.e. some sense impressions or affective stimuli, as if the actual stimuli were present. This is strong evidence that semiosis is intermodal: i.e. it involves presentational and discursive forms of knowing in tandem. The term that is used to characterize this intermodality is *synesthesia*. So, the above sensations associated with touch, smell, etc., but evoked by verbal descriptions, constitute synesthetic reactions.

Painting, sculpture, photography, music, and all the other arts are designed presentationally. The question of what the function of art is all about has become part of a general social debate as contemporary art galleries routinely put controversial "abstract" paintings and sculptures on display. One of the most famous versions of this debate was initiated by Andy Warhol (1928–1987), the American pop artist who produced paintings and silk-screen prints of commonplace images, such as soup cans and photographs of celebrities. When asked *what* does it mean, people will either: (1) say that it means nothing; or (2) give responses such as "It is a symbol of our consumer society;" "It represents the banality and triviality of contemporary life" etc. The latter pattern of responses suggests that we typically tend to interpret human-made artifacts as "works of art" because meanings and values are attributed to them by those who make them, by the society in which they live, and by those who look at them in later years.

Langer comes from the intellectual lineage initiated by the eigh-
teenth-century German philosopher Immanuel Kant (1724–1804), who
proposed that objects can be judged as beautiful when they satisfy a disinterested desire: one that does not involve personal interests or needs.
Beautiful objects have no specific purpose, claimed Kant, and judg-
ments of beauty are not expressions of mere personal preference but
universal intuitions. Although one cannot be certain that others will be
satisfied by the objects one judges to be beautiful, one can at least say
that others ought to be satisfied. Art should give the same disinterested
satisfaction as natural beauty does. Paradoxically, art can accomplish
one thing Nature cannot. It can offer ugliness and beauty in one object
—a fine painting of an ugly face is still beautiful aesthetically.

6. *Roman Jakobson*

The Moscow-born linguist and semiotician, Roman Jakobson
(1896–1982) carried out most of his work in the United States. Among
his contributions to semiotics, linguistics, and communication theory is
his widely-used model that identifies the main functions and components of human communication.

People commonly think of language as the primary means of *communication*. Semiotics, however, sees it as part of social communication,
a code that is used in tandem with nonverbal modes of message-mak-
ing. To explain the relation, Jakobson posited six "constituents" that
characterize all speech acts (Jakobson 1960):

1. an *addresser* who initiates a communication;
2. a *message* that he or she recognizes must refer to something other than
   itself;
3. an *addressee* who is the intended receiver of the message;
4. a *context* that permits the addressee to recognize that the message is
   referring to something other than itself: e.g. if someone were crying
   out "Help," lying motionless on the ground, then one would easily
   understand that the message is referring to a concrete situation;
5. a mode of *contact* by which a message is delivered (the physical channel) and the primary social and psychological connections that are
   established between the addresser and addressee;
6. a *code* providing the signs and structural patterns for constructing
   and deciphering messages.

Jakobson then pointed out that each of these constituents determines a different communicative function:
1. *emotive*, which refers to the witting or unwitting presence of the
   addresser's emotions, attitudes, social status, etc. in the message;

2. *conative,* which refers to the intended effect—physical, psychological, social, etc.—that the message is expected to have on the addressee;

3. *referential,* which refers to a message constructed to convey information ("Main Street is two blocks north of here").

4. *poetic,* which refers to a message constructed to deliver meanings effectively, like poetry ("Roses are red, violets are blue, and how's it going with you?");

5. *phatic,* which refers to a message designed to establish social contact ("Hi, how's it going?");

6. *metalingual,* which refers to a message designed to refer to the code used ("The word noun is a noun.").

Jakobson's analysis of verbal communication suggests that discourse goes well beyond a situation of simple information transfer. It involves determining *who* says *what* to *whom*; *where* and *when* it is said; and *how* and *why* it is said: i.e. it is motivated and shaped by the setting, the message contents, the participants, and the goals of each interlocutor. Discourse makes an emotional claim on everyone in the social situation. It is a form of acting, of presenting persona through language.

7. Émile Benveniste

The French linguist Émile Benveniste (1902–1976) claimed that language cannot be studied apart from how it is put to use in daily life. Benveniste thus emphasized the study of *parole* (language as it is used) in order to understand how the system of *langue* (the grammar) is constructed in the native speaker's mind. In this passage, Benveniste challenges the Saussurean view of the sign as something arbitrary, pointing out that there is much more to signification.

To understand Benveniste's argument, it is essential to open a parenthesis here and discuss a basic dichotomy of signification—that between denotation and connotation. *Denotation* is the initial meaning a sign *intends* to capture. But the *denotated referent*, or *denotatum*, Y, is not something specific in the world, but rather a prototypical *category* of something. For instance, the word *cat* does not refer to a specific "cat," although it can, but to the *category* of animals that we recognize as having the quality "catness." The denotative meaning of *cat* is, therefore, really *catness*, a prototypical mental picture marked by specific *distinctive features* such as [mammal], [retractile claws], [long tail], etc. This composite mental picture allows us to determine if a specific real or imaginary animal under consideration will fall within the category of *catness*. Similarly, the word *square* does not denote a specific "square," but rather a figure consisting of four equal straight lines that meet at right angles. It is irrelevant if the lines are thick, dotted, 2 meters long,

80 feet long, or whatever. So long as the figure can be seen to have the distinctive features [four equal straight lines] and [meeting at right angles], it is identifiable denotatively as a *square*.

Now, the meaning of a sign invariably encompasses other kinds of referents and meanings that appear, by association or analogy, to have something in common with the denotatum. This process is known as *connotation*. The use of *cat* in "You've let the cat out of the bag," is an example of connotative meaning associated with cats. The various *connotata* of signs are much greater than their denotata. Connotation is the operative mode in the production and decipherment of creative texts such as poems, novels, musical compositions, art works—in effect, of most of the non-mathematical and non-scientific texts that a culture produces. Mathematical and scientific texts, on the other hand, are interpreted primarily in denotative ways. But this does not mean that meaning in science is encoded necessarily denotatively. On the contrary, many of the theories and models of science, as the philosopher Max Black argued in 1962[1], are born of metaphorical thinking, even though they end up being interpreted denotatively over time. The theory of atomic structure, for instance, is presented as a tiny universe, with a sun (nucleus) and orbiting planets (electrons, protons, etc.). The end result is a theory that extends a model that at the time it was fashioned was already familiar to scientists.

In order to capture the power of language as a highly productive connotative system Benveniste sets out the formal principles of language pointing out that meaning systems are largely associative in structure and interconnected with nonverbal ones. As mentioned, semioticians seek answers to the *what*, the *how*, and the *why* of meaning. But what is *meaning*? And indeed what happens when we define the *meaning* of a sign? Take the dictionary definition of *cat* as "a small carnivorous mammal domesticated since early times as a catcher of rats and mice and as a pet and existing in several distinctive breeds and varieties." The first problem that emerges with this definition is the use of *mammal* to define cat—i.e. it makes the unwarranted assumption that one is familiar with this term. But, then, what is a *mammal*? Once again, the dictionary definition is of little use because it defines *mammal* as "any of various warm-blooded vertebrate animals of the class Mammalia." And this leads to the question: What is an *animal*? The dictionary defines an *animal* as an *organism*, which it defines as an individual form of *life*, which it defines as the property that distinguishes living *organisms*. At this point the dictionary has gone into a loop—i.e. it has started to employ an already-used word, *organism*, to define *life*! This inbuilt circularity in definitions is even more apparent when the refer-

---

[1]*Models and Metaphors* (Ithaca: Cornell University Press, 1962).

ent is abstract.

So, like the axioms of arithmetic or geometry, the notion of *meaning* is best left undefined, and a system of principles or techniques set up to flesh out the meaning of words: e.g. by contrasting *love* with *hate*, *good* with *evil* it is possible to infer what the "meaning" of each is, *in relation to one another*. Benveniste suggests that in semiotics the term *meaning* entails, more specifically, the system of images and feelings that a sign elicits. These are shaped, on the one side, by previous experience with the sign's referent and, on the other side, by the social view of the referent. The *meaning* that a sign evokes is really a sign itself, or as Charles Peirce called it, an *interpretant* of the sign. The interpretant encompasses the specific designations, emotions, feelings, ideas, etc. that the sign evokes for a person at a certain point in time. As Peirce put it: "A sign addresses somebody, that is, creates in the mind of that person an equivalent sign, or perhaps a more developed sign." So, while *signification* designates a formal relation existing within the sign, *meaning* implies something external, namely, the responses that a specific sign elicits in the human being.

8. *Louis Hjelmslev*

The Danish linguist, Louis Hjelmslev (1899–1965), elaborated Saussurean theory into a framework known as *glossematics*, formalizing the Saussurean notions in a synthetic way. But, like Benveniste, Hjelmslev also emphasized that signs encompass not only internal denotative meaning, but a mass of information coming from outside the sign itself: namely, the historical meanings and connotations associated with the sign.

Essentially, Hjelmslev claims that the signifier or *expression* mode and the signified or *content* mode of signification have both paradigmatic and syntagmatic properties that, in tandem, generate meaning. To understand why a system of analysis is required in understanding a verbal structure such as a word, let us consider the phenomenon of the word itself. What is a word? Consider the word *green*. First, note that it is a legitimate signifier structurally—i.e. it is made up with legitimate English sounds (known as *phonemes*), connected in an appropriate fashion (according to English *syllable structure*). The signifier *çeñ*, on the other hand, is not an acceptable signifier because it contains two phonemes, represented by the alphabet characters *ç* and *ñ*, that do not exist in English. It violates paradigmatic structure. Nor is *gpeen* a legitimate signifier, even though each of its sounds are acceptable phonemes, because it violates syntagmatic syllable structure (the sequence *gp* does not occur in English to start a syllable). Now, consider what *green* denotes. It refers, of course, to a specific gradation on the light spectrum. The story of *green* is not complete, however, until we consider its connotations: e.g. *envy* ("She's *green* with envy"), *hope* ("The grass is always *greener* on the other side"), *youthfulness* ("He's at the *green* age of eighteen"), etc. This is how words function in all languages. But language is not just a collection of words. When words are used in verbal representation and communication they allow people to deliver messages in the form of *sentences* and *discourses*. These too exhibit such structural and signifying properties as paradigmaticity, syntagmaticity, denotation, connotation, and so on.

9. *Claude Lévi-Strauss*

The Belgian-born anthropologist based in Paris all his life, Claude Lévi-Strauss, proposes a theory of culture as an external manifestation of sign systems. Using kinship systems, Lévi-Strauss shows how structuralism can shed light on a variety of interconnected cultural phenomena.

Lévi-Strauss's argument is a crucial one. To elaborate upon structuralist method, as propounded by Lévi-Strauss, without taking away from a first-hand engagement in the reading, we take an illustrative digression here in the realm of food, so as to exemplify the method in our own terms.

At a biological level, survival without food is impossible. So, at a denotative level food is a survival substance. But, once again, given the representational instinct in the human species, food and eating invariably take on a whole range of connotations in social settings. The term that is often used to designate the connotations that food entails is *cuisine*. This refers to *what* we eat, *how* we make it, and *what* it tells us about the makers and eaters. At the level of culture, cuisine is perhaps more precisely definable as the agglomeration of the *food codes* that are found in the culture. So food denotes, first, bodily survival; second, it takes on specific connotative meanings in social settings; and, third, these meanings cohere into the various food codes (cuisine) that characterize what and how people eat in specific social settings.

Claude Lévi-Strauss himself traced the origin of food as a signifying system to the evolutionary distinction that he termed "the raw" vs. "the cooked." Cooked food is food that has been transformed by culture into something more than a survival substance. According to Lévi-Strauss this transformation was accomplished by two processes—roasting and boiling—both of which were among the first significant technological advances made by humans. Roasting is more primitive than boiling because it implies a direct contact between the food and a fire. So, it is slightly above "the raw" in evolutionary terms. But boiling reveals an advanced form of technological thinking, since the cooking process in this case is mediated by a pot and a cooking process. Boiling was the event that led to "the cooked" form of eating. This dichotomy has hardly disappeared. In some parts of the world it has been enshrined into the social system to connote social relations. In the Hindu caste system, for instance, the higher castes may receive only raw food from the lower castes; whereas the lower castes are allowed to accept any kind of cooked food from any caste.

Raw food is tied to survival and cooked food to culture. Indeed, it might even be claimed, as do some anthropologists, that the cooking of food was *the* event that laid the foundations of culture. When especially favorable food sources became available, early humans settled in permanent, year-round communities, learning to domesticate plants and animals for food, transportation, clothing, and other uses. With greater population concentrations and permanent living sites, cultural institutions developed, united by religious ceremonies and food exchanges. These early hunting-gathering societies soon developed complex belief systems with regard to the supernatural world, the so-called *forces of Nature*, and the behaviors of spirits and gods. Food thus became a part of ritual and a staple of symbolic life. Early food symbolism still reverberate in our perception of food. Indeed, the world's religious ceremonies are still centered on food. The *raison d'être* of the Catholic Mass, for instance, is to partake symbolically of the consecrated body and blood of Christ. Specific types of food are served and eaten traditionally at Thanksgiving, Easter, Christmas, and so on. Food invariably is a primary constituent of all kinds of ceremonies and rituals, from feasts (weddings, Bar Mitzvahs, etc.) to simple social gatherings. We schedule "breakfast," "lunch," and "dinner" events on a daily basis. Indeed, we plan our days around meals. Even going out on a common date would be virtually unthinkable without some eating component associated with this courtship ritual (ranging from the popcorn eaten at movie theaters to the elaborate meals consumed at trendy restaurants).

The essence of structuralist method is to oppose things to each other in order to get a sense of their cultural valence. In the domain of food, the relevant opposition is *edibility* vs. *inedibility*. The fact that in our culture rabbits, cats, and dogs, for instance, are felt to be "household pets," forces us to perceive cooked rabbit, cat, and dog meat as "inedible." Unless one is a vegetarian, this does not mean that one considers all meat inedible. In our culture, bovine meat (beef steaks, hamburgers, etc.), lamb meat, and poultry meat are eaten routinely, with few negative perceptions. The animals that are slaughtered, cooked, and eaten regularly are hardly perceived in the same way as are rabbits, cats, and dogs. Predictably, such cultural perceptions are not universal. In India, a cow is classified as "sacred" and, therefore, as "inedible"—incidentally, this is the basis of our expression *sacred cow* to refer to something unassailable and revered. Anglo-American culture does not classify foxes or dogs as edible food items; but the former is reckoned a delicacy in Russia, and the latter a delicacy in China. Need it be mentioned that some people even eat human meat (known technically as *anthropophagitism* or *cannibalism*)?

So, edibility turns out to be more a product of Culture than of Nature. Outside of those which have a demonstrably harmful effect on the human organism, the species of flora and fauna that are considered to be edible or inedible is very much an arbitrary cultural decision. Perceptions of edibility have a basis in history, not digestive processes. We cannot get nourishment from eating tree bark, grass, or straw. But we certainly could get it from eating frogs, ants, earthworms, silkworms, lizards, and snails. Most people in our culture would, of course, respond with disgust and revulsion at the thought of eating such potential food items. However, there are cultures where they are not only eaten for nourishment, but also considered to be delicacies. Our expression *to develop a taste* for some "strange" food reveals how closely tied edibility is to cultural perception.

10. *Charles Morris*

The American Charles Morris (1901–1979) divided semiotics into the study of the relations between a sign and other signs, which he called *syntactics*; the relations between signs and their denotative meanings, which he called *semantics*; and the relations between signs and interpreters, which he called *pragmatics*.

The relation between language, thought in behavior is the essence of the Morris agenda. Without delving into the reading here, we take a brief excursion into the nature of this relation here. Do linguistic categories influence or determine how people view the world? This idea is called the Whorfian hypothesis, after the American anthropological linguist Benjamin Lee Whorf (1897–1941), even though versions can be found before Whorf. Morris' analysis starts by classifying linguistic structures according to a common range of meaning which is said to constitute a semantic domain. Such a domain is characterized by the distinctive features that differentiate individual items in the domain from one another, and also by features shared by all the items in the domain. For example, in the domain where "seat" occurs in English can be found the words "chair," "sofa," "loveseat," and "bench." These can be distinguished from one another according to how many people are accommodated and whether a back support is included. At the same time all these items share the common component, or feature, of meaning "something on which to sit."

In structuralism, the hope is to identify a universal set of such semantic features, from which are drawn the different sets of features that characterize different languages. This idea of universal semantic features has been applied to the analysis of systems of myth and kinship in various cultures, as we saw, by Lévi-Strauss, who showed that people organize their societies and interpret their place in these societies in ways that, despite apparent differences, have remarkable underlying similarities. More importantly, such linguists claim that these features predispose an individual to attend to certain objects and events in the world. In a phrase, they influence or shape the individual's thinking and, above all else, behavior.

Morris suggests that the structure of language not only has an effect on what we do and believe, but upon the ways in which we respond to verbal forms. In effect, language predisposes its users to view certain things, events, people, etc. in terms of categories imprinted in verbal signs.

11. *Roland Barthes*

The French semiotician Roland Barthes (1915–1980) has become widely known for claiming that systems of representation are largely based on mythical concepts which manifest themselves in the content of everyday discourses, spectacles, performances, and common-sensical notions. Barthes studied popular culture extensively, demonstrating how common conversations, performances, and spectacles recall the ancient myths through connotation. Recreational wrestling, for instance, is far from being just a sport, Barthes emphasized. Rather, it is a complex spectacle grafted from the mythic connotations associated with the bodily shapes, facial expressions, excessive gestures, and speech of the wrestlers. Taking his cue from Hjelmslev, Barthes argued that connotation is the operative principle in all forms of cultural meaning-making.

Barthes is also associated with the so-called *New Criticism*, a literary movement in Europe and the United States, prominent after World War II, which emphasized interpreting the written text in itself, apart from considerations of a biographical, cultural, or historical nature.

In this passage he deals with the language vs. speech or *langue* vs. *parole* dichotomy. Again, without intruding into the reader's engagement with the text, we would like to comment simply that this dichotomy has always been a critical one in semiotics and linguistics. *Langue* was the term used by Saussure to refer to the largely unconscious knowledge that speakers of a language share about what forms and grammatical structures are appropriate in that language; *parole* was the use of language in various situations. He made an analogy to the game of chess to clarify the crucial difference between these two terms. The ability to play chess, he observed, is dependent upon knowledge of its langue, i.e. of the rules of movement of the pieces—no matter how brilliantly or poorly someone plays, what the chess board or pieces are made of, what the color and size of the pieces are. *Langue* is a mental code that is independent of such variables. Now, the actual ways in which a person plays a specific game—why he or she made the moves that he or she did, how she or he used his or her past knowledge of the game to plan his or her strategies and tactics, etc.—are dependent instead on the person's particular execution abilities, i.e. on his or her control of *parole*. In an analogous fashion, Saussure suggested, the ability to speak and understand a language is dependent upon knowing the rules of the language game (langue); whereas the actual use of the rules in certain situations is dependent instead upon execution (psychological, social, and communicative) factors (*parole*).

Barthes and others argue that the two are interconnected, one suggesting the other, rather than separate or autonomous dimensions of language. A true semiology of language, therefore, would take both into account.

12. *Thomas A. Sebeok*

The late American semiotician and linguist, Thomas A. Sebeok (1920–2001), was famous for his work on animal communication, sign theory, and the establishment of the fields of zoosemiotics and biosemiotics. Sebeok was instrumental in showing the relevance of semiotics to those working in cognate disciplines.

His study of semiosis is especially insightful. Known as the *biosemiotic* or *global semiotic* movement, the Sebeokean agenda is starting to attract an increasing larger cadre of semioticians and scholars in cognate disciples. The basic message of that movement is that that *life is semiosis*—and thus largely implanted in the innate tendency for producing and understanding signs. The signs that we produce are thus hardly arbitrarily-conceived artifacts, but rather they are structures that emanate from bodily experiences. They are "signs of life," so to say. People and animals are so vastly different, yet, paradoxically, very much the same. That is the contradiction of life. No life science other than biosemiotics is capable of penetrating this contradiction, as Sebeok, so cogently argued throughout his illustrious career.

The crucial distinction that Sebeok made in his writings was between *semiosis* as a product of biological processes, and *representation* as the activity of capturing, portraying, simulating, or relaying impressions, sensations, perceptions, ideas, etc. in conventionalized ways—through language, art, music, etc. Semiosis is a product of Nature, representation of Culture. Representational strategies allow human beings to refer to virtually anything they notice or find interesting in their world. Indeed, representation is so powerful cognitively, that human beings rarely fail to differentiate themselves from their representational forms. In chapter 3 of his 1986 book *I Think I Am a Verb* (1986), Sebeok brought this out by explaining the title of his book, which refers to a phrase uttered by the eighteenth President of the United States, Ulysses S. Grant, just before he died. For Sebeok it encapsulated the fact that human beings see themselves as signs. Verbs refer to actions, change, existence; they are perfect instantiations of sign activity, of the infinite capacity to generate signification—literally the "making of signs"—in order to construct models of reality. Grant's phrase thus nicely captures the essence of the human condition—the urgent need to capture, represent, and interpret the dynamic flux of the world in the form of signs, including the mystery of the Self. Sebeok's work is useful for examining the dynamics and manifestations of this very condition.

Readings

Marcel Danesi and Paul Perron

1
The Sign

St. Augustine[1]

Just as I began, when I was writing about things, by warning that no one should consider them except as they are, without reference to what they signify beyond themselves, now when I am discussing signs I wish it understood that no one should consider them for what they are but rather for their value as signs which signify something else. A sign is a thing which causes us to think of something beyond the impression the thing itself makes upon the senses. Thus if we see a track, we think of the animal that made the track; if we see smoke, we know that there is a fire which causes it; if we hear the voice of a living being, we attend to the emotion it expresses; and when a trumpet sounds, a soldier should know whether it is necessary to advance or to retreat, or whether the battle demands some other response.

Among signs, some are natural and others are conventional. Those are natural which, without any desire or intention of signifying, make us aware of something beyond themselves, like smoke which signifies fire. It does this without any will to signify, for even when smoke appears alone, observation and memory of experience with things bring a recognition of an underlying fire. The track of a passing animal belongs to this class, and the face of one who is wrathful or sad signifies his emotion even when he does not wish to show that he is wrathful or sad, just as other emotions are signified by the expression even when we do not deliberately set out to show them. But it is not proposed here to discuss signs of this type. Since the class formed a division of my subject, I could not disregard it completely, and this notice of it will suffice.

Conventional signs are those which living creatures show to one another for the purpose of conveying, in so far as they are able, the motion of their spirits or something which they have sensed or understood. Nor is there any other reason for signifying, or for giving signs, except for bringing forth and transferring to another mind the action of the mind in the person who makes the sign. We propose to consider and to discuss this class of signs in so far as men are connected with it, for even signs given by God and contained in the Holy Scriptures are of

---

[1] *On Christian Doctrine* (c. 427), book II, trans. by D. W. Robertson, Jr. (New York: Macmillan, 1986); and *On the Trinity*, bk. XV, 10, 15, trans. by A. W. Haddan, *Basic Writings of Saint Augustine*, ed. by W. J. Oates (New York: Random House, 1948), vol. 2.

41

this type also, since they were presented to us by the men who wrote them. Animals also have signs which they use among themselves, by means of which they indicate their appetites. For a cock who finds food makes a sign with his voice to the hen so that she runs to him. And the dove calls his mate with a cry or is called by her in turn, and there are many similar examples which may be adduced. Whether these signs, or the expression or cry of a man in pain, express the motion of the spirit without intention of signifying or are truly shown as signs is not in question here and does not pertain to our discussion, and we remove this division of the subject from this work as superfluous.

Among the signs by means of which men express their meanings to one another, some pertain to the sense of sight, more to the sense of hearing, and very few to the other senses. For when we nod, we give a sign only to the sight of the person whom we wish by that sign to make a participant in our will. Some signify many things through the motions of their hands, and actors give signs to those who understand with the motions of all their members as if narrating things to their eyes. And banners and military standards visibly indicate the will of the captains. And all of these things are like so many visible words. More signs, as I have said, pertain to the ears, and most of these consist of words. But the trumpet, the flute, and the harp make sounds which are not only pleasing but also significant, although as compared with the number of verbal signs the number of signs of this kind are few. For words have come to be predominant among men for signifying whatever the mind conceives if they wish to communicate it to anyone. However, Our Lord gave a sign with the odor of the ointment with which His feet were anointed; and the taste of the sacrament of His body and blood signified what He wished; and when the woman was healed by touching the hem of His garment, something was signified. Nevertheless, a multitude of innumerable signs by means of which men express their thoughts is made up of words. And I could express the meaning of all signs of the type here touched upon in words, but I would not be able at all to make the meanings of words clear by these signs.

But because vibrations in the air soon pass away and remain no longer that they sound, signs of words have been constructed by means of letters.Thus words are shown to the eyes, not in themselves but through certain signs which stand for them. These signs could not be common to all peoples because of the sin of human dissension which arises when one people seizes the leadership for itself. A sign of this pride is that tower erected in the heavens where impious men deserved that not only their minds but also their voices should be dissonant.

Whoever, then, is able to understand a word, not only before it is uttered in sound, but also before the images of its sounds are considered in thought—for this it is which belongs to no tongue, to wit, of those which are called the tongues of nations, of which our Latin tongue is one—whoever, I say, is able to understand this, is able now to see through this glass and in this enigma some likeness of that Word of whom it is said, "In the beginning was the Word, and the Word was with God, and the Word was God." For of necessity, when we speak what is true, i.e. speak what we know, there is born from the knowledge itself which the memory retains, a word that is altogether of the same kind with that knowledge from which it is born. For the thought that is formed by the thing which we know, is the word which we speak in the heart: which word is neither Greek nor Latin, nor of any other tongue. But when it is needful to convey this to the knowledge of those to whom we speak, then some sign is assumed whereby to signify it. And generally a sound, sometimes a nod, is exhibited, the former to the ears, the latter to the eyes, that the word which we bear in our mind may become known also by bodily signs to the bodily senses. For what is to nod or beckon, except to speak in some way to the sight? And Holy Scripture gives its testimony to this; for we read in the *Gospel according to John:* "Verily, verily, I say *unto you,* that one of you shall betray me. Then the disciples looked one upon another, doubting of whom He spake. Now there was leaning on Jesus' breast one of His disciples whom Jesus loved. Simon Peter therefore beckons to him, and says to him, Who is it of whom He speaks?" Here he spoke by beckoning what he did not venture to speak by sounds. But whereas we exhibit these and the like bodily signs either to ears or eyes of persons present to whom we speak, letters have been invented that we might be able to converse also with the absent; but these are signs of words, as words themselves are signs in our conversation of those things which we think.

And hence it comes to pass, that if there can be in the mind any knowledge that is eternal, while the thought of that knowledge cannot be eternal, and any inner and true word of ours is only said by our thought, then God alone can be understood to have a Word that is eternal, and co-eternal with Himself unless, perhaps, we are to say that the very possibility of thought—since that which is known is capable of being truly thought, even at the time when it is not being thought—constitutes a word as perpetual as the knowledge itself is perpetual. But how is that a word which is not yet formed in the vision of the thought? How will it be like the knowledge of which it is born, if it has not the form of that knowledge, and is only now called a word because it can have it? For it is much as if one were to say that a word is to be so called because it can be a word. But what is this that can be a word, and is therefore already held worthy of the name of a word? What, I say, is this thing that is formable, but not yet formed, except a something in our mind, which we toss to and fro by revolving it this way or that, while we think of first one thing and then another, according as they are found by or occur to us? And the true word then comes into being, when, as I said, that which we toss to and fro by revolving it arrives at that which we know, and is formed by that, in taking its entire likeness; so that in what manner each thing is known, in that manner also it is thought, i.e. is said in this manner in the heart, without articulate sound, without thought of articulate sound, such as no doubt belongs to some particular tongue. And hence if we even admit, in order not to dispute laboriously about a name, that this something of our mind, which can be formed from our knowledge, is to be already called a word, even before it is so formed, because it is, so to say, already formable, who would not see how great would be the unlikeness between it and that Word of God, which is so in the form of God, as not to have been formable before it was formed, or to have been capable at any time of being formless, but is a simple form, and simply equal to Him from whom it is, and with whom it is wonderfully co-eternal?

2
Signification

John Poinsot[1]

A term, no less than a statement and a proposition, and any other logical instrument, is defined by means of signification. This is due to the fact that the understanding knows by means of the signification of concepts, and expresses what it knows by means of the signification of sounds, so that, without exception, all the instruments which we use for knowing and speaking are signs. Therefore, if the student of logic is to know his tools—namely, terms and statements—in an exact manner, it is necessary that he should also know what a sign is. *The sign*, therefore *admits of the following general definition:* "That which represents something other than itself to a cognitive power."

To better understand this definition, one must consider that there is a fourfold cause of knowledge namely, a productive, objective, formal, and instrumental cause. The productive or efficient cause is the power itself which elicits an act of knowledge, for example, the eye, the ear, the understanding. The object is the thing which stimulates or toward which a cognition tends, as when I see a stone or a man. The formal cause is the awareness itself whereby a power is rendered cognizant, as the sight itself of the stone or of the man. The instrumental cause is the means by which the object is represented to the power, as a picture of Caesar represents Caesar. The object is threefold, to wit, stimulative only, terminative only, both stimulative and terminative at once. An object that is only a stimulus is one that arouses a power to form an awareness not of the stimulating object itself, but of another object, as, for example, the picture of the emperor, which moves the power to know the emperor. An object that is terminative only is a thing known through an awareness produced by some other object, for example, the emperor known through the picture. An object that is simultaneously terminative and stimulative is one that arouses a power to form a cognition of the very object stimulating, as when the wall is seen in itself.

Thus, "making cognizant" has wider extension than does "representing", and "representing" more than "signifying". For *to make cognizant* is said of every cause concurring in the production of knowledge; and so it is said in *four* ways, namely, effectively, objectively, formally,

---

[1] John of St. Thomas, *Ars Logica* (1632), Parts I and II, trans. by John Deely, *Tractatus de Signis: The Semiotic of John Poinsot* (Berkeley: University of California Press, 1985), pp. 25-27, 135-137. Permission granted from John Deely.

and instrumentally. *Effectively,* as of the power itself eliciting cognition and of the causes concurring in that production, as of God moving, the understanding, acting or producing, specifying forms, the inclinations of habit, etc. *Objectively,* as of the very thing which is known. For example, if I know a man, the man as an object makes himself known by presenting himself to the power. *Instrumentally,* as of the awareness itself, which as a form, makes the power know *instrumentally,* as of the very medium or means bearing object to power, as the picture of the emperor conveys the emperor to the understanding as a medium, and this means we call the instrument. To *represent* is said of each factor which makes anything become present to a power, and so is said in *three* ways, namely, *objectively, formally,* and *instrumentally.* For an object such as the wall represents itself objectively, an awareness represents formally, a footprint instrumentally. To *signify* is said of that by which something distinct from itself becomes present, and so is said in only *two* ways, namely, formally and instrumentally.

Hence arises the twofold *division of the sign.* For insofar as signs are ordered *to a power,* they are divided into formal and instrumental signs; but insofar as signs are ordered *to something signified,* they are divided according to the cause of that ordering into natural and stipulative and customary. A formal sign is the formal awareness which represents of itself, not by means of another. An instrumental sign is one that represents something other than itself from a pre-existing cognition of itself as an object, as the footprint of an ox represents an ox. And this definition is usually given for signs generally. A natural sign is one that represents from the nature of a thing, independently of any stipulation and custom whatever, and so it represents the same for all, as smoke signifies a fire burning. A stipulated sign is one that represents something owing to an imposition by the will of a community, like the linguistic expression "man". A customary sign is one that represents from use alone without any public imposition, as napkins upon the table signify a meal.

To get to the point of difficulty, it is necessary to distinguish the several relations which can concur in a sign. There is no doubt that some of these relations could exist in a natural sign independently of mind, yet they are not the formal and definitive relation of sign. A sign by its definition is "that which represents something to a knowing power." If the sign is outside the cognitive power, in order to represent another it must have in itself the rationale of an object knowable in itself, so that the cognitive power might arrive at another by knowing the sign. If, on the other hand, the sign is a formal sign and within the power, in order to represent another it must be an intentional representation independent of being itself known objectively, which in the physical order is a kind of quality, yet one with a relation of similitude to that of which it is a representation, and with an order to the power.

Similarly, for a sign to be said to represent this rather than that, there has to be in it some congruence or proportion and connection with the given significate. This proportion or congruence can take several forms. Sometimes it is one of an effect to a cause or of cause to effect, as, for example, smoke as an effect signifies fire, clouds or wind as a cause signify rain. Sometimes it is one of similitude or of an image or of whatever other proportion. But in the case of stipulated signs, it is the imposition and appointment, the acceptance, by common usage. In a word: since a sign functions relative to a significate and to a cognitive power, the respects or rationales which habilitate it to the power or those which habilitate it to the signified can precede the forming of the rationale of a sign. But the formal and definitive rationale of a sign does not consist in these, nor does its relation to the thing signified, since indeed they can be separated and found apart from the rationale of a sign. For the rationale of an object is found without the rationale of a sign; and the rationale of an effect or cause or similitude or image can also be found apart from the rationale of a sign. Again because a relation to some thing bespeaks diverse fundaments and formal rationales, as, for example: the relation to an effect or a cause, which is founded on an action; or the relation of an image, which is founded on a similarity of imitation without an order to a cognitive power; or the relation of a sign, which is founded on the measured's being relative to its measure in the mode of a representative substituting for another in an order to a cognitive power, which the other relations do not respect.

We ask, therefore, whether that formal and most proper sign-relation which is found in addition to or as arising from all those involved in the habilitation of a sign to its significate or to a cognitive power, is a mind independent relation in the case of physical or natural signs. And we certainly acknowledge that the relation of object to power, which precedes the sign-relation in the case of the instrumental sign, whether by way of stimulating or of terminating, is not a mind-independent relation, because an object does not respect a power by a relation that is mind-independent according to the way it has being, but rather the power respects the object and depends upon and is specified by it. And supposing that the relation of object to power were mind-independent, and that the object reciprocally respects the power in just the way that the power respects the object (which is certainly an assumption contrary to fact, since the object is the measure and the power the measured), this relation still would not be the relation nor the rationale of the sign, because the rationale of an object formally and directly respects or is respected by the power in such a way that the respect between the two is immediate; but the rationale of a sign directly respects a signified and a power indirectly, because it respects the thing signified as that which is to be manifested to a cognitive power. There-

fore there is a different fine and order of respecting in an object inasmuch as it is an object, and in a sign inasmuch as it is a sign, although
for it to be a sign, an object must be supposed.

I answer the question before us therefore by saying: The relation of
a natural sign to its significate by which the sign is constituted in being
as a sign, is mind-independent and not mind-dependent, considered in
itself and by virtue of its fundament and presupposing the existence of
the terminus and the other conditions for a mind- independent or physical relation.

3

A Theory of the Sign

Charles S. Peirce[1]

I. *What is a* Sign? *Three Divisions of Logic*

Logic, in its general sense, is, as I believe I have shown, only another
name for *semiotic* (σημειωτική), the quasi-necessary, or formal, doctrine
of signs. By describing the doctrine as "quasi-necessary," or formal, I
mean that we observe the characters of such signs as we know, and
from such an observation, by a process which I will not object to naming Abstraction, we are led to statements, eminently fallible, and therefore in one sense by no means necessary, as to what *must be* the characters of all signs used by a "scientific" intelligence, that is to say, by an
intelligence capable of learning by experience. As to that process of
abstraction, it is itself a sort of observation. The faculty which I call
abstractive observation is one which ordinary people perfectly recognize, but for which the theories of philosophers sometimes hardly leave
room. It is a familiar experience to every human being to wish for something quite beyond this present means, and to follow that wish by the
question, "Should I wish for that thing just the same, if I had ample
means to gratify it?" To answer that question, he searches this heart,
and in doing so makes what I term an abstractive observation. He
makes in this imagination a sort of skeleton diagram, or outline sketch,
of himself, considers what modifications the hypothetical state of things
would require to be made in that picture, and then examines it, that is,
observes what he has imagined, to see whether the same ardent desire is
there to be discerned. By such a process, which is at bottom very much
like mathematical reasoning, we can reach conclusions as *to* what *would
be* true of signs in all cases, so long as the intelligence using them was
scientific. The modes of thought of a God, who should possess an intuitive omniscience superseding reason, are put out of the question. Now
the whole process of development among the community of students of
those formulations by abstractive observation and reasoning of the
truths which *must* hold good of all signs used by a scientific intelligence
is an observational science, like any other positive science, notwithstanding its strong contrast to all the special sciences which arises from
its aiming to find out what *must be* and not merely what is in the actual
world.

---

[1] Charles S. Peirce, *The Collected Papers of Charles Sanders Peirce*, Volumes I and II, edited
by Charles Hartshorne and Paul Wiess (Cambridge, Mass.: Harvard University Press,
1931–1958).

A sign, or *representamen,* is something which stands to somebody for something in some respect or capacity. It addresses somebody, that is, creates in the mind of that person an equivalent sign, or perhaps a more developed sign. That sign which it creates I call the *interpretant* of the first sign. The sign stands for something, its *object.* It stands for that object, not in all respects, but in reference to a sort of idea, which I have sometimes called the *ground* of the representamen. "Idea" is here to be understood in a sort of Platonic sense, very familiar in everyday talk; I mean in that sense in which we say that one man catches another man's idea, in which we say that when a man recalls what he was thinking of at some previous time, he recalls the same idea, and in which when a man continues to think anything, say for a tenth of a second, in so far as the thought continues to agree with itself during that time, that is to have a *like* content, it is the same idea, and is not at each instant of the interval a new idea.

In consequence of every representamen being thus connected with three things, the ground, the object, and the interpretant, the science of semiotic has three branches. The first is called by Duns Scotus *grammatica speculativa.* We may term it *pure grammar.* It has for its task to ascertain what must be true of the representamen used by every scientific intelligence in order that they may embody any *meaning.* The second is logic proper. It is the science of what is quasi-necessarily true of the representamens of any scientific intelligence in order that they may hold good of any *object,* that is, may be true. Or say, logic proper is the formal science of the conditions of the truth of representations. The third, in imitation of Kant's fashion of preserving old associations of words in finding nomenclature for new conceptions, I call *pure rhetoric.* Its task is to ascertain the laws by which in every scientific intelligence one sign gives birth to another, and especially one thought brings forth another.

A *Sign,* or *Representamen,* is a First which stands in such a genuine triadic relation to a Second, called its *Object,* as to be capable of determining a Third, called its *Interpretant,* to assume the same triadic relation to its Object in which it stands itself to the same Object. The triadic relation is *genuine,* that is its three members are bound together by it in a way that does not consist in any complexus of dyadic relations. That is the reason the Interpretant, or Third, cannot stand in a mere dyadic relation to the Object, but must stand in such a relation to it as the Representamen itself does. Nor can the triadic relation in which the Third stands be merely similar to that in which the First stands, for this would make the relation of the Third to the First a degenerate Secondness merely. The Third must indeed stand in such a relation, and thus must be capable of determining a Third of its own; but besides that, it must have a second triadic relation in which the Representamen, or rather the relation thereof to its Object, shall be its own (the Third's) Object, and must be capable of determining a Third to this relation. All this must equally be true of the Third's Thirds and so on endlessly; and this, and more, is involved in the familiar idea of a Sign; and as the term Representamen is here used, nothing more is implied. A *Sign* is a Representamen with a mental Interpretant. Possibly there may be Representamens that are not Signs. Thus, if a sunflower, in turning toward the sun, becomes by that very act fully capable, without further condition, of reproducing a sunflower which turns in precisely corresponding ways toward the sun, and of doing so with the same reproductive power, the sunflower would become a Representamen of the sun. But *thought* is the chief, if not the only, mode of representation.

The Sign can only represent the Object and tell about it. It cannot furnish acquaintance with or recognition of that Object; for that is what is meant in this volume by the Object of a Sign; namely, that with which it presupposes an acquaintance in order to convey some further information concerning it. No doubt there will be readers who will say they cannot comprehend this. They think a Sign need not relate to anything otherwise known, and can make neither head nor tail of the statement that every sign must relate to such an Object. But if there be anything that conveys information and yet has absolutely no relation nor reference to anything with which the person to whom it conveys the information has, when he comprehends that information, the slightest acquaintance, direct or indirect—and a very strange sort of information that would be—the vehicle of that sort of information is not, in this volume, called a Sign.

Two men are standing on the seashore looking out to sea. One of them says to the other, "That vessel there carries no freight at all, but only passengers." Now, if the other, himself, sees no vessel, the first information he derives from the remark has for its Object the part of the sea that he does see, and informs him that a person with sharper eyes than his, or more trained in looking for such things, can see a vessel there; and then, that vessel having been thus introduced to this acquaintance, he is prepared to receive the information about it that it carries passengers exclusively. But the sentence as a whole has, for the person supposed, no other Object than that with which it finds him already acquainted. The Objects—for a Sign may have any number of them—may each be a single known existing thing or thing believed formerly to have existed or expected to exist, or a collection of such things, or a known quality or relation or fact, which single Object may be a collection, or whole of parts, or it may have some other mode of being, such as some act permitted whose being does not prevent its negation from being equally permitted, or something of a general nature desired, required, or invariably found under certain general circumstances.

2. *Three Trichotomies of Signs*

Signs are divisible by three trichotomies; first, according as the sign in itself is a mere quality, is an actual existent, or is a general law; secondly, according as the relation of the sign to its object consists in the sign's having some character in itself, or in some existential relation to that object, or in its relation to an interpretant; thirdly, according as its Interpretant represents it as a sign of possibility or as a sign of fact or a sign of reason.

I

According to the first division, a Sign may be termed a *Qualisign*, a *Sinsign*, or a *Legisign*.

A *Qualisign is* a quality which is a Sign. It cannot actually act as a sign until it is embodied; but the embodiment has nothing to do with its character as a sign.

A *Sinsign* (where the syllable *sin is* taken as meaning "being only once," as in *single, simple,* Latin *semel,* etc.) is an actual existent thing or event which is a sign. It can only be so through its qualities; so that it involves a qualisign, or rather, several qualisigns. But these qualisigns are of a peculiar kind and only form a sign through being actually embodied.

A Legisign is a law that is a Sign. This law is usually established by men. Every conventional sign is a legisign [but not conversely]. It is not a single object, but a general type which, it has been agreed, shall be significant. Every legisign signifies through an instance of its application, which may be termed a *Replica* of it. Thus, the word "the" will usually occur from fifteen to twenty-five times on a page. It is in all these occurrences one and the same word, the same legisign. Each single instance of it is a Replica. The Replica is a Sinsign. Thus, every Legisign requires Sinsigns. But these are not ordinary Sinsigns, such as are peculiar occurrences that are regarded as significant. Nor would the Replica be significant if it were not for the law which renders it so.

II

According to the second trichotomy, a Sign may be termed an *Icon*, an *Index*, or a *Symbol*.

An *Icon is* a sign which refers to the Object that it denotes merely by virtue of characters of its own, and which it possesses, just the same, whether any such Object actually exists or not. It is true that unless there really is such an Object, the Icon does not act as a sign; but this has nothing to do with its character as a sign. Anything whatever, be it quality, existent individual, or law, is an Icon of anything, in so far as it is like that thing and used as a sign of it.

An *Index* is a sign which refers to the Object that it denotes by virtue of being really affected by that Object. It cannot, therefore, be a Qualisign, because qualities are whatever they are independently of anything else. In so far as the Index is affected by the Object, it necessarily has some Quality in common with the Object, and it is in respect to these that it refers to the Object. It does, therefore, involve a sort of Icon, although an Icon of a peculiar kind; and it is not the mere resemblance of its Object, even in these respects which makes it a sign, but it is the actual modification of it by the Object.

A *Symbol* is a sign which refers to the Object that it denotes by virtue of a law, usually an association of general ideas, which operates to cause the Symbol to be interpreted as referring to that Object. It is thus itself a general type or law, that is, is a Legisign. As such it acts through a Replica. Not only is it general itself, but the Object to which it refers is of a general nature Now that which is general has its being in the instances which it will determine. There must, therefore, be existent instances of what the Symbol denotes, although we must here understand by "existent," existent in the possibly imaginary universe to which the Symbol refers. The Symbol will indirectly, through the association or other law, be affected by those instances; and thus the Symbol will involve a sort of Index, although an Index of a peculiar kind. It will not, however, be by any means true that the slight effect upon the Symbol of those instances accounts for the significant character of the Symbol.

III

According to the third trichotomy, a Sign may be termed a *Rheme*, a *Dicisign* or *Dicent Sign* (that is, a proposition or quasiproposition), or an *Argument*.

A *Rheme* is a Sign which, for its Interpretant, is a Sign of qualitative Possibility, that is, is understood as representing such and such a kind of possible Object. Any Rheme, perhaps, will afford some information; but it is not interpreted as doing so.

A *Dicent Sign*, is a Sign, which, for its Interpretant, is a Sign of actual existence. It cannot, therefore, be an Icon, which affords no "round for an interpretation of it as referring to actual existence. A Dicisign necessarily involves, as a part of it, a Rheme, to describe the fact which it is interpreted as indicating. But this is a peculiar kind of Rheme; and while it is essential to the Dicisign, it by no means constitutes it.

An *Argument* is a Sign which, for its Interpretant, is a Sign of law. Or we may say that a Rheme is a sign which is understood to represent its object in its characters merely; that a Dicisign is a sign which is understood to represent its object in respect to actual existence; and that an Argument is a Sign which is understood to represent its Object in its character as Sign. Since these definitions touch upon points at this time much in dispute, a word may be added in defence of them. A question often put is: What is the essence of a Judgment? A judgment is the mental act by which the judges seeks to impress upon himself the truth of a proposition. It is much the same as an act of asserting the proposition, or going before a notary and assuming formal responsibility for *its* truth, except that those acts are intended to affect others, while the judgment is only intended to affect oneself. However, the logician, as such, cares not what the psychological nature of the act of judging may be. The question for him is: What is the nature of the sort of sign of which a principal variety is called a proposition, which is the master upon which the act of judging is exercised? The proposition need not be asserted or judged. It may be contemplated as a sign capable of being asserted or denied. This sign itself retains its full meaning whether it be actually asserted or not. The peculiarity of it, therefore, lies in its mode of meaning; and to say this is to say that its peculiarity lies in its relation to its interpretant. The proposition professes to be really affected by the actual existent or real law to which it refers. The argument makes the same pretension, but that is not the principal pretension of the argument. The rheme makes no such pretension.

3. *Icon, Index, and Symbol*

A. SYNOPSIS

A sign is either an *icon,* an *index,* or a *symbol.* An *icon* is a sign which would possess the character which renders it significant, even though its object had no existence; such as a lead-pencil streak as representing a geometrical fine. An *index* is a sign which would, at once, lose the character which makes it a sign if its object were removed, but would not lose that character if there were no interpretant. Such, for instance, is a piece of mould with a bullet-hole in it as sign of a shot; for without the shot there would have been no hole; but there is a hole there, whether anybody has the sense to attribute it to a shot or not. A *symbol* is a sign which would lose the character which renders it a sign if there were no interpretant. Such is any utterance of speech which signifies what it does only by virtue of its being understood to have that signification.

B. ICON

. . . While no Representamen actually functions as such until it actually determines an Interpretant, yet it becomes a Representamen as soon as it is fully capable of doing this; and its Representative Quality is not necessarily dependent upon its ever actually determining an Interpretant, nor even upon its actually having an Object.

An *Icon* is a Representamen whose Representative Quality is a First-ness of it as a First. That is, a quality that it has *qua* thing renders it fit to be a representamen. Thus, anything is fit to be a *Substitute* for anything that it is like. (The conception of "substitute" involves that of a purpose, and thus of genuine thirdness.) Whether there are other kinds of sub-stitutes or not we shall see. A Representamen by Firstness alone can only have a similar Object. Thus, a Sign by Contrast denotes its object only by virtue of a contrast, or Secondness, between two qualifies. A sign by Firstness is an image of its object and, more strictly speaking, can only be an *idea*. For it must produce an Interpretant idea; and an external object excites an idea by a reaction upon the brain. But most strictly speaking, even an idea, except in the sense of a possibility, or firstness, cannot be an Icon. A possibility alone is an Icon purely by virtue of its quality; and its object can only be a Firstness. But a sign may be *iconic*, that is, may represent its object mainly by its similarity, no matter what its mode of being. If a substantive be wanted, an iconic rep-resentamen may be termed a *hypoicon*. Any material image, as a paint-ing, is largely conventional in its mode of representation; but in itself, without legend or label it may be called a *hypoicon*.

Hypoicons may be roughly divided according to the mode of First-ness of which they partake. Those which partake of simple qualities, or First Firstnesses, are *images;* those which represent the relations, mainly dyadic, or so regarded, of the parts of one thing by analogous relations in their own parts, are *diagrams;* those which represent the representa-tive character of a representamen by representing a parallelism in some-thing else, are *metaphors.*

The only way of directly communicating an idea is by means of an icon; and every indirect method of communicating an idea must depend for its establishment upon the use of an icon. Hence, every assertion must contain an icon or set of icons, or else must contain signs whose meaning is only explicable by icons. The idea which the set of icons (or the equivalent of a set of icons) contained in an assertion sig-nifies may be termed the *predicate* of the assertion.

Turning now to the rhetorical evidence, it is a familiar fact that there are such representations as icons. Every picture (however conventional its method) is essentially a representation of that kind. So is every dia-gram, even although there be no sensuous resemblance between it and its object, but only an analogy between the relations of the parts of each. Particularly deserving of notice are icons in which the likeness is aided by conventional rules. Thus, an algebraic formula is an icon, rendered such by the rules of commutation, association, and distribution of the symbols. It may seem at first glance that it is an arbitrary classification to call an algebraic expression an icon; that it might as well, or better, be regarded as a compound conventional sign. But it is not so. For a great distinguishing property of the icon is that by the direct observation of it other truths concerning its object can be discovered than those which suffice to determine its construction. Thus, by means of two photographs a map can be drawn, etc. Given a conventional or other general sign of an object, to deduce any other truth than that which it explicitly signifies, it is necessary, in all cases, to replace that sign by an icon. This capacity of revealing unexpected truth is precisely that wherein the utility of algebraical formulae consists, so that the iconic character is the prevailing one.

That icons of the algebraic kind, though usually very simple ones, exist in all ordinary grammatical propositions is one of the philosophic truths that the Boolean logic brings to light. In all primitive writing, such as the Egyptian hieroglyphics, there are icons of a non-logical kind, the ideographs. In the earliest form of speech, there probably was a large element of mimicry. But in all languages known, such representations have been replaced by conventional auditory sings. These, however, are such that they can only be explained by icons. But in the syntax of every language there are logical icons of the kind that are aided by conventional rules....

Photographs, especially instantaneous photographs, are very instructive, because we know that they are in certain respects exactly like the objects they represent. But this resemblance is due to the photographs having been produced under such circumstances that they were physically forced to correspond point by point to nature. In that aspect, then, they belong to the second class of signs, those by physical connection. The case is different if I surmise that zebras are likely to be obstinate, or otherwise disagreeable animals, because they seem to have a general resemblance to donkeys, and donkeys are self-willed. Here the donkey serves precisely as a probable likeness of the zebra. It is true we suppose that resemblance has a physical cause in heredity; but then, this hereditary affinity is itself only an inference from the likeness between the two animals, and we have not (as in the case of the photograph) any independent knowledge of the circumstances of the production of the two species. Another example of the use of a likeness is the design an artist draws of a statue, pictorial composition, architectural elevation, or piece of decoration, by the contemplation of which he can ascertain whether what he proposes will be beautiful and satisfactory. The question asked is thus answered almost with certainty because it relates to how the artist will himself be affected. The reasoning of mathematicians will be found to turn chiefly upon the use of likenesses, which are the very hinges of the gates of their science. The utility of likenesses to mathematicians consists in their suggesting in a very precise way, new aspects of supposed states of things....

Many diagrams resemble their objects not at all in looks; it is only in respect to the relations of their parts that their likeness consists. Thus, we may show the relation between the different kinds of signs by a brace, thus:

$$\text{Signs}: \left\{ \begin{array}{l} \text{Icons,} \\ \text{Indices} \\ \text{Symbols} \end{array} \right.$$

This is an icon. But the only respect in which it resembles its object is that the brace shows the classes of *icons, indices,* and *symbols* to be related to one another and to the general class of signs, as they really are, in a general way. When, in algebra, we write equations under one another in a regular array, especially when we put resembling letters for corresponding coefficients, the array is an icon. Here is an example:

$$a_1x+b_1y=n_1,$$
$$a_2x+b_2y=n_2.$$

This is an icon, in that it makes quantities look alike which are in analogous relations to the problem. In fact, every algebraical equation is an icon, in so far as it *exhibits*, by means of the algebraical signs (which are not themselves icons), the relations of the quantities concerned.

It may be questioned whether all icons are likenesses or not. For example, if a drunken man is exhibited in order to show, by contrast, the excellence of temperance, this is certainly an icon, but whether it is a likeness or not may be doubted. The question seems somewhat trivial.

C. INDEX

[An index is] a sign, or representation, which refers to its object not so much because of any similarity or analogy with it, nor because it is associated with general characters which that object happens to possess, as because it is in dynamical (including spatial) connection both with the individual object, on the one hand, and with the senses of memory of the person for whom it serves as a sign, on the other hand.... While demonstrative and personal pronouns are, as ordinarily used, "genuine indices," relative pronouns are "degenerate indices"; for though they may, accidentally and indirectly, refer to existing things, they directly refer, and need only refer, to the images in the mind which previous words have created.

Indices may be distinguished from other signs, or representations, by three characteristic marks: first, that they have no significant resemblance to their objects; second, that they refer to individuals, single units, single collections of units, or single continua; third, that they direct the attention to their objects by blind compulsion. But it would be difficult, if not impossible, to instance an absolutely pure index, or to find any sign absolutely devoid of the indexical quality. Psychologically, the action of indices depends upon association by contiguity, and not upon association by resemblance or upon intellectual operations.

An *Index* of *Seme* (σῆμα) is a Representamen whose Representative character consists in its being an individual second. If the Secondness is an existential relation, the Index is *genuine*. If the Secondness is a reference, the Index is *degenerate*. A genuine Index and its Object must be existent individuals (whether things or facts), and its immediate Interpretant must be of the same character. But since every individual must have characters, it follows that a genuine Index may contain a Firstness, and so an Icon as a constituent part of it. Any individual is a degenerate Index of its own characters.

Subindices or *Hyposemes* are signs which are rendered such principally by an actual connection with their objects. Thus a proper name, personal demonstrative, or relative pronoun or the letter attached to a diagram, denotes what it does owing to a real connection with its object, but none of these is an Index, since it is not an individual.

Let us examine some examples of indices. I see a man with a rolling gait. This is a probable indication that he is a sailor. I see a bowlegged man in corduroys, gaiters, and a jacket. These are probable indications that he is a jockey or something of the sort. A sundial or a clock *indicates* the time of day. Geometricians mark letters against the different parts of their diagrams and then use these letters to indicate those parts. Letters are similarly used by lawyers and others. Thus, we may say: If A and B are married to one another and C is their child while D is brother of A, then D is uncle of C. Here A, B, C, and D fulfill the office of relative pronouns, but are more convenient since they require no special collocation of words. A rap on the door is an index. Anything which focusses the attention is an index. Anything which startles us is an index, in so far as it marks the junction between two portions of experience. Thus a tremendous thunderbolt indicates that *something* considerable happened, though we may not know precisely what the event was. But it may be expected to connect itself with some other experience.

. . . A low barometer with a moist air is an index of rain; that is we suppose that the forces of nature establish a probable connection between the low barometer with moist air and coming rain. A weathercock is an index of the direction of the wind; because in the first place it really takes the self-same direction as the wind, so that there is a real connection between them, and in the second place we are so constituted that when we see a weathercock pointing in a certain direction it draws our attention to that direction, and when we see the weathercock veering with the wind, we are forced by the law of mind to think that direction is connected with the wind. The pole star is an index, or pointing finger, to shown us which way is north. A spirit-level, or a plumb bob, is an index of the vertical direction. A yard-stick might seem, at first sight, to be an icon of a yard; and so it would be, if it were merely intended to show a yard as near as it can be seen and estimated to be a yard. But the very purpose of a yard- stick is to show a yard nearer than it can be estimated by its appearance. This it does in consequence of an accurate mechanical comparison made with the bar in London called the yard. Thus it is a real connection which gives the yardstick its value as a representamen; and thus it is an *index*, not a mere *icon*.

When a driver to attract the attention of a foot passenger and cause him to save himself, calls out "Hi!" so far as this is a significant word, it is, as will be seen below, something more than an index; but so far as it is simply intended to act upon the hearer's nervous system and to rouse him to get out of the way, it is an index, because it is meant to put him in real connection with the object, which is this situation relative to the approaching horse. Suppose two men meet upon a country road and one of them says to the other, "The chimney of that house is on fire." The other looks about him and descries a house with green blinds and a verandah having a smoking chimney. He walks on a few miles and meets a second traveller. Like a Simple Simon he says, "The chimney of that house is on fire." "What house?" asks the other. "Oh, a house with green blinds and a verandah," replies the simpleton. "Where is the house?" asks the stranger. He desires some *index* which shall connect this apprehension with the house meant. Words alone cannot do this. The demonstrative pronouns, "this" and "that," are indices. For they call upon the hearer to use this powers of observation, and so establish a real connection between this mind and the object; and if the demonstrative pronoun does that—without which its meaning is not understood—it goes to establish such a connection; and so is an index. The relative pronouns, *who* and *which,* demand observational activity in much the same way, only with them the observation has to be directed to the words that have gone before. Lawyers use A, B, C, practically as very effective relative pronouns. To show how effective they are, we may note that Messrs. Allen and Greenough, in their admirable (though in the edition of 1877 [?], too small) Latin Grammar, declare that no conceivable syntax could wholly remove the ambiguity of the following sentence, "A replied to B that he thought C (his brother) more unjust to himself than to this own friend." Now, any lawyer would state that will perfect clearness, by using A, B, C, as relatives, thus:

$$\text{A replied to B that he } \left\{ \begin{matrix} A \\ B \end{matrix} \right\}, \text{ thought C (his } \left\{ \begin{matrix} A's \\ B's \end{matrix} \right\} \text{ brother)}$$

$$\text{more unjust to himself, } \left\{ \begin{matrix} A \\ B \\ C \end{matrix} \right\} \text{ than to his } \left\{ \begin{matrix} A's \\ B's \\ C's \end{matrix} \right\} \text{ own friend.}$$

The terminations which in any inflected language are attached to words "governed" by other words, and which serve to show which the governing word is, by repeating what is elsewhere expressed in the same form, are likewise *indices* of the same relative pronoun character. Any bit of Latin poetry illustrates this, such as the twelve-line sentence beginning, *"Jam satis terris."* Both in these terminations and in the A, B, C, a likeness is relied upon to carry the attention to the right object. But this does not make them icons, in any important way; for it is of no consequence how the letters A, B, C, are shaped or what the terminations are. It is not merely that one occurrence of an A is like a previous occurrence that is the important circumstance, but that *there is an understanding that like letters shall stand for the same thing,* and this acts as a force carrying the attention from one occurrence of A to the previous one. A possessive pronoun is two ways an index: first it indicates the possessor, and, second, it has a modification which syntactically carries the attention to the word denoting the thing possessed.

Some indices are more or less detailed directions for what the hearer is to do in order to place himself in direct experiential or other connection with the thing meant. Thus, the Coast Survey issues "Notices to Mariners," giving the latitude and longitude, four or five bearings or prominent objects, etc., and saying *there is* a rock, or shoal, or buoy, or lightship. Although there will be other elements in such directions, yet in the main they are indices.

Along with such indexical directions of what to do to find the object meant, ought to be classed those pronouns which should be entitled *selective* pronouns [or quantifiers] because they inform the hearer how he is to pick out one of the objects intended, but which grammarians call by the very indefinite designation of *indefinite* pronouns. Two varieties of these are particularly important in logic; the *universal selectives,* such as *quivis, quilibet, quisquam, ullus, nullus, nemo, quisque, uterque,* and in English, *any, every, all, no, none, whatever, whoever, everybody, anybody, nobody.* These mean that the hearer is at liberty to select any instance he likes within limits expressed or understood, and the assertion is intended to apply to that one. The other logically important variety consists of the *particular selectives, quis, quispiam, nescio quis, aliquis, quidam,* and in English, *some, something, somebody, a, a certain, some or other, a suitable, one.*

Allied to the above pronouns are such expressions as *all but one, one or two, a few, nearly all, every other one,* etc. Along with pronouns are to be classed adverbs of place and time, etc.

Not very unlike these are, *the first, the last, the seventh, two-thirds of, thousands of,* etc.

Other indexical words are prepositions, and prepositional phrases, such as, "on the right (or left) of." Right and left cannot be distinguished by any general description. Other prepositions signify relations which may, perhaps, be described; but when they refer, as they do oftener than would be supposed, to a situation relative to the observed, or assumed to be experientially known, place and attitude of the speaker relatively to that of the hearer, then the indexical element is the dominant element.

Icons and indices assert nothing. If an icon could be interpreted by a sentence, that sentence must be in a "potential mood," that is, it would merely say, "Suppose a figure has three sides," etc. Were an index so interpreted, the mood must be imperative, or exclamatory, as "See there!" or "Look out!" But the kind of signs which we are now coming to consider are, by nature, in the "indicative," or, as it should be called, the *declarative* mood. Of course, they can go to the expression of any other mood, since we may declare assertions to be doubtful, or mere interrogations, or imperatively requisite.

D. SYMBOL

A Symbol is a Representamen whose Representative character consists precisely in its being a rule that will determine its Interpretant. All words, sentences, books, and other conventional signs are Symbols. We speak of writing or pronouncing the word "man"; but it is only a *replica*, or embodiment of the word, that is pronounced or written. The word itself has no existence although it has a real being, *consisting in* the fact that existents *will* conform to it. It is a general mode of succession of three sounds or representamens of sounds, which becomes a sign only in the fact that a habit, or acquired law, will cause replicas of it to be interpreted as meaning a man or men. The word and its meaning are both general rules; but the word alone of the two prescribes the qualifies of its replicas in themselves. Otherwise the "word" and its "meaning" do not differ, unless some special sense be attached to "meaning."

A Symbol is a law, or regularity of the indefinite future. Its Interpretant must be of the same description; and so must be also the complete immediate Object, or meaning. But a law necessarily governs, or "is embodied in" individuels, and prescribes some of their qualifies. Consequently, a constituent of a Symbol may be an Index, and a constituent may be an Icon. A man walking with a child points this arm up into the air and says, "There is a balloon." The pointing arm is an essential part of the symbol without which the latter would convey no information. But if the child asks, "What is a balloon," and the man replies, "It is something like a great big soap bubble," he makes the image a part of the symbol. Thus, while the complete object of a symbol, that is to say, its meaning, is of the nature of a law, it must *denote* an individual, and must *signify* a character. A *genuine* symbol is a symbol that has a general meaning. There are two kinds of degenerate symbols, the *Singular Symbol* whose Object is an existent individual, and which signifies only such characters as that individual may realize; and the *Abstract Symbol,* whose only Object is a character.

Although the immediate Interpretant of an Index must be an Index, yet since its Object may be the Object of an Individual [Singular] Symbol, the Index may have such a Symbol for its indirect Interpretant. Even a genuine Symbol may be an imperfect Interpretant of it. So an *icon* may have a degenerate Index, or an Abstract Symbol, for an indirect Interpretant, and a genuine Index or Symbol for an imperfect Interpretant.

A *Symbol* is a sign naturally fit to declare that the set of objects which is denoted by whatever set of indices may be in certain ways attached to it is represented by an icon associated with it. To show what this complicated definition means, let us take as an example of a symbol the word "loveth." Associated with this word is an idea, which is the mental icon of one person loving another. Now we are to understand that "loveth" occurs in a sentence; for what it may mean by itself, if it means anything, is not the question. Let the sentence, then, be "Ezekiel loveth Huldah." Ezekiel and Huldah must, then, be or contain indices; for without indices it is impossible to designate what one is talking about. Any mere description would leave it uncertain whether they were not mere characters in a ballad; but whether they be so or not, indices can designate them. Now the effect of the word "loveth" is that the pair of objects denoted by the pair of indices Ezekiel and Huldah is represented by the icon, or the image we have in our minds of a lover and his beloved.

The same thing is equally true of every verb in the declarative mood; and indeed of every verb, for the other moods are merely declarations of a fact somewhat different from that expressed by the declarative mood. As for a noun, considering the meaning which it has in the sentence, and not as standing by itself, it is most conveniently regarded as a portion of a symbol. Thus the sentence, "every man loves a woman" is equivalent to "whatever is a man loves something that is a woman." Here "whatever" is a universal selective index, "is a man" is a symbol, "loves" is a symbol, "something that" is a particular selective index, and "is a woman" is a symbol....

The word *Symbol* has so many meanings that it would be an injury to the language to add a new one. I do not think that the signification I attach to it, that of a conventional sign, or one depending upon habit (acquired or inborn), is so much a new meaning as a return to the original meaning. Etymologically, it should mean a thing thrown together, just as ἔμβολον, (embolum) is a thing thrown into something, a bolt, and παράβολον (parabolum) is a thing thrown besides, collateral security, and ὑπόβολον (hypobolum) is a thing thrown underneath, an antenuptial gift. It is usually said that in the word *symbol* the throwing together is to be understood in the sense of "to conjecture"; but were that the case, we ought to find that *sometimes* at least it meant a conjecture, a meaning for which literature may be searched in vain. But the Greeks used "thrown together" (συμβάλλειν) very frequently to signify the making of a contract or convention. Now, we do find symbol (σύμβολον) early and often used to mean a convention or contract. Aristotle calls a noun a "symbol," that is, a conventional sign. In Greek, watchfire is a "symbol," that is, a signal agreed upon; a standard or ensign is a "symbol," a watchfire is a "symbol," a badge is a "symbol"; a church creed is called a "symbol," because it serves as a badge or shibboleth; a theatre ticket is called a "symbol"; any ticket or check entitling one to receive anything is a "symbol." Moreover, any expression of sentiment was called a "symbol." Such were the principal meanings of the word in the original language. The reader will judge whether they suffice to establish my claim that I am not seriously wrenching the word in employing it as I propose to do.

Any ordinary word, as "give," "bird," "marriage," is an example of a symbol. It is *applicable to whatever may be found to realize the idea connected with the word;* it does not, in itself, identify those things. It does not show us a bird, nor enact before our eyes a giving or a marriage, but supposes that we are able to imagine those things, and have associated the word with them.

A regular progression of one, two, three may be remarked in the three orders of signs, Icon, Index, Symbol. The Icon has no dynamical connection with the object it represents; it simply happens that its qualities resemble those of that object, and excite analogous sensations in the mind for which it is a likeness. But it really stands unconnected with them. The index is physically connected with its object; they make an organic pair, but the interpreting mind has nothing to do with this connection, except remarking it, after it is established. The symbol is connected with its object by virtue of the idea of the symbol-using mind, without which no such connection would exist.

Every physical force reacts between a pair of particles, either of which may serve as an index of the other. On the other hand, we shall find that every intellectual operation involves a triad of symbols.

A symbol, as we have seen, cannot indicate any particular thing; it denotes a kind of thing. Not only that, but it is itself a kind and not a single thing. You can write clown the word "star," but that does not make you the creator of the word, nor if you erase it have you destroyed the word. The word lives in the minds of those who use it. Even if they are all asleep, it exists in their memory. So we may admit, if there be reason to do so, that generals are mere words without at all saying, as Ockham supposed, that they are really individuals.

Symbols grow. They come into being by development out of other signs, particularly from icons, or from mixed signs partaking of the nature of icons and symbols. We think only in signs. These mental signs are of mixed nature; the symbol-parts of them are called concepts. if a man makes a new symbol, it is by thoughts involving concepts. So it is only out of symbol that a new symbol can grow. *Omne symbolum de symbolo.* A symbol, once in being, spreads among the peoples. In use and in experience, its meaning grows. Such words as *force, law, wealth, marriage,* bear for us very different meanings from those they bore to our barbarous ancestors. The symbol may, with Emerson's sphynx, say to man,

Of thine eye I am eyebeam.

4. *Ten Classes of Signs*

The three trichotomies of Signs result together in dividing Signs into TEN CLASSES OF SIGNS, of which numerous subdivisions have to be considered. The ten classes are as follows:

First: A Qualisign [e.g., a feeling of "red"] is any quality in so far as it is a sign. Since a quality is whatever it is positively in itself, a quality can only denote an object by virtue of some common ingredient or similarity; so that a Qualisign is necessarily an Icon. Further, since a quality is a mere logical possibility, it can only be interpreted as a sign of essence, that is, as a Rheme.

Second: An Iconic Sinsign [e.g., an individual diagram] is any object of experience in so far as some quality of it makes it determine the idea of an object. Being an Icon, and thus a sign by likeness purely, of whatever it may be like, it can only be interpreted as a sign of essence, or Rheme. It will embody a Qualisign.

Third: A Rhematic indexical Sinsign [e.g., a spontaneous cry] is any object of direct experience so far as it directs attention to an Object by which its presence is caused. It necessarily involves an Iconic Sinsign of a peculiar kind, yet is quite different since it brings the attention of the interpreter to the very Object denoted.

Fourth: A Dicent Sinsign [e.g., a weathercock] is any object of direct experience, in so far as it is a sign, and, as such, affords information concerning its Object. This it can only do by being really affected by its Object; so that it is necessarily an Index. The only information it can afford is of actual fact. Such a Sign must involve an Iconic Sinsign to embody the information and a Rhematic Indexical Sinsign to indicate the Object to which the information refers. But the mode of combination, or *Syntax*, of these two must also be significant.

Fifth: An Iconic Legisign [e.g., a diagram, apart from its factual individuality] is any general law or type, in so far as it requires each instance of it to embody a definite quality which renders it fit to call up in the mind the idea of a like object. Being an Icon, it must be a Rheme. Being a Legisign, its mode of being is that of governing single Replicas, each of which will be an Iconic Sinsign of a peculiar kind.

Sixth: A Rhematic Indexical Legisign [e.g., a demonstrative pronoun] is any general type or law, however established, which requires each instance of it to be really affected by its Object in such a manner as merely to draw attention to that Object. Each Replica of it will be a Rhematic Indexical Sinsign of a peculiar kind. The Interpretant of a Rhematic Indexical Legisign represents it as an Iconic Legisign; and so it is, in a measure—but in a very small measure.

Seventh: A Dicent Indexical Legisign [e.g., a street cry] is any general type or law, however established, which requires each instance of it to be really affected by its Object in such a manner as to furnish definite information concerning that Object. It must involve an Iconic Legisign to signify the information and a Rhematic Indexical Legisign to denote the subject of that information. Each Replica of it will be a Dicent Sinsign of a peculiar kind.

Eighth: A Rhematic Symbol or Symbolic Rheme [e.g., a common noun] is a sign connected with its Object by an association of general ideas in such a way that its Replica calls up an image in the mind, which image, owing to certain habits or dispositions of that mind, tends to produce a general concept, and the Replica is interpreted as a Sign of an Object that is an instance of that concept. Thus, the Rhematic Symbol either is, or is very like, what the logicians call a General Term. The Rhematic Symbol, like any Symbol, is necessarily itself of the nature of a general type, and is thus a Legisign. Its Replica, however, is a Rhematic Indexical Sinsign of a peculiar kind, in that the image it suggests to the mind acts upon a Symbol already in that mind to give rise to a General Concept. In this it differs from other Rhematic Indexical Sinsigns, including those which are Replicas of Rhematic Indexical Legisigns. Thus, the demonstrative pronoun "that" is a Legisign, being a general type; but it is not a Symbol, since it does not signify a general concept. Its Replica draws attention to a single Object, and is a Rhematic Indexical Sinsign. A Replica of the word "camel" is likewise a Rhematic Indexical Sinsign, being really affected, through the knowledge of camels, common to the speaker and auditor, by the real camel it denotes, even if this one is not individually known to the auditor; and it is through such real connection that the word "camel" calls up the idea of a camel. The same thing is true of the word "phoenix." For although no phoenix really exists, real descriptions of the phoenix are well known to the speaker and his auditor; and thus the word is really affected by the Object denoted. But not only are the Replicas of Rhematic Symbols very different from ordinary Rhematic Indexical Sinsigns, but so likewise are Replicas of Rhematic Indexical Legisigns. For the thing denoted by "that" has not affected the replica of the word in any such direct and simple manner as that in which, for example, the ring of a telephone-bell is affected by the person at the other end who wants to make a communication. The Interpretant of the Rhematic Symbol often represents it as a Rhematic Indexical Legisign; at other times as an Iconic Legisign; and it does in a small measure partake of the nature of both.

Ninth: A Dicent Symbol, or ordinary Proposition, is a sign connected with its object by an association of general ideas, and acting like a Rhematic Symbol, except that its intended interpretant represents the Dicent Symbol as being, in respect to what it signifies, really affected by its Object, so that the existence or law which it calls to mind must be actually connected with the indicated Object. Thus, the intended Interpretant looks upon the Dicent Symbol as a Dicent Indexical Legisign; and if it be true, it does partake of this nature, although this does not represent its whole nature. Like the Rhematic Symbol, it is necessarily a Legisign. Like the Dicent Sinsign it is composite inasmuch as it necessarily involves a Rhematic Symbol (and thus is for its Interpretant an Iconic Legisign) to express its information and a Rhematic Indexical Legisign to indicate the subject of that information. But its Syntax of these is significant. The Replica of the Dicent Symbol is a Dicent Sinsign of a peculiar kind. This is easily seen to be true when the information the Dicent Symbol conveys is of actual fact. When that information is of a real law, it is not true in the same fullness. For a Dicent Sinsign cannot convey information of law. It is, therefore, true of the Replica of such a Dicent Symbol only in so far as the law has its being in instances.

Tenth: An Argument is a sign whose interpretant represents its object as being an ulterior sign through a law, namely, the law that the passage from all such premises to such conclusions tends to the truth. Manifestly, then, its object must be general; that is, the Argument must be a Symbol. As a Symbol it must, further, be a Legisign. Its Replica is a Dicent Sinsign.

The affinities of the ten classes are exhibited by arranging their designations in the triangular table here shown, which has heavy boundaries between adjacent squares that are appropriated to classes alike in only one respect. All other adjacent squares pertain to classes alike in two respects. Squares not adjacent pertain to classes alike in one respect only, except that each of the three squares of the vertices of the triangle pertains to a class differing in all three respects from the classes to which the squares along the opposite side of the triangle are appropriated. The lightly printed designations are superfluous.

In the course of the above descriptions of the classes, certain subdivisions of some of them have been directly or indirectly referred to. Namely, beside the normal varieties of Sinsigns, Indices, and Dicisigns, there are others which are Replicas of Legisigns, Symbols, and Arguments, respectively. Beside the normal varieties of Qualisigns, Icons, and Rhemes, there are two series of others; to wit, those which are

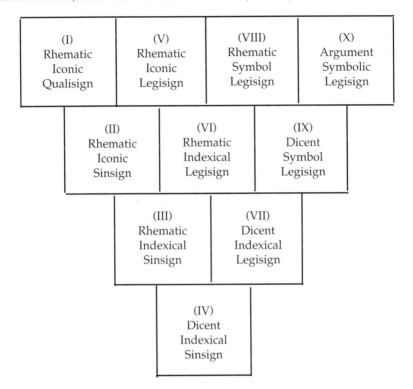

directly involved in Sinsigns, Indices, and Dicisigns, respectively, and also those which are indirectly involved in Legisigns, Symbols, and Arguments, respectively. Thus, the ordinary Dicent Sinsign is exemplified by a weathercock and its veering and by a photograph. The fact that the latter is known to be the effect of the radiations from the object renders it an index and highly informative. A second variety is a Replica of a Dicent Indexical Legisign. Thus any given street cry, since its tone and theme identifies the individual, is not a symbol, but an Indexical Legisign; and any individual instance of it is a Replica of it which is a Dicent Sinsign. A third variety is a Replica of a Proposition. A fourth variety is a Replica of an Argument. Beside the normal variety of the Dicent Indexical Legisign, of which a street cry is an example, there is a second variety, which is that sort of proposition which has the name of a well-known individuel as its predicate; as if one is asked, "Whose statue is this?" the answer may be, "It is Farragut." The meaning of this answer is a Dicent Indexical Legisign. A third variety may be a premiss of an argument. A Dicent Symbol, or ordinary proposition, insofar as it is a premiss of an Argument, takes on a new force, and becomes a second variety of the Dicent Symbol. It would not be worth while to go through all the varieties; but it may be well to consider the varieties of one class more. We may take the Rhematic Indexical Legisign. The shout of "Hullo!" is an example of the ordinary variety—meaning, not an individual shout, but this shout "Hullo!" in general—this type of shout. A second variety is a constituent of a Dicent Indexical Legisign; as the word "that" in the reply, "that is Farragut." A third variety is a particular application of a Rhematic Symbol; as the exclamation "Hark!" A fourth and fifth variety are in the peculiar force a general word may have in a proposition or argument. It is not impossible that some varieties are here overlooked. It is a nice problem to say to what class a given sign belongs; since all the circumstances of the case have to be considered. But it is seldom requisite to be very accurate; for if one does not locate the sign precisely, one will easily come near enough to its character for any ordinary purpose of logic.

4

The Linguistic Sign

Ferdinand de Saussure[1]

The Object of Linguistics

DEFINITION OF LANGUAGE

What is both the integral and concrete object of linguistics? The question is especially difficult; later we shall see why; here I wish merely to point up the difficulty.

Other sciences work with objects that are given in advance and that can then be considered from different viewpoints; but not linguistics. Someone pronounces the French word *nu* 'bare': a superficial observer would be tempted to call the word a concrete linguistic object; but a more careful examination would reveal successively three or four quite different things, depending on whether the word is considered as a sound, as the expression of an idea, as the equivalent of Latin *nudum*, etc. Far from it being the object that antedates the viewpoint, it would seem that it is the viewpoint that creates the object; besides, nothing tells us in advance that one way of considering the fact in question takes precedence over the others or is in any way superior to them.

Moreover, regardless of the viewpoint that we adopt, the linguistic phenomenon always has two related sides, each deriving its values from the other. For example:

I) Articulated syllables are acoustical impressions perceived by the ear, but the sounds would not exist without the vocal organs; an *n*, for example, exists only by virtue of the relation between the two sides. We simply cannot reduce language to sound or detach sound from oral articulation; reciprocally, we cannot define the movements of the vocal organs without taking into account the acoustical impression.

2) But suppose that sound were a simple thing: would it constitute speech? No, it is only the instrument of thought; by itself, it has no existence. At this point a new and redoubtable relationship arises: a sound, a complex acoustical-vocal unit, combines in turn with an idea to form a complex physiological-psychological unit. But that is still not the complete picture.

---

[1] Ferdinand de Saussure, *Course in General Linguistics,* edited by Charles Bally and Albert Sechehaye translated by Wade Baskin (New York: Philosophical Library, 1959).

3) Speech has both an individual and a social side, and we cannot conceive of one without the other. Besides:

4) Speech always implies both an established system and an evolution; at every moment it is an existing institution and a product of the past. To distinguish between the system and its history, between what it is and what it was, seems very simple at first glance; actually the two things are so closely related that we can scarcely keep them apart. Would we simplify the question by studying the linguistic phenomenon in its earliest stages—if we began, for example, by studying the speech of children? No, for in dealing with speech, it is completely misleading to assume that the problem of early characteristics differs from the problem of permanent characteristics. We are left inside the vicious circle.

From whatever direction we approach the question, nowhere do we find the integral object of linguistics. Everywhere we are confronted with a dilemma: if we fix our attention on only one side of each problem, we run the risk of failing to perceive the dualities pointed out above; on the other hand, if we study speech from several viewpoints simultaneously, the object of linguistics appears to us as a confused mass of heterogeneous and unrelated things. Either procedure opens the door to several sciences—psychology, anthropology, normative grammar, philology, etc.— which are distinct from linguistics, but which might claim speech, in view of the faulty method of linguistics, as one of their objects.

As I see it there is only one solution to all the foregoing difficulties: *from the very outset we must put both feet on the ground of language and use language as the norm of all other manifestations of speech.* Actually, among so many dualities, language alone seems to fend itself to independent definition and provide a fulcrum that satisfies the mind.

But what is language [*langue*]? It is not to be confused with human speech [*langage*], of which it is only a definite part, though certainly an essential one. It is both a social product of the faculty of speech and a collection of necessary conventions that have been adopted by a social body to permit individuals to exercise that faculty. Taken as a whole, speech is many-sided and heterogeneous; straddling several areas simultaneously—physical, physiological, and psychological—it belongs both to the individual and to society; we cannot put it into any category of human facts, for we cannot discover its unity.

Language, on the contrary, is a self-contained whole and a principle of classification. As soon as we give language first place among the facts of speech, we introduce a natural order into a mass that lends itself to no other classification.

One might object to that principle of classification on the ground that since the use of speech is based on a natural faculty whereas language is something acquired and conventional, language should not take first place but should be subordinated to the natural instinct.

That objection is easily refuted.

First, no one has proved that speech, as it manifests itself when we speak, is entirely natural, i.e. that our vocal apparatus was designed for speaking just as our legs were designed for walking. Linguists are far from agreement on this point. For instance Whitney, to whom language is one of several social institutions, thinks that we use the vocal apparatus as the instrument of language purely through luck, for the sake of convenience: men might just as well have chosen gestures and used visual symbols instead of acoustical symbols. Doubtless his thesis is too dogmatic; language is not similar in all respects to other social institutions; moreover, Whitney goes too far in saying that our choice happened to fall on the vocal organs; the choice was more or less imposed by nature. But on the essential point the American linguist is right: language is a convention, and the nature of the sign that is agreed upon does not matter. The question of the vocal apparatus obviously takes a secondary place in the problem of speech.

One definition of *articulated speech* might confirm that conclusion. In Latin, *articulus* means a member, part, or subdivision of a sequence; applied to speech, articulation designates either the subdivision of a spoken chain into syllables or the subdivision of the chain of meanings into significant units; *gegliederte Sprache* is used in the second sense in German. Using the second definition, we can say that what is natural to mankind is not oral speech but the faculty of constructing a language, i.e. a system of distinct signs corresponding to distinct ideas.

Broca discovered that the faculty of speech is localized in the third left frontal convolution; his discovery has been used to substantiate the attribution of a natural quality to speech. But we know that the same part of the brain is the center of *everything* that has to do with speech, including writing. The preceding statements, together with observations that have been made in different cases of aphasia resulting from lesion of the centers of localization, seem to indicate: (I) that the various disorders of oral speech are bound up in a hundred ways with those of written speech; and (2) that what is lost in all cases of aphasia or agraphia is less the faculty of producing a given sound or writing a given sign than the ability to evoke by means of an instrument, regardless of what it is, the signs of a regular system of speech. The obvious implication is that beyond the functioning of the various organs there exists a more general faculty which governs signs and which would be the linguistic faculty proper. And this brings us to the same conclusion as above.

To give language first place in the study of speech, we can advance a final argument: the faculty of articulating words—whether it is natural or not—is exercised only with the help of the instrument created by a collectivity and provided for its use; therefore, to say that language gives unity to speech is not fanciful.

PLACE OF LANGUAGE IN THE FACTS OF SPEECH

In order to separate from the whole of speech the part that belongs to language, we must examine the individual act from which the speaking circuit can be reconstructed. The act requires the presence of at least two persons; that is the minimum number necessary to complete the circuit. Suppose that two people, A and B, are conversing with each other:

A   B

Suppose that the opening of the circuit is in A's brain, where mental facts (concepts) are associated with representations of the linguistic sounds (sound-images) that are used for their expression. A given concept unlocks a corresponding sound-image in the brain; this purely *psychological* phenomenon is followed in turn by a *physiological* process: the brain transmits an impulse corresponding to the image to the organs used in producing sounds. Then the sound waves travel from the mouth of A to the ear of B: a purely *physical* process. Next, the circuit continues in B, but the order is reversed: from the ear to the brain, the physiological transmission of the sound-image; in the brain, the psychological association of the image with the corresponding concept. If B then speaks, the new act will follow—from his brain to A's—exactly the same course as the first act and pass through the same successive phases, which I shall diagram as follows:

Audition   Phonation

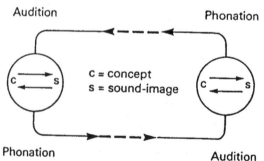

c = concept
s = sound-image

Phonation   Audition

The preceding analysis does not purport to be complete. We might also single out the pure acoustical sensation, the identification of that sensation with the latent sound-image, the muscular image of phonation, ect. I have included only the elements thought to be essential, but the drawing brings out at a glance the distinction between the physical (sound waves), physiological (phonation and audition), and psychological parts (word-images and concepts). Indeed, we should not fail to note that the word-image stands apart from the sound itself and that it is just as psychological as the concept which is associated with it.

The circuit that I have outlined can be further divided into:

(*a*) an outer part that includes the vibrations of the sounds which travel from the mouth to the ear, and an inner part that includes everything else;

(*b*) a psychological and a nonpsychological part, the second including the physiological productions of the vocal organs as well as the physical facts that are outside the individual;

(*c*) an active and a passive part: everything that goes from the associative center of the speaker to the ear of the listener is active, and everything that goes from the ear of the listener to his associative center is passive;

(*d*) finally, everything that is active in the psychological part of the circuit is executive ($c \rightarrow s$), and everything that is passive is receptive ($s \rightarrow c$).

We should also add the associative and co-ordinating faculty that we find as soon as we leave isolated signs; this faculty plays the dominant role in the organization of language as a system.

But to understand clearly the role of the associative and co-ordinating faculty, we must leave the individual act, which is only the embryo of speech, and approach the social fact.

Among all the individuals that are linked together by speech, some sort of average will be set up: all will reproduce—not exactly of course, but approximately—the same signs united with the same concepts.

How does the social crystallization of language come about? Which parts of the circuit are involved? For all parts probably do not participate equally in it.

The nonpsychological part can be rejected from the outset. When we hear people speaking a language that we do not know, we perceive the sounds but remain outside the social fact because we do not understand them.

Neither is the psychological part of the circuit wholly responsible: the executive side is missing, for execution is never carried out by the collectivity. Execution is always individual, and the individual is always its master: I shall call the executive side *speaking* [*parole*].

Through the functioning of the receptive and co-ordinating faculties, impressions that are perceptibly the same for all are made on the minds of speakers. How can that social product be pictured in such a way that language will stand apart from everything else? If we could embrace the sum of word-images stored in the minds of all individuals, we could identify the social bond that constitutes language. It is a storehouse filled by the members of a given community through their active use of speaking, a grammatical system that has a potential existence in each brain, or, more specifically, in the brains of a group of individuals. For language is not complete in any speaker; it exists perfectly only within a collectivity.

In separating language from speaking we are at the same time separating: (1) what is social from what is individual, and (2) what is essential from what is accessory and more or less accidental.

Language is not a function of the speaker; it is a product that is passively assimilated by the individual. It never requires premeditation, and reflection enters in only for the purpose of classification, which we shall take up later.

Speaking, on the contrary, is an individual act. It is wilful and intellectual. Within the act, we should distinguish between: (1) the combinations by which the speaker uses the language code for expressing his own thought; and (2) the psychophysical mechanism that allows him to exteriorize those combinations.

Note that I have defined things rather than words; these definitions are not endangered by certain ambiguous words that do not have identical meanings in different languages. For instance, German *Sprache* means both "language" and "speech"; *Rede* almost corresponds to "speaking" but adds the special connotation of "discourse." Latin *sermo* designates both "speech" and "speaking," while *lingua* means "language," etc. No word corresponds exactly to any of the notions specified above ; that is why all definitions of words are made in vain; starting from words in defining things is a bad procedure.

To summarize, these are the characteristics of language:

(1) Language is a well-defined object in the heterogeneous mass of speech facts. It can be localized in the limited segment of the speaking circuit where an auditory image becomes associated with a concept. It is the social side of speech, outside the individual who can never create nor modify it by himself; it exists only by virtue of a sort of contract signed by the members of a community. Moreover, the individual must always serve an apprenticeship in order to learn the functioning of language; a child assimilates it only gradually. It is such a distinct thing that a man deprived of the use of speaking retains it provided that he understands the vocal signs that he hears.

(2) Language, unlike speaking, is something that we can study separately. Although dead languages are no longer spoken, we can easily assimilate their linguistic organisms. We can dispense with the other elements of speech; indeed, the science of language is possible only if the other elements are excluded.

(3) Whereas speech is heterogeneous, language, as defined, is homogeneous. It is a system of signs in which the only essential thing is the union of meanings and sound-images, and in which both parts of the sign are psychological.

(4) Language is concrete, no less so than speaking; and this is a help in our study of it. Linguistic signs, though basically psychological, are not abstractions; associations which bear the stamp of collective approval—and which added together constitute language—are realities that have their seat in the brain. Besides, linguistic signs are tangible; it is possible to reduce them to conventional written symbols, whereas it would be impossible to provide detailed photographs of acts of speaking [*actes de parole*]; the pronunciation of even the smallest word represents an infinite number of muscular movements that could be identified and put into graphic form only with great difficulty. In language, on the contrary, there is only the sound-image, and the latter can be translated into a fixed visual image. For if we disregard the vast number of movements necessary for the realization of sound-images in speaking, we see that each sound image is nothing more than the sum of a limited number of elements or phonemes that can in turn be called up by a corresponding number of written symbols. The very possibility of putting the things that relate to language into graphic form allows dictionaries and grammars to represent it accurately, for language is a storehouse of sound-images, and writing is the tangible form of those images.

PLACE OF LANGUAGE IN HUMAN FACTS: SEMIOLOGY

The foregoing characteristics of language reveal an even more important characteristic. Language, once its boundaries have been marked off within the speech data, can be classified among human phenomena, whereas speech cannot.

We have just seen that language is a social institution; but several features set it apart from other political, legal, etc. institutions. We must call in a new type of facts in order to illuminate the special nature of language.

Language is a system of signs that express ideas, and is therefore comparable to a system of writing, the alphabet of deaf-mutes, symbolic rites, polite formulas, military signals, etc. But it is the most important of all these systems.

A science that studies the life of signs within society is conceivable; it would be a part of social psychology and consequently of general psychology; I shall call it *semiology*[2] (from Greek *sēmeîon* 'sign'). Semiology

---

[2] Semiology should not be confused with semantics, which studies changes in meaning, and which Saussure did not treat methodically.

would show what constitutes signs, what laws govern them. Since the science does not yet exist, no one can say what it would be; but it has a right to existence, a place staked out in advance. Linguistics is only a part of the general science of semiology; the laws discovered by semiology will be applicable to linguistics, and the latter will circumscribe a well-defined area within the mass of anthropological facts.

To determine the exact place of semiology is the task of the psycholgist.[3] The task of the linguist is to find out what makes language a special system within the mass of semiological data. This issue will be taken up again later; here I wish merely to call attention to one thing: if I have succeeded in assigning linguistics a place among the sciences, it is because I have related it to semiology.

Why has semiology not yet been recognized as an independent science with its own object like all the other sciences? Linguists have been going around in circles: language, better than anything else, offers a basis for understanding the semiological problem; but language must, to put it correctly, be studied in itself; heretofore language has almost always been studied in connection with something else, from other viewpoints.

There is first of all the superficial notion of the general public: people see nothing more than a name-giving system in language, thereby prohibiting any research into its true nature.

Then there is the viewpoint of the psychologist, who studies the sign-mechanism in the individual; this is the easiest method, but it does not lead beyond individual execution and does not reach the sign, which is social.

Or even when signs are studied from a social viewpoint, only the traits that attach language to the other social institutions—those that are more or less voluntary—are emphasized; as a result, the goal is by-passed and the specific characteristics of semiological systems in general and of language in particular are completely ignored. For the distinguishing characteristic of the sign—but the one that is least apparent at first sight—is that in some way it always eludes the individual or social will.

In short, the characteristic that distinguishes semiological systems from all other institutions shows up clearly only in language where it manifests itself in the things which are studied least, and the necessity or specific value of a semiological science is therefore not clearly recognized. But to me the language problem is mainly semiological, and all developments derive their significance from that important fact. If we are to discover the true nature of language we must learn what it has in

---

[3] *Cf.* A. Naville, *Classification des Sciences* (2nd. ed.), p. 104. [Editorial note to French edition.]

common with all other semiological systems; linguistic features that seem very important at first glance (e.g., the role of the vocal apparatus) will receive only secondary consideration if they serve only to set language apart from the other systems. This procedure will do more than to clarify the linguistic problem. By studying rites, customs, etc. as signs, I believe that we shall throw new light on the facts and point up the need for including them in a science of semiology and explaining them by its laws.

Nature of the Linguistic Sign

SIGN, SIGNIFIED, SIGNIFIER

Some people regard language, when reduced to its elements, as a naming-process only—a list of words, each corresponding to the thing that it names. For exemple:

This conception is open to criticism at several points. It assumes that ready-made ideas exist before words; it does not tell us whether a name is vocal or psychological in nature (*arbor,* for instance, can be considered from either viewpoint); finally, it lets us assume that the linking of a name and a thing is a very simple operation—an assumption that is anything but true. But this rather naive approach can bring us near the truth by showing us that the linguistic unit is a double entity, one formed by the associating of two terms.

We have seen in considering the speaking-circuit (p. 72) that both terms involved in the linguistic sign are psychological and are united in the brain by an associative bond. This point must be emphasized.

The linguistic sign unites, not a thing and a name, but a concept and a sound-image.[4] The latter is not the material sound, a purely physical thing, but the psychological imprint of the sound, the impression that it makes on our senses. The sound-image is sensory, and if I happen to call it "material," it is

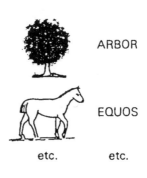

ARBOR

EQUOS

etc.   etc.

---

[4] The term sound-image may seem to be too restricted inasmuch as beside the representation of the sounds of a word there is also than of its articulation, the muscular image of the phonational act. But for F. de Saussure language is essentially a depository, a thing received from without (see p. [74 of this book]).

only in that sense, and by way of opposing it to the other term of the association, the concept, which is generally more abstract.

The psychological character of our sound-images becomes apparent when we observe our own speech. Without moving our lips or tongue, we can talk to ourselves or recite mentally a selection of verse. Because we regard the words of our language as sound-images, we must avoid speaking of the "phonemes" that make up the words. This term, which suggests vocal activity, is applicable to the spoken word only, to the realization of the inner image in discourse. We can avoid that misunderstanding by speaking of the *sounds* and *syllables* of a word provided we remember that the names refer to the sound-image.

The linguistic sign is then a two-sided psychological entity that can be represented by the drawing:

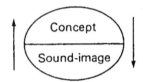

The two elements are intimately united, and each recalls the other. Whether we try to find the meaning of the Latin word *arbor* or the word that Latin uses to designate the concept "tree," it is clear that only the associations sanctioned by that language appear to us to conform to reality, and we disregard whatever others might be imagined.

Our definition of the linguistic sign poses an important question of terminology. I call the combination of a concept and a sound-image a *sign,* but in current usage the term generally designates only a sound-image, a word, for example *(arbor,* etc.). One tends to forget that *arbor* is called a sign only because it carries the concept "tree, with the result that the idea of the sensory part implies the idea of the whole.

Ambiguity would disappear if the three notions involved here were designated by three names, each suggesting and opposing the others. I propose to retain the word *sign* [*signe*] to designate the whole and to replace *concept* and *sound-image* respectively by *signified* [*signifié*] and *signifier* [*signifiant*]; the last two terms have the advantage of indicating the opposition that separates them from each other and from the whole of which they are parts. As regards *sign*, if I am satisfied with it, this is simply because I do not know of any word to replace it, the ordinary language suggesting no other.

The linguistic sign, as defined, has two primordial characteristics. In enunciating them I am also positing the basic principles of any study of this type.

PRINCIPLE I: THE ARBITRARY NATURE OF THE SIGN

The bond between the signifier and the signified is arbitrary. Since I mean by sign the whole that results from the associating of the signifier with the signified, I can simply say: *the linguistic sign is arbitrary.*

The idea of "sister" is not linked by any inner relationship to the succession of sounds s-ö-r which serves as its signifier in French; that it could be represented equally by just any other sequence is proved by differences among languages and by the very existence of different languages: the signified "ox" has as its signifier b-ö-f on one side of the border and o-k-s (*Ochs*) on the other.

No one disputes the principle of the arbitrary nature of the sign, but it is often easier to discover a truth than to assign to it its proper place. Principle I dominates all the linguistics of language; its consequences are numberless. It is true that not all of them are equally obvious at first glance; only after many detours does one discover them, and with them the primordial importance of the principle.

One remark in passing: when semiology becomes organized as a science, the question will arise whether or not it properly includes modes of expression based on completely natural signs, such as pantomime. Supposing that the new science welcomes them, its main concern will still be the whole group of systems grounded on the arbitrariness of the sign. In fact, every means of expression used in society is based, in principle, on collective behavior or—what amounts to the same thing—on convention. Polite formulas, for instance, though often imbued with a certain natural expressiveness (as in the case of a Chinese who greets his emperor by bowing down to the ground nine times), are nonetheless fixed by rule; it is this rule and not the intrinsic value of the gestures that obliges one to use them. Signs that are wholly arbitrary realize better than the others the ideal of the semiological process; that is why language, the most complex and universal of all systems of expression, is also the most characteristic; in this sense linguistics can become the master-pattern for all branches of semiology although language is only one particular semiological system.

The word *symbol* has been used to designate the linguistic sign, or more specifically, what is here called the signifier. Principle I in particular weighs against the use of this term. One characteristic of the symbol is that it is never wholly arbitrary; it is not empty, for there is the rudiment of a natural bond between the signifier and the signified. The symbol of justice, a pair of scales, could not be replaced by just any other symbol, such as a chariot.

The word *arbitrary* also calls for comment. The term should not imply that the choice of the signifier is left entirely to the speaker (we shall see below that the individual does not have the power to change a sign in any way once it has become established in the linguistic community); I mean that it is unmotivated, i.e. arbitrary in that it actually has no natural connection with the signified.

In concluding let us consider two objections that might be raised to the establishment of Principle 1:

1) *Onomatopoeia* might be used to prove that the choice of the signifier is not always arbitrary. But onomatopoeic formations are never organic elements of a linguistic system. Besides, their number is much smaller than is generally supposed. Words like French *fouet* 'whip' or *glas* 'knell' may strike certain ears with suggestive sonority, but to see that they have not always had this property we need only examine their Latin forms (*fouet* is derived from *fāgus* 'beech-tree,' *glas* from *classicum* 'sound of a trumpet'). The quality of their present sounds, or rather the quality that is attributed to them, is a fortuitous result of phonetic evolution.

As for authentic onomatopoeic words (e.g. *glug-glug*, *tick-tock*, etc.), not only are they limited in number, but also they are chosen somewhat arbitrarily, for they are only approximate and more or less conventional imitations of certain sounds (cf. English *bow-wow* and French *ouaoua*). In addition, once these words have been introduced into the language, they are to a certain extent subjected to the same evolution—phonetic, morphological, etc.—that other words undergo (cf. *pigeon*, ultimately from Vulgar Latin *pīpiō*, derived in turn from an onomatopoeic formation): obvious proof that they lose something of their original character in order to assume that of the linguistic sign in general, which is unmotivated.

2) *Interjections*, closely related to onomatopoeia, can be attacked on the same grounds and come no closer to refuting our thesis. One is tempted to see in them spontaneous expressions of reality dictated, so to speak, by natural forces. But for most interjections we can show that there is no fixed bond between their signified and their signifier. We need only compare two languages on this point to see how much such expressions differ from one language to the next (e.g. the English equivalent of French *aïe!* is *ouch!*). We know, moreover, that many interjections were once words with specific meanings (cf. French *diable!* 'darn!' *mordieu!* 'golly!' from *mort Dieu* 'God's death,' etc.).[5]

---

[5] Cf. English *goodness!* and *sounds!* (from *God's wounds*). [Translator's note.]

Onomatopoeic formations and interjections are of secondary importance, and their symbolic origin is in part open to dispute.

PRINCIPLE II: THE LINEAR NATURE OF THE SIGNIFIER

The signifier, being auditory, is unfolded solely in time from which it gets the following characteristics: (a) it represents a span, and (b) the span is measurable in a single dimension; it is a line.

While Principle II is obvious, apparently linguists have always neglected to state it, doubtless because they found it too simple; nevertheless, it is fundamental, and its consequences are incalculable. Its importance equals that of Principle 1; the whole mechanism of language depends upon it. In contrast to visual signifiers (nautical signals, etc.) which can offer simultaneous groupings in several dimensions, auditory signifiers have at their command only the dimension of time. Their elements are presented in succession; they form a chain. This feature becomes readily apparent when they are represented in writing and the spatial line of graphic marks is substituted for succession in time.

Sometimes the linear nature of the signifier is not obvious. When I accent a syllable, for instance, it seems that I am concentrating more than one significant element on the same point. But this is an illusion; the syllable and its accent constitute only one phonational act. There is no duality within the act but only different oppositions to what precedes and what follows.

Immutability and Mutability of the Sign

IMMUTABILITY

The signifier, though to all appearances freely chosen with respect to the idea that it represents, is fixed, not free, with respect to the linguistic community that uses it. The masses have no voice in the matter, and the signifier chosen by language could be replaced by no other. This fact, which seems to embody a contradiction, might be called colloquially "the stacked deck." We say to language: "Choose!" but we add: "It must be this sign and no other." No individual, even if he willed it, could modify in any way at all the choice that has been made; and what is more, the community itself cannot control so much as a single word; it is bound to the existing language.

No longer can language be identified with a contract pure and simple, and it is precisely from this viewpoint that the linguistic sign is a particularly interesting object of study; for language furnishes the best proof that a law accepted by a community is a thing that is tolerated and not a rule to which all freely consent.

Let us first see why we cannot control the linguistic sign and then draw together the important consequences that issue from the phenomenon.

No matter what period we choose or how far back we go, language always appears as a heritage of the preceding period. We might conceive of an act by which, at a given moment, names were assigned to things and a contract was formed between concepts and sound-images; but such an act has never been recorded. The notion that things might have happened like that was prompted by our acute awareness of the arbitrary nature of the sign.

No society, in fact, knows or has ever known language other than as a product inherited from preceding generations, and one to be accepted as such. That is why the question of the origin of speech is not so important as it is generally assumed to be. The question is not even worth asking; the only real object of linguistics is the normal, regular life of an existing idiom. A particular language-state is always the product of historical forces, and these forces explain why the sign is unchangeable, i.e. why it resists any arbitrary substitution.

Nothing is explained by saying that language is something inherited and leaving it at that. Can not existing and inherited laws be modified from one moment to the next?

To meet that objection, we must put language into its social setting and frame the question just as we would for any other social institution. How are other social institutions transmitted? This more general question includes the question of immutability. We must first determine the greater or lesser amounts of freedom that the other institutions enjoy; in each instance it will be seen that a different proportion exists between fixed tradition and the free action of society. The next step is to discover why in a given category, the forces of the first type carry more weight or less weight than those of the second. Finally, coming back to language, we must ask why the historical factor of transmission dominates it entirely and prohibits any sudden widespread change.

There are many possible answers to the question. For example, one might point to the fact that succeeding generations are not superimposed on one another like the drawers of a piece of furniture, but fuse and interpenetrate, each generation embracing individuals of all ages—with the result that modifications of language are not tied to the succession of generations. One might also recall the sum of the efforts required for learning the mother language and conclude that a general change would be impossible. Again, it might be added that reflection does not enter into the active use of an idiom—speakers are largely unconscious of the laws of language; and if they are unaware of them, how could they modify them? Even if they were aware of these laws, we may be sure that their awareness would seldom lead to criticism, for people are generally satisfied with the language they have received.

The foregoing considerations are important but not topical. The following are more basic and direct, and all the others depend on them.

(1) *The arbitrary nature of the sign.* Above, we had to accept the theoretical possibility of change; further reflection suggests that the arbitrary nature of the sign is really what protects language from any attempt to modify it. Even if people were more conscious of language than they are, they would still not know how to discuss it. The reason is simply that any subject in order to be discussed must have a reasonable basis. It is possible, for instance, to discuss whether the monogamous form of marriage is more reasonable than the polygamous form and to advance arguments to support either side. One could also argue about a system of symbols, for the symbol has a rational relationship with the thing signified (see p. 80); but language is a system of arbitrary signs and lacks the necessary basis, the solid ground for discussion. There is no reason for preferring *soeur* to *sister*, *Ochs* to *boeuf*, etc.

(2) *The multiplicity of signs necessary to form any language.* Another important deterrent to linguistic change is the great number of signs that must go into the making of any language. A system of writing comprising twenty to forty letters can in case of need be replaced by another system. The same would be true of language if it contained a limited number of elements; but linguistic signs are numberless.

(3) *The over-complexity of the system.* A language constitutes a system. In this one respect (as we shall see later) language is not completely arbitrary but is ruled to some extent by logic; it is here also, however, that the inability of the masses to transform it becomes apparent. The system is a complex mechanism that can be grasped only through reflection; the very ones who use it daily are ignorant of it. We can conceive of a change only through the intervention of specialists, grammarians, logicians, etc.; but experience shows us that all such meddlings have failed.

(4) *Collective inertia toward innovation.* Language—and this consideration surpasses all the others—is at every moment everybody's concern; spread throughout society and manipulated by it, language is something used daily by all. Here we are unable to set up any comparison between it and other institutions. The prescriptions of codes, religious rites, nautical signals, etc., involve only a certain number of individuals simultaneously and then only during a limited period of time; in language, on the contrary, everyone participates at all times, and that is why it is constantly being influenced by all. This capital fact suffices to show the impossibility of revolution. Of all social institutions, language is least amenable to initiative. It blends with the life of society, and the latter, inert by nature, is a prime conservative force.

But to say that language is a product of social forces does not suffice to show clearly that it is unfree; remembering that it is always the heritage of the preceding period, we must add that these social forces are linked with time. Language is checked not only by the weight of the collectivity but also by time. These two are inseparable. At every moment solidarity with the past checks freedom of choice. We say man and dog. This does not prevent the existence in the total phenomenon of a bond between the two antithetical forces—arbitrary convention by virtue of which choice is free and time which causes choice to be fixed. Because the sign is arbitrary, it follows no law other than that of tradition, and because it is based on tradition, it is arbitrary.

MUTABILITY

Time, which insures the continuity of language, wields another influence apparently contradictory to the first: the more or less rapid change of linguistic signs. In a certain sense, therefore, we can speak of both the immutability and the mutability of the sign.[6]

In the last analysis, the two facts are interdependent: the sign is exposed to alteration because it perpetuates itself. What predominates in all change is the persistence of the old substance; disregard for the past is only relative. That is why the principle of change is based on the principle of continuity.

Change in time takes many forms, on any one of which an important chapter in linguistics might be written. Without entering into detail, let us see what things need to be delineated.

First, let there be no mistake about the meaning that we attach to the word change. One might think that it deals especially with phonetic changes undergone by the signifier, or perhaps changes in meaning which affect the signified concept. That view would be inadequate. Regardless of what the forces of change are, whether in isolation or in combination, they always result in a *shift in the relationship between the signified* and *the signifier.*

Here are some examples. Latin *necāre* 'kill' became *noyer* 'drown' in French. Both the sound-image and the concept changed; but it is useless to separate the two parts of the phenomenon; it is sufficient to state with respect to the whole that the bond between the idea and the sign was loosened, and that there was a shift in their relationship. If instead of comparing Classical Latin *nĕcare* with French *noyer*, we contrast the for-

---

[6] It would be wrong to reproach F. de Saussure for being illogical or paradoxical in attributing two contradictory qualities to language. By opposing two striking terms, he wanted only to emphasize the fact that language changes in spite of the inability of speakers to change it. One can also say that it is intangible but not unchangeable. [Editorial note to French edition.]

mer term with *necāre* of Vulgar Latin of the fourth or fifth century, meaning 'drown' the case is a little different; but here again, although there is no appreciable change in the signifier, there is a shift in the relationship between the idea and the sign.[7]

Old German *dritteil* 'one-third' became *Drittel* in Modern German. Here, although the concept remained the same, the relationship was changed in two ways: the signifier was changed not only in its material aspect but also in its grammatical form; the idea of *Teil* 'part' is no longer implied; *Drittel* is a simple word. In one way or another there is always a shift in the relationship.

In Anglo-Saxon the preliterary form *fot* 'foot' remained while its plural *fōti* became *fēt* (Modern English *feet*). Regardless of the other changes that are implied, one thing is certain: there was a shift in their relationship; other correspondences between the phonetic substance and the idea emerged.

Language is radically powerless to defend itself against the forces which from one moment to the next are shifting the relationship between the signified and the signifier. This is one of the consequences of the arbitrary nature of the sign.

Unlike language, other human institutions—customs, laws, etc.— are all based in varying degrees on the natural relations of things; all have of necessity adapted the means employed to the ends pursued. Even fashion in dress is not entirely arbitrary; we can deviate only slightly from the conditions dictated by the human body. Language is limited by nothing in the choice of means, for apparently nothing would prevent the associating of any idea whatsoever with just any sequence of sounds.

To emphasize the fact that language is a genuine institution, Whitney quite justly insisted upon the arbitrary nature of signs; and by so doing, he placed linguistics on its true axis. But he did not follow through and see that the arbitrariness of language radically separates it from all other institutions. This is apparent from the way in which language evolves. Nothing could be more complex. As it is a product of both the social force and time, no one can change anything in it, and on the other hand, the arbitrariness of its signs theoretically entails the freedom of establishing just any relationship between phonetic substance and ideas. The result is that each of the two elements united in the sign maintains its own life to a degree unknown elsewhere, and that language changes, or rather evolves, under the influence of all the forces which can affect either sounds or meanings. The evolution is inevitable; there is no example of a single language that resists it. After a certain

---

[7] From May to July of 1911, Saussure used interchangeably the old terminology *(idea* and *sign)* and the new *(signified* and *signifier)*. [*Translator's* note.]

period of time, some obvious shifts can always be recorded.

Mutability is so inescapable that it even holds true for artificial languages. Whoever creates a language controls it only so long as it is not in circulation; from the moment when it fulfills it mission and becomes the property of everyone, control is lost. Take Esperanto as an exemple; if it succeeds, will it escape the inexorable law? Once launched, it is quite likely that Esperanto will enter upon a fully semiological life; it will be transmitted according to laws which have nothing in common with those of its logical creation, and there will be no turning backwards. A man proposing a fixed language that posterity would have to accept for what it is would be like a hen hatching a duck's egg: the language created by him would be borne along, willy-nilly, by the current that engulfs all languages.

Signs are governed by a principle of general semiology: continuity in time is coupled to change in time; this is confirmed by orthographic systems, the speech of deaf-mutes, etc.

But what supports the necessity for change? I might be reproached for nor having been as explicit on this point as on the principle of immutability. This is because I failed to distinguish between the different forces of change. We must consider their great variety in order to understand the extent to which they are necessary.

The causes of continuity are *a priori* within the scope of the observer, but the causes of change in time are not. It is better not to attempt giving an exact account at this point, but to restrict discussion to the shifting of relationships in general. Time changes all things; there is no reason why language should escape this universal law.

Let us review the main points of our discussion and relate them to the principles set up in the Introduction.

I) Avoiding sterile word definitions, within the total phenomenon represented by speech we first singled out two parts: language and speaking. Language is speech less speaking. It is the whole set of linguistic habits which allow an individual to understand and to be understood.

2) But this definition still leaves language outside its social context; it makes language something artificial since it includes only the individual part of reality; for the realization of language, a community of speakers [*masse parlante*] is necessary. Contrary to all appearances, language never exists apart from the social fact, for it is a semiological phenomenon. Its social nature is one of its inner characteristics. Its complete definition confronts us with two inseparable entities, as shown in this drawing:

But under the conditions described language is not living—it has only potential life; we have considered only the social, not the historical, fact.

3) The linguistic sign is arbitrary; language, as defined, would therefore seem to be a system which, because it depends solely on a rational principle, is free and can be organized at will. Its social nature,considered

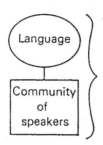

independently, does not definitely rule out this viewpoint. Doubtless it is not on a purely logical basis that group psychology operates; one must consider everything that deflects reason in actual contacts between individuals. But the thing which keeps language from being a simple convention that can be modified at the whim of interested parties is not its social nature; it is rather the action of time combined with the social force. If time is left out, the linguistic facts are incomplete and no conclusion is possible.

If we considered language in time, without the community of speakers—imagine an isolated individual living for several centuries—we probably would notice no change; time would not influence language. Conversely, if we considered the community of speakers without considering time, we would not see the effect of the social forces that influence language. To represent the actual facts, we must then add to our first drawing a sign to indicate passage of time:

Language is no longer free, for time will allow the social forces at work on it to carry out their effects. This brings us back to the principle

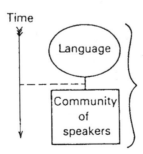

of continuity, which cancels freedom. But continuity necessarily implies change, varying degrees of shifts in the relationship between the signified and the signifier.

5

Forms

Susanne K. Langer[1]

The logical theory on which this whole study of symbols is based is essentially that which was set forth by Wittgenstein, some twenty years ago, in his *Tractatus Logico-Philosophicus:*

"One name stands for one thing, and another for another thing, and they are connected together. And so the whole, like a living picture, presents the atomic fact. (4.032)

"At the first glance the proposition—say as it stands printed on paper— does not seem to be a picture of the reality of which it treats. But neither does the musical score appear at first sight to be a picture of a musical piece; nor does our phonetic spelling (letters) seem to be a picture of our spoken language.... (4.011)

"In the fact that there is a general rule by which the musician is able to read the symphony out of the score, and that there is a rule by which one could reconstruct the symphony from the line on a phonograph record and from this again—by means of the first rule—construct the score, herein lies the internal similarity between the things which at first sight seem to be entirely different. And the rule is the law of projection which projects the symphony into the language of the musical score. It is the rule of translation of this language into the language of the gramophone record." (4.0141)

"Projection" is a good word, albeit a figurative one, for the process by which we draw purely *logical* analogies. Geometric projection is the best instance of a perfectly faithful representation which, without knowledge of some logical rule, appears to be a misrepresentation. A child looking at a map of the world in Mercator projection cannot help believing that Greenland is larger than Australia; he simply finds it larger. The projection employed is not the usual principle of copying which we use in all visual comparisons or translations, and his training in the usual rule makes him unable to "see" by the new one. It takes sophistication to "see" the relative sizes of Greenland and Australia on a Mercator map. Yet a mind educated to appreciate the projected image brings the eye's habit with it. After a while, we genuinely "see" the thing as we apprehend it.

---

[1] Susanne K. Langer, *Philosophy in a New Key* (Cambridge, Mass.: Harvard University Press, 1942).

Language, our most faithful and indispensable picture of human experience, of the world and its events, of thought and life and all the march of time, contains a law of projection of which philosophers are sometimes unaware, so that their reading of the presented "facts" is obvious and yet wrong, as a child's visual experience is obvious yet deceptive when his judgment is ensnared by the trick of the flattened map. The transformation which facts undergo when they are rendered as propositions is that the relations in them are turned into something like *objects*. Thus, "A killed B" tells of a way in which A and B were unfortunately combined; but our only means of expressing this way is to *name* it, and presto!—a new entity, "killing," seems to have added itself to the complex of A and B. The event which is "pictured" in the proposition undoubtedly involved a *succession* of acts by A and B, but not the succession which the proposition seems to exhibit—first A, then "killing," then B. Surely A and B were simultaneous with each other and with the killing. But words have a linear, discrete, successive order; they are strung one after another like beads on a rosary; beyond the very limited meanings of inflections, which can indeed be incorporated in the words themselves, we cannot talk in simultaneous bunches of names. We must name one thing and then another, and symbols that are not names must be stuck between or before or after, by convention. But these symbols, holding proud places in the chain of names, are apt to be mistaken for names, to the detriment of many a metaphysical theory. Lord Russell regrets that we cannot construct a language which would express all relations by analogous relations; then we would not be tempted to misconstrue language, as a person who knows the meaning of the Mercator map, but has not used one freely enough to "see" in its terms, misconstrues the relative sizes of its areas.

"Take, say, that lightning precedes thunder," he says. "To express this by a language closely reproducing the structure of the fact, we should have to say simply: 'lightning, thunder,' where the fact that the first word precedes the second means that what the first word means precedes what the second word means. But even it we adopted his method for temporal order, we should still need words for all other relations, because we could not without intolerable ambiguity symbolize them by the order of our words."[2]

It is a mistake, I think, to symbolize things by entities too much like themselves; to let words in temporal order represent things in temporal order. If relations such as temporal order are symbolized at all, let the symbols not be those same relations themselves. A structure cannot include as *part of a symbol* something that should properly be *part of the meaning*. But it is unfortunate that names and syntactical indicators look

---

[2] *Philosophy*, p. 264.

so much alike in language; that we cannot represent objects by words, and relations by pitch, loudness, or other characteristics of speech.[3]

As it is, however, all language has a form which requires us to string out our ideas even though their objects rest one within the other; as pieces of clothing that are actually worn one over the other have to be strung side by side on the clothesline. This property of verbal symbolism is known as *discursiveness;* by reason of it, only thoughts which can be arranged in this peculiar order can be spoken at all; any idea which does not lend itself to this "projection" is ineffable, incommunicable by means of words. That is why the laws of reasoning, our clearest formulation of exact expression, are sometimes known as the "laws of discursive thought."

There is no need of going further into the details of verbal symbolism and its poorer substitutes, hieroglyphs, the deaf-and-dumb language, Morse Code, or the highly developed drum-telegraphy of certain jungle tribes. The subject has been exhaustively treated by several able men, as the many quotations in this chapter indicate; I can only assent to their findings. The relation between word- structures and their meanings is, I believe, one of logical analogy, whereby, in Wittgenstein's phrase, "we make ourselves pictures of facts." This philosophy of language lends itself, indeed, to great technical development, such as Wittgenstein envisaged:

"In the language of everyday life it very often happens that the same word signifies in different ways—and therefore belongs to two different symbols—or that two words, which signify in different ways, are apparently applied in the same way in the proposition. (3.323)

"In order to avoid these errors, we must employ a symbolism which excludes them, by not applying the same sign in different symbols and by not applying signs in the same way which signify in different ways. A symbolism, that is to say, which obeys the rules of *logical* grammar—of logical syntax.

"(The logical symbolism of Frege and Russell is such a language, which, however, does still not exclude all errors.)" (3.325)[4]

Carnap's admirable book, *The Logical Syntax of Language*, carries out the philosophical program suggested by Wittgenstein. Here an actual, detailed technique is developed for determining the *capacity for expres-*

---

[3] In the same chapter from which I have just quoted, Lord Russell attributes the power of language to represent *events* to the fact that, like events, it is a temporal series. I cannot agree with him in this matter. It is by virtue of *names for relations* that we can depict dynamic relations. We do not mention past events earlier in a sentence than present ones, but subject temporal order to the same projection" as, for instance, attribution or classification; temporal order is usually rendered by the syntactical (nontemporal) device of *tense*.

[4] *Tractatus.*

sion of any given linguistic system, a technique which predicts the limit of all combinations to be made in that system, shows the equivalence of certain forms and the differences among others which might be mistaken for equivalents, and exhibits the conventions to which any thought or experience must submit in order to become conveyable by the symbolism in question. The distinctions between scientific language and everyday speech, which most of us can feel rather than define, are clearly illumined by Carnap's analysis; and it is surprising to find how little of our ordinary communication measures up to the standard of "meaning" which a serious philosophy of language, and hence a logic of discursive thought, set before us.

In this truly remarkable work the somewhat diffuse apprehension of our intellectual age, that *symbolism* is the key to epistemology and "naturel knowledge," finds precise and practical corroboration. The Kantian challenge: "What can I know?" is shown to be dependent on the prior question: "What can I ask?" And the answer, in Professor Carnap's formulation, is clear and direct. I can ask whatever language will express; I can know whatever experiment will answer. A proposition which could not, under any (perhaps ideal, impracticable) conditions, be verified or refuted, is a pseudo-proposition, it has no literal meaning. It does not belong to the framework of knowledge that we call logical conception; it is not true or false, but *unthinkable,* for it falls outside the order of symbolism.

Since an inordinate amount of our talk, and therefore (we hope) of our cerebration too, defies the canons of literal meaning, our philosophers of language—Russell, Wittgenstein, Carnap, and others of similar persuasions—are faced with the new question: What is the true function of those verbal combinations and other pseudo-symbolic structures that have no real significance, but are freely used as though they meant something?

According to our logicians, those structures are to be treated as "expressions" in a different sense, namely as "expressions" of emotions, feelings, desires. They are not symbols for thought, but symptoms of the inner life, like tears and laughter, crooning, or profanity.

"Many linguistic utterances," says Carnap, "are analogous to laughing in that they have only an expressive function, no representative function. Examples of this are cries like 'Oh, Oh,' or, on a higher level, lyrical verses. The aim of a lyrical poem in which occur the words 'sunshine' and 'clouds,' is not to inform us of certain meteorological facts, but to express certain feelings of the poet and to excite similar feelings in us.... Metaphysical propositions—like lyrical verses—have only an expressive function, but no representative function. Metaphysical propositions are neither true nor false, because they assert nothing.... But they are, like laughing, lyrics and music, expressive. They express not so much temporary feelings as permanent emotional and volitional dispositions."[5]

Lord Russell holds a very similar view of other people's metaphysics: "I do not deny," he says, "the importance or value, within its own sphere, of the kind of philosophy which is inspired by ethical notions. The ethical work of Spinoza, for instance, appears to me of the very highest significance, but what is valuable in such a work is not any metaphysical theory as to the nature of the world to which it may give rise, nor indeed anything that can be proved or disproved by argument. What is valuable is the indication of some new way of feeling toward life and the world, some way of feeling by which our own existence can acquire more of the characteristics which we must deeply desire."[6]

And Wittgenstein:

"Most propositions and questions, that have been written about philosophical matters, are not false, but senseless. We cannot, therefore, answer questions of this kind at all, but only state their senselessness. Most questions and propositions of the philosophers result from the fact that we do not understand the logic of our language. (4.003)"

"A proposition presents the existence and non-existence of atomic facts. (4. 1)

"The totality of true propositions is the total of natural science (or the totality of the natural sciences). (4. 11)

"Everything that can be thought at all can be thought clearly. Everything that can be said can be said clearly." (4. 116)[7]

In their criticism of metaphysical propositions, namely that such propositions are usually pseudo-answers to pseudo-questions, these logicians have my full assent; problems of "First Cause" and "Unity" and "Substance," and all the other time-honored topics, are insoluble, because they arise from the fact that we attribute to the world what really belongs to the "logical projection" in which we conceive it, and by misplacing our questions we jeopardize our answers. This source of bafflement has been uncovered by the philosophers of our day, through their interest in the functions and nature of symbolism. The discovery marks a great intellectual advance. But it does not condemn philosophical inquiry as such; it merely requires *every philosophical problem to be recast*, to be conceived in a different form. Many issues that seemed to concern the *sources* of knowledge, for instance, now appear to turn partly or wholly on the *form* of knowledge, or even the forms of expression, of symbolism. The center of philosophical inrerest has shifted once more, as it has shifted several times in the past. That does not mean,

---

[5] *Philosophy and Logical Syntax*, p. 28.

[6] "Scientific Method in Philosophy," in *Mysticism and Logic* (1918), p.109.

[7] *Op. cit.*

however, that rational people should now renounce metaphysics. The recognition of the intimate relation between symbolism and experience, on which our whole criticism of traditional problems is based, is itself a metaphysical insight. For metaphysics is, like every philosophical pursuit, a study of *meaning*. From it spring the special sciences, which can develop their techniques and verify their propositions one by one, *as soon as their initial concepts are clear enough to allow systematic handling* i.e. as soon as the philosophical work behind them is at least tentatively accomplished.[8] Metaphysics is not itself a science with fixed presuppositions, but progresses from problem to problem rather than from premise to consequence. To suppose that we have outgrown it is to suppose that all "the sciences" are finally established, that human language is complete, or at least soon to be completed, and additional facts are all we lack of the greatest knowledge ever possible to man; and though this knowledge may be small, it is all that we shall ever have.

This is, essentially, the attitude of those logicians who have investigated the limits of language. Nothing that is not "language" in the sense of their technical definition can possess the character of symbolic expressiveness (though it may be "expressive" in the symptomatic way). Consequently nothing that cannot be "projected" in discursive form is accessible to the human mind at all, and any attempt to understand anything but demonstrable fact is bootless ambition. The knowable is a clearly defined field, governed by the requirement of discursive projectability. Outside this domain is the inexpressible realm of feeling, of formless desires and satisfactions, immediate experience, forever incognito and incommunicado. A philosopher who looks in that direction is, or should be, a mystic, from the ineffable sphere nothing but nonsense can be conveyed, since language, our only possible semantic, will not clothe experiences that elude the discursive form.

But intelligence is a slippery customer; if one door is closed to it, it finds, or even breaks, another entrance to the world. If one symbolism is inadequate, it seizes another; there is no eternal decree over its means and methods. So I will go with the logisticians and linguists as far as they like, but do not promise to go no further. For there is an unexplored possibility of genuine semantic beyond the limits of discursive language.

This logical "beyond," which Wittgenstein calls the "unspeakable," both Russell and Carnap regard as the sphere of subjective experience, emotion, feeling, and wish, from which only *symptoms* come to us in the form of metaphysical and artistic fancies. The study of such products they relegate to psychology, not semantics. And here is the point of my

---

[8] I have presented a fuller discussion of philosophy as the "mother of sciences" in *The Practice of Philosophy* (1930), ch. ii.

radical divergence from them. Where Carnap speaks of "cries like 'Oh, Oh, 'or, on a higher level, lyrical verses," I can see only a complete failure to apprehend a fundamental distinction. Why should we cry our feelings at such high levels that anyone would think we were *talking?*[9] Clearly, poetry means more than a cry; it has reason for being articulate; and metaphysics is more than the croon with which we might cuddle up to the world in a comfortable attitude. We are dealing with symbolisms here, and what they express is often highly intellectual. Only, the form and function of such symbolisms are not those investigated by logicians, under the heading of "language." The field of semantics is wider than that of language, as certain philosophers—Schopenhauer, Cassirer, Delacroix, Dewey, Whitehead, and some others—have discovered; but it is blocked for us by the two fundamental tenets of current epistemology, which we have just discussed.

These two basic assumptions go hand in hand: (1) That *language*[10] *is the only means of articulating thought,* and (2) That *everything which is not speakable thought, is feeling.* They are linked together because all genuine thinking is symbolic, and the limits of the expressive medium are, therefore, really the limits of our conceptual powers. Beyond these we can have only blind feeling, which records nothing and conveys nothing, but has to be discharged in action or self-expression, in deeds or cries or other impulsive demonstrations.

But if we consider how difficult it is to construct a meaningful language that shall meet neo-positivistic standards, it is quite incredible that people should ever *say* anything at all, or understand each other's propositions. At best, human thought is but a tiny, grammar-bound island, in the midst of a sea of feeling expressed by "Oh-oh" and sheer babble. The island has a periphery, perhaps, of mud—factual and hypothetical concepts broken down by the emotional tides into the "material mode," a mixture of meaning and nonsense. Most of us live the better part of our lives on this mudflat; but in artistic moods we take to the deep, where we flounder about with symptomatic cries that sound like-propositions about life and death, good and evil, substance, beauty, and other nonexistent topics.

So long as we regard only scientific and "material" (semi-scientific) thought as really cognitive of the world, this peculiar picture of mental life must stand. And so *long as we admit only discursive symbolism as a bearer of ideas, "thought" in this restricted sense must be regarded as our only intellectual activity.* It begins and ends with language; without the elements, at least, of scientific grammar, conception must be impossible.

---

[9] *Cf.* Urban, *Language and Reality,* p. 164.

[10] Including, of course, its refinements in mathematical and scientific symbolisms, and its approximations by gesture, hieroglyphics, or graphs.

A theory which implies such peculiar consequences is itself a suspicious character. But the error which it harbors is not in its reasoning. It is in the very premise from which the doctrine proceeds, namely that all articulate symbolism is discursive. As Lord Russell, with his usual precision and directness, has stated the case, "it is clear that anything that can be said in an inflected language can be said in an uninflected language; therefore, anything that can be said in language can be said by means of a temporal series of uninflected words. This places a limitation upon what can be expressed in words. It may well be that there are facts which do not lend themselves to this very simple schema; if so, they cannot be expressed in language. Our confidence in language is due to the fact that it . . . shares the structure of the physical world, and therefore can express that structure. But if there be a world which is not physical, or not in space-time, it may have a structure which we can never hope to express or to know.... Perhaps that is why we know so much physic and so little of anything else."[11]

Now, I do not believe that "there is a world which is not physical, or not in space-time," but I do believe that in this physical, space-time world of our experience there are things which do not fit the grammatical scheme of expression. But they are not necessarily blind, inconceivable, mystical affairs; they are simply matters which require to be conceived through some symbolistic schema other than discursive language. And to demonstrate the possibility of such a non-discursive pattern one needs only to review the logical requirements for any symbolic structure whatever. Language is by no means our only articulate product.

Our merest sense-experience is a process of *formulation*. The world that actually meets our senses is not a world of "things," about which we are invited to discover facts as soon as we have codified the necessary logical language to do so; the world of pure sensation is so complex, so fluid and full, that sheer sensitivity to stimuli would only encounter what William James has called (in characteristic phrase) "a blooming, buzzing confusion." Out of this bedlam our sense-organs must select certain predominant forms, if they are to make report of *things* and not of mere dissolving sensa. The eye and the ear must have their logic—their "categories of understanding," if you like the Kantian idiom, or their "primary imagination," in Coleridge's version of the same concept."[12] An object is not a datum, but a form construed by the sensitive and intelligent organ, a form which is at once an experienced individual thing and a symbol for the concept of it, for *this sort of thing*.

---

[11] *Philosophy*, p. 265.

[12] An excellent discussion of Coleridge's philosophy may be found in D. G. James, *Skepticism and Poetry* (1937), a book well worth reading in connection with this chapter.

A tendency to organize the sensory field into groups and patterns of sense-data, to perceive forms rather than a flux of light-impressions, seems to be inherent in our receptor apparatus just as much as in the higher nervous centers with which we do arithmetic and logic. But this unconscious appreciation of forms is the primitive root of all abstraction, which in turn is the keynote of rationality; so it appears that the conditions for rationality lie deep in our pure animal experience—in our power of perceiving, in the elementary functions of our eyes and ears and fingers. Mental life begins with our mere physiological constitution. A little reflection shows us that, since no experience occurs more than once, so-called "repeated" experiences are really *analogous* occurrences, all fitting a form that was abstracted on the first occasion. Familiarity, is nothing but the quality of fitting very neatly into the form of a previous experience. I believe our ingrained habit of hypostatizing impressions, of seeing *things* and not sense-data, rests on the fact that we promptly and unconsciously abstract a form from each sensory experience, and use this form to *conceive* the experience as a whole, as a "thing."

No matter what heights the human mind may attain, it can work only with the organs it has and the functions peculiar to them. Eyes that did not see forms could never furnish it with *images;* ears that did not hear articulated sounds could never open it to *words.* Sense-data, in brief, would be useless to a mind whose activity is "through and through a symbolic process," were they not *par excellence* receptacles of meaning. But meaning, as previous considerations have shown, accrues essentially to forms. Unless the *Gestalt*-psychologists are right in their belief that *Gestaltung* is of the very nature of perception, I do not know how the hiatus between perception and conception, sense-organ and mind-organ, chaotic stimulus and logical response, is ever to be closed and welded. A mind that works primarily with meanings must have organs that supply it primarily with forms.

The nervous system is the organ of the mind; its center is the brain, its extremities the sense-organs; and any characteristic function it may possess must govern the work of all its parts. In other words, the activity of our senses is "mental" not only when it reaches the brain, but in its very inception, whenever the alien world outside impinges on the furthest and smallest receptor. All sensitivity bears the stamp for mentality. "Seeing," for instance, is not a passive process, by which meaningless impressions are stored up for the use of an organizing mind, which construes forms out of these amorphous data to suit its own purposes. "Seeing" is itself a process of formulation; our understanding of the visible world begins in the eye.[13]

---

[13] For a general account of the *Gestalt*-theory, see Wolfgang Kohler, *Gestalt Psychology* (1929), from which the following relevant passage is taken:

This psychological insight, which we owe to the school of Wertheimer, Köhler, and Koffka, has far-reaching philosophical consequences, if we take it seriously; for it carries rationality into processes that are usually deemed pre-rational, and points to the existence of forms, i.e. of *possible symbolic material*, at a level where symbolic activity has certainly never been looked for by any epistemologist. The eye and the ear make their own abstractions, and consequently dictate their own peculiar forms of conception. But these forms are derived from exactly the same world that furnished the totally different forms known to physics. There is, in fact, no such thing as *the* form of the "real" world; physics is one pattern which may be found in it, and "appearance," or the pattern of *things* with their qualities and characters, is another. One construction may indeed preclude the other; but to maintain that the consistency and universality of the one brands the other as *false* is a mistake. The fact that physical analysis does not rest in a final establishment of irreducible "qualities" does not refute the belief that there are red, blue, and green things, wet or oily or dry substances, fragrant flowers, and shiny surfaces in the real world. These concepts of the "material mode" are not approximations to "physical" notions at all. Physical concepts owe their origin and development to the application of *mathematics* to the world of "things," and mathematics never—even in the beginning—dealt with qualities of objects. It measured their proportions, but never treated its concepts—triangularity, circularity, etc.—as qualities of which *so-and-so much* could become an ingredient of certain objects. Even though an elliptical race-track may approximate a circle, it is not to be improved by the addition of more circularity. On the other hand, wine which is not sweet enough requires more sweetening, paint which is not bright enough is given an ingredient of more white or more color. The world of physics is essentially the real world construed by mathematical abstractions, and the world of sense is the real world construed by the abstractions which the sense-organs immediately furnish. To suppose that the "material mode" is a primitive and groping attempt at physical conception is a fatal error in epistemology, because it cuts off all interest in the developments of which sensuous conception is capable, and the intellectual uses to which it might be put.

"It is precisely the original organization and segregation of circumscribed wholes which make it possible for the sensory world to appear so utterly imbued with meaning to the adult because, in its gradual entry into the sensory field, meaning follows the lines drawn by natural organization. It usually enters into segregated wholes....

"Where 'form' *exists* originally, it acquires a meaning very easily. But here a whole with its form is given first and then a meaning 'creeps into it.' That meaning automatically produces a form where beforehand there is none, has not been shown experimentally in a single case, as for as I know" (p. 208).

See also Max Wertheimer, *Drei Abhandlungen zur Gestalttheorie* (1925), and Kurt Koffka, *Principles of Gestalt Psychology* (1935).

These intellectual uses lie in a field which usually harbors a slough of despond for the philosopher, who ventures into it because he is too honest to ignore it, though really he knows no path around its pitfalls. It is the field of "intuition," "deeper meaning," "artistic truth," "insight," and so forth. A dangerous-looking sector, indeed, for the advance of a rational spirit! To date, I think, every serious epistemology that has regarded mental life as greater than discursive reason, and has made concessions to "insight" or "intuition," has just so far capitulated to *unreason*, to mysticism and irrationalism. Every excursion beyond propositional thought has dispensed with thought altogether, and postulated some inmost soul of pure feeling in direct contact with a Reality unsymbolized, unfocused, and incommunicable (with the notable exception of the theory set forth by L. A. Reid in the last chapter of his *Knowledge and Truth*, which admits the facts of non-propositional conception in a way that invites rather than precludes logical analysis).

The abstractions made by the ear and the eye—the forms of direct perception—are our most primitive instruments of intelligence. They are genuine symbolic materials, media of understanding, by whose office we apprehend a world of *things*, and of events that are the histories of things. To furnish such conceptions is their prime mission. Our sense-organs make their habitual, unconscious abstractions, in the interest of this "reifying" function that underlies ordinary recognition of objects, knowledge of signals, words, tunes, places, and the possibility of classifying such things in the outer world according to their kind. We recognize the elements of this sensuous analysis in all sorts of combination; we can use them imaginatively, to conceive prospective changes in familiar scenes.

Visual forms—fines, colors, proportions, etc.—are just as capable of *articulation*, i.e. of complex combination, as words. But the laws that govern this sort of articulation are altogether different from the laws of syntax that govern language. The most radical difference is that *visual forms are not discursive*. They do not present their constituants successively, but simultaneously, so the relations determining a visual structure are grasped in one act of vision. Their complexity, consequently, is not limited, as the complexity of discourse is limited, by what the mind can retain from the beginning of an apperceptive act to the end of it. Of course such a restriction on discourse sets bounds to the complexity of speakable ideas. An idea that contains too many minute yet closely related parts, too many relations within relations, cannot be "projected" into discursive form; it is too subtle for speech. A language-bound theory of mind, therefore, rules it out of the domain of understanding and the sphere of knowledge.

But the symbolism furnished by our purely sensory appreciation of forms is a *non-discursive symbolism*, peculiarly well suited to the expression of ideas that defy linguistic "projection." Its primary function, that of conceptualizing the flux of sensations, and giving us concrete *things* in place of kaleidoscopic colors or noises, is itself an office that no language born thought can replace. The understanding of space which we owe to sight and touch could never be developed, in all its detail and definiteness, by a discursive knowledge of geometry. Nature speaks to us, first of all, through our senses; the forms and qualities we distinguish, remember, imagine, or recognize are symbols of entities which exceed and outlive our momentary experience. Moreover, the same symbols—qualities, lines, rhythms—may occur in innumerable presentations; they are abstractable and combinatory. It is quite natural, therefore, that philosophers who have recognized the symbolical character of so-called "sense-data," especially in their highly developed uses, in science and art, often speak of a "language" of the senses, a "language" of musical tones, of colors, and so forth.

Yet this manner of speaking is very deceptive. Language is a special mode of expression, and not every sort of semantic can be brought under this rubric; by generalizing from linguistic symbolism to symbolism as such, we are easily led to misconceive all other types, and overlook their most interesting features. Perhaps it were well to consider, here, the salient characteristics of true language, or discourse.

In the first place, *every language has a vocabulary and a syntax*. Its elements are words with fixed meanings. Out of these one can construct, according to the rules of the syntax, composite symbols with resultant new meanings.

Secondly, in a language, some words are equivalent to whole combinations of other words, so that most meanings can be expressed in several different ways. This makes it possible *to define the meanings of the ultimate single words*, i.e., to construct a dictionary.

Thirdly, there may be alternative words for the same meaning. When two people systematically use different words for almost everything, they are said to speak different languages. But the two languages are roughly equivalent; with a little artifice, an occasional substitution of a phrase for a single word, etc., the propositions enunciated by one person, in his system, may be *translated* into the conventional system of the other.

Now consider the most familiar sort of non-discursive symbol, a picture. Like language, it is composed of elements that represent various respective constituants in the object; but these elements are not units with independent meanings. The areas of light and shade that constitute a portrait, a photograph for instance, have no significance by themselves. In isolation we would consider them simply blotches. Yet they are faithful representatives of visual elements composing the visual object. However, they do not represent, item for item, those elements which have *names;* there is not one blotch for the nose, one for the mouth, etc.; their shapes, in quite indescribable combinations, convey a total picture in which nameable features may be pointed out. The gradations of light and shade cannot be enumerated. They cannot be correlated, one by one, with parts or characteristics by means of which we might *describe* the person who posed for the portrait. The "elements" that the camera represents are not the "elements" that language represents. They are a thousand times more numerous. For this reason the correspondance between a word-picture and a visible object can never be as close as that between the object and its photograph. Given all at once to the intelligent eye, an incredible wealth and detail of information is conveyed by the portrait, where we do not have to stop to construe verbal meanings. That is why we use a photograph rather than a description on a passport or in the Rogues' Gallery.

Clearly, a symbolism with so many elements, such myriad relationships, cannot be broken up into basic units. It is i⸻ ⸻nd the smallest independent symbol, and recognize its identity when the same unit is met in other context. Photography, therefore, *has no vocabulary.* The same is obviously true of painting, drawing, etc. There is, of course, a technique of picturing objects, but the law governing this technique cannot properly be called a "syntax," since there are no items that might be called, metaphorically, the "words" of portraiture.

Since we have no words, there can be no dictionary of meanings for lines, shadings, or other elements of pictorial technique. We may well pick out some line, say a certain curve, in a picture, which serves to represent one nameable item; but in another place the same curve would have an entirely different meaning. It has no fixed meaning apart from its context. Also, there is no complex of other elements that is equivalent to it at all times, as "2+2" is equivalent to "4." Non- discursive symbols cannot be defined in terms of others, as discursive symbols can.

If there can be no defining dictionary, of course we have no translating dictionary, either. There are different media of graphic representation, but their respective elements cannot be brought into one-to-one correlation with each other, as in languages: *"chien"* = *"dog,"* *"moi"* = *"me,"* etc. There is no standard key for translating sculpture into painting, or drawing into ink-wash, because their equivalence rests on their common *total reference,* not on bit-for-bit equivalences of parts such as underlie a literal translation.

Furthermore, verbal symbolism, unlike the non-discursive kinds, has primarily a *general* reference. Only convention can assign a proper name—and then there is no way of preventing some other convention from assigning the same proper name to a different individual. We may name a child as oddly as we will, yet we cannot guarantee that no one else will ever bear that designation. A description may fit a scene ever so closely, but it takes some known proper name to refer it without possible doubt to one and only one place. Where the names of persons and places are withheld, we can never *prove* that a discourse refers—not merely applies—to a certain historic occasion. In the non-discursive mode that speaks directly to sense, however, there is no intrinsic generality. It is first and foremost a direct *presentation* of an individual object. A picture has to be schematized if it is to be capable of various meanings. In itself it represents just one object—real or imaginary, but still a unique object. The definition of a triangle fits triangles in general, but a drawing always presents a triangle of some specific kind and size. We have to abstract from the conveyed meaning in order to conceive triangularity in general. Without the help of words this generalization, if possible at all, is certainly incommunicable.

It appears, then, that although the different media of non-verbal representation are often referred to as distinct "languages," this is really a loose terminology. Language in the strict sense is essentially discursive; it has permanent units of meaning which are combinable into larger units; it has fixed equivalences that make definition and translation possible; its connotations are general, so that it requires non-verbal acts, like pointing, looking, or emphatic voice-inflections, to assign specific denotations to its terms. In all these salient characters it differs from wordless symbolism, which is non-discursive and untranslatable does not allow of definitions within its own system, and cannot directly convey generalities. The meanings given through language are successively understood, and gathered into a whole by the process called discourse; the meanings of all other symbolic elements that compose a larger, articulate symbol are understood only through the meaning of the whole, through their relations within the total structure. Their very functioning as symbols depends on the fact that they are involved in a simultaneous, integral presentation. This kind of semantic may be called "presentational symbolism," to characterize its essential distinction from discursive symbolism, or "language" proper.[14]

The recognition of presentational symbolism as a normal and prevalent vehicle of meaning widens our conception of rationality far beyond the traditional boundaries, yet never breaks faith with logic in the strictest sense. Wherever a symbol operates, there is a meaning; and conversely, different classes of experience—say, reason, intuition,

---

[14] It is relevant here to note that "picture language," which uses *separate pictures in place of words,* is a discursive symbolism, though each "word" is a presentational symbol; and that all codes, e.g., the conventional gestures of deaf-mutes or the drum communications of African tribes, are discursive systems.

appreciation—correspond to different types of symbolic mediation. No symbol is exempt from the office of logical formulation, of *conceptualizing* what it conveys; however simple its import, or however great, this import is a *meaning*, and therefore an element for understanding. Such reflection invites one to tackle anew, and with entirely different expectations, the whole problem of the limits of reason, the much-disputed life of feeling, and the great controversial topics of fact and truth, knowledge and wisdom, science and art. It brings within the compass of reason much that has been traditionally relegated to "emotion," or to that crepuscular depth of the mind where "intuitions" are supposed to be born, without any midwifery of symbols, without due process of thought, to fill the gaps in the edifice of discursive, or "rational," judgment.

The symbolic materials given to our senses, the *Gestalten* or fundamental perceptual forms which invite us to construe the pandemonium of sheer impression into a world of things and occasions, belong to the "presentational" order. They furnish the elementary abstractions in terms of which ordinary sense-experience is understood.'[15] This kind of understanding is directly reflected in the pattern of *physical reaction*, impulse and instinct. May not the order of perceptual forms, then, be a possible principle for symbolization, and hence the conception, expression, and apprehension, of impulsive, instinctive, and sentient life? May not a nondiscursive symbolism of light and color, or of tone, be formulative of that life? And is it not possible that the sort of "intuitive" knowledge which Bergson extols above all rational knowledge because it is supposedly not mediated by any formulating (and hence deforming) symbol'[16] is itself perfectly rational, but not to be conceived through language—a product of that presentational symbolism which the mind reads in a flash, and preserves in a disposition or an attitude?

This hypothesis, though unfamiliar and therefore somewhat difficult, seems to me well worth exploring. For, quite apart from all questions of the authenticity of intuitive, inherited, or inspired knowledge,

---

[15] Kant thought that the *principles* of such formulation were supplied by a faculty of the mind, which he called *Verstand;* but his somewhat dogmatic delimitation of the field of knowledge open to *Verstand,* and the fact that he regarded the mind-engendered forms as *constitutive* of experience rather than *interpretative* (as principles must be), prevented logicians from taking serious note of such forms as possible machinery of reason. They abode by the forms of *Vernunft,* which are, roughly speaking, the forms of discourse. Kant himself exalted *Vernunft* as the special gift and glory of man. When an epistemology of medium and meaning began to crowd out the older epistemology of percept and concept, his *Verstandesformen,* in their role of *Conceptual ingredients* of phenomena, were lumped with his metaphysical doctrines, and eclipsed by "metalogical" interests.

[16] See Henri Bergson, *La pensée et le mouvement* (1934), esp. essays ii ("De la position des problèmes") and iv ("L'intuition philosophique"): also his *Essai sur les données immédiates de la conscience* (1889), and *Introduction to Metaphysics* (1912).

about which I do not wish to cavil, the very idea of a *non-rational source* of any knowledge vitiates the concept of mind as an organ of understanding. "The power of reason is simply the power of the whole mind at its fullest stretch and compass," said Professor Creighton, in an essay that sought to stem the great wave of irrationalism and emotionalism following the World War.[17] This assumption appears to me to be a basic one in any study of mentality. Rationality is the essence of mind, and symbolic transformation its elementary process. It is a fundamental error, therefore, to recognize it only in the phenomenon of systematic, explicit reasoning. That is a mature and precarious product.

Rationality, however, is embodied in every mental act, not only when the mind is "at its fullest stretch and compass." It permeates the peripheral activities of the human nervous system, just as truly as the cortical functions.

"The facts of perception and memory maintain themselves only in so for as they are mediated, and thus given significance beyond their mere isolated existence.... What falls in any way within experience partakes of the rational form of the mind. As mental content, any part of experience is something more than a particular impression having only the attributes of existence. As already baptized into the life of the mind, it partakes of its logical nature and moves on the plane of universality....

"No matter how strongly the unity and integrity of the mind is asserted, this unity is nothing more than verbal if the mind is not in principle the expression of reason. For it can be shown that all attempts to render comprehensible the unity of the mental life in terms of an alogical principle fail to attain their goal."[18]

The title of Professor Creighton's trenchant little article is "Reason and Feeling." Its central thesis is that if there is something in our mental life besides "reason," by which he means, of course, discursive thinking, then it cannot be an alogical factor, but must be in essence cognitive, too; and since the only alternative to this reason is feeling (the author does not question that axiom of epistemology), feeling itself must somehow participate in knowledge and understanding.

All this may be granted. The position is well taken. But the most crucial *problem* is barely broached: this problem is epitomized in the word "somehow." *Just how* can feelings be conceived as possible ingredients of rationality? We are not told, but we are given a generous hint, which in the light of a broader theory of symbolism points to explanation.

"In the development of mind," he says, "feeling does not remain a static element, constant in form and content at all levels, but . . . is trans-

[17] J. E. Creighton, "Reason and Feeling," *Philosophical Review, XXX* (1921),5: 465– 481. See p. 469.
[18] *Ibid.,* pp. 470–472.

formed and disciplined through its interplay with other aspects of experience.... Indeed, the character of the feeling in any experience may be
taken as an index of the mind's grasp of its object; at the lower levels of
experience, where the mind is only partially or superficially involved,
feeling appears as something isolated and opaque, as the passive
accompaniment of mere bodily sensations.... In the higher experiences,
the feelings assume an entirely different character, just as do the sensations and the other contents of mind."[19]

The significant observation voiced in this passage is that *feelings
have definite forms, which become progressively articulated.* Their development is effected through their "interplay with the other aspects of experience"; but the nature of that interplay is not specified. Yet it is here, I
think, that cogency for the whole thesis must be sought. *What* character
of feeling is "an index of the mind's grasp of its object," and by what
tokens is it so? If feeling has articulate forms, what are they like? For
what these are *like* determines by what symbolism we might understand them. Everybody knows that language is a very poor medium for
expressing our emotional nature. It merely names certain vaguely and
crudely conceived stases, but fails miserably in any attempt to convey
the evermoving patterns, the ambivalences and intricacies of inner
experience, the interplay of feelings with thoughts and impressions,
memories and echoes of memories, transient fantasy, or its mere runic
traces, all turned into nameless, emotional stuff. If we say that we
understand someone else's feeling in a certain matter, we mean that we
understand why he should be sad or happy, excited or indifferent, in a
general way; that we can see due cause for his attitude. We do not mean
that we have insight into the actual flow and balance of his feelings, into
that "character" which "may be taken as an index of the mind's grasp
of its object." Language is quite inadequate to articulate such a conception. Probably we would not impart our actual, inmost feelings even if
they could be spoken. We rarely speak in detail of entirely personal
things.

There is, however, a kind of symbolism peculiarly adapted to the
explication of "unspeakable" things, though it lacks the cardinal virtue
of language, which is denotation. The most highly developed type of
such purely connotational semantic is music. We are not talking nonsense when we say that a certain musical progression is significant, or
that a given phrase lacks meaning, or a player's rendering fails to convey the import of a passage. Yet such statements make sense only to
people with a natural understanding of the medium, whom we
describe, therefore, as "musical." Musicality is often regarded as an
essentially unintellectual, even a biologically sportive trait. Perhaps that

---

[19] *Ibid.*, pp. 478–479.

is why musicians, who know that it is the prime source of their mental life and the medium of their clearest insight into humanity, so often feel called upon to despise the more obvious forms of understanding, that claim practical virtues under the names of reason, logic, etc. But in fact, musical understanding is not hampered by the possession of an active intellect, nor even by that love of pure reason which is known as rationalism or intellectualism; and *vice versa*, common-sense and scientific acumen need not defend themselves against any "emotionalism" that is supposed to be inherent in a respect for music. Speech and music have essentially different functions, despite their oft-remarked union in song. Their original relationship lies much deeper than any such union (of which more will be said in a subsequent chapter), and can be seen only when their respective natures are understood.

The problem of meaning deepens at every turn. The longer we delve into its difficulties, the more complex it appears. But in a central philosophical concept, this is a sign of health. Each question answered leads to another which previously could not be even entertained: the logic of symbolism, the possible types of representation, the fields proper to them, the actual functions of symbols according to their nature, their relationships to each other, and finally our main theme, their integration in human mentality.

Of course it is not possible to study every known phenomenon in the realm of symbolism. But neither is this necessary even in an intimate study. The logical structures underlying all semantic functions, which I have discussed in this chapter, suggest a general principle of division. Signs are logically distinct from symbols; discursive and presentational patterns show a formal difference. There are further natural divisions due to various ways of *using* symbols, no less important than the logical distinctions. Altogether, we may group meaning-situations around certain outstanding types, and make these several types the subjects of individual studies. Language, ritual, myth, and music, representing four respective modes, may serve as central topics for the study of actual symbolisms; and I trust that further problems of significance in art, in science or mathematics, in behavior or in fantasy and dream, may receive some light by analogy, and by that most powerful human gift, the adaptation of ideas.

6

Linguistics and Poetics

Roman Jakobson[1]

Sometimes we hear that poetics, in contradistinction to linguistics, is concerned with evaluation. This separation of the two fields from each other is based on a current but erroneous interpretation of the "contrast" between the structure of poetry and other types of verbal structure: the latter are said to be opposed by their "casual," designless nature to the "noncasual," purposeful character of poetic language. In point of fact, any verbal behavior is goal-directed, but the aims are different and the conformity of the means used to the effect aimed at is a problem that evermore preoccupies inquirers into the diverse kinds of verbal communication. There is a close correspondence, much closer than critics believe, between the question of linguistic phenomena expanding in space and time and the spatial and temporal spread of literary models. Even such discontinuous expansion as the resurrection of neglected or forgotten poets—for instance, the posthumous discovery and subsequent canonization of Gerard Manley Hopkins (d. 1889), the tardy fame of Lautréamont (d. 1870) among surrealist poets, and the salient influence of the hitherto ignored Cyprian Norwid (d. 1883) on Polish modern poetry—find a parallel in the history of standard languages which are prone to revive outdated models sometimes long forgotten, as was the case in literary Czech which toward the beginning of the nineteenth century leaned to sixteenth-century models.

Unfortunately the terminological confusion of "literary studies" with "criticism" tempts the student of literature to replace the description of the intrinsic values of a literary work by a subjective, censorious verdict. The label "literary critic" applied to an investigator of literature is as erroneous as "grammatical (or lexical) critic" would be applied to a linguist. Syntactic and morphologic research cannot be supplanted by a normative grammar, and likewise no manifesto, foisting a critic's own tastes and opinions on creative literature, may act as substitute for an objective scholarly analysis of verbal art. This statement is not to be mistaken for the quietist principle of *laissez faire;* any verbal culture involves programmatic, planning, normative endeavors. Yet why is a clear-cut discrimination made between pure and applied linguistics or

[1] Roman Jakobson, "Linguistics and poetics," in *Style in Language* ed. Thomas A. Sebeok (Cambridge, Mass.: Harvard University Press, 1960).

between phonetics and orthoepy but not between literary studies and criticism?

Literary studies, with poetics as their focal point, consist like linguistics of two sets of problems: synchrony and diachrony. The synchronic description envisages not only the literary production of any given stage but also that part of the literary tradition which for the stage in question has remained vital or has been revived. Thus, for instance, Shakespeare on the one hand and Donne, Marvell, Keats, and Emily Dickinson on the other are experienced by the present English poetic world, whereas the works of James Thomson and Longfellow, for the time being, do not belong to viable artistic values. The selection of classics and their reinterpretation by a novel trend is a substantial problem of synchronic literary studies. Synchronic poetics, like synchronic linguistics, is not to be confused with statics; any stage discriminates between more conservative and more innovatory forms. Any contemporary stage is experienced in its temporal dynamics, and, on the other hand, the historical approach both in poetics and in linguistics is concerned not only with changes but also with continuous, enduring, static factors. A thoroughly comprehensive historical poetics or history of language is a superstructure to be built on a series of successive synchronie descriptions.

Insistence on keeping poetics apart from linguistics is warranted only when the field of linguistics appears to be illicitly restricted, for example, when the sentence is viewed by some linguists as the highest analyzable construction or when the scope of linguistics is confined to grammar alone or uniquely to nonsemantic questions of external form or to the inventory of denotative devices with no reference to free variations. Voegelin has clearly pointed out the two most important and related problems which face structural linguistics, namely, a revision of "the monolithic hypothesis of language" and a concern with "the interdependence of diverse structures within one language." No doubt, for any speech community, for any speaker, there exists a unity of language, but this over-all code represents a system of interconnected subcodes; each language encompasses several concurrent patterns which are each characterized by a different function.

Obviously we must agree with Sapir that, on the whole, "ideation reigns supreme in language...[2]," but this supremacy does not authorize linguistics to disregard the "secondary factors." The emotive elements of speech which, as Joos is prone to believe, cannot be described "with a finite number of absolute categories," are classified by him "as non-linguistic elements of the real world." Hence, "for us they remain

---

[2] Edward Sapir, *Language: An Introduction to the Study of Speech* (New York: Harcourt, Brace, 1921).

vague, protean, fluctuating phenomena," he concludes, "which we refuse to tolerate in our science[3]." Joos is indeed a brilliant expert in reduction experiments, and his emphatic requirement for an "expulsion" of the emotive elements "from linguistic science" is a radical experiment in reduction — *reductio ad absurdum*.

Language must be investigated in all the variety of its functions. Before discussing the poetic function we must define its place among the other functions of language. An outline of these functions demands a concise survey of the constitutive factors in any speech event, in any act of verbal communication. The ADDRESSER sends a MESSAGE to the ADDRESSEE. To be operative the message requires a CONTEXT referred to ("referent" in another, somewhat ambiguous, nomenclature), seizable by the addressee, and either verbal or capable of being verbalized; a CODE fully, or at least partially, common to the addresser and addressee (or in other words, to the encoder and decoder of the message); and, finally, a CONTACT, a physical channel and psychological connection between the addresser and the addressee, enabling both of them to enter and stay in communication. All these factors inalienably involved in verbal communication may be schematized as follows:

CONTEXT

ADDRESSER   MESSAGE   ADDRESSEE
....

CONTACT

CODE

Each of these six factors determines a different function of language. Although we distinguish six basic aspects of language, we could, however, hardly find verbal messages that would fulfill only one function. The diversity lies not in a monopoly of some one of these several functions but in a different hierarchical order of functions. The verbal structure of a message depends primarily on the predominant function. But even though a set *(Einstellung)* toward the referent, an orientation toward the CONTEXT—briefly the so-called REFERENTIAL, "denotative," "cognitive" function—is the leading task of numerous messages, the accessory participation of the other functions in such messages must be taken into account by the observant linguist.

The so-called EMOTIVE or "expressive" function, focused on the ADDRESSER, aims a direct expression of the speaker's attitude toward what he is speaking about. It tends to produce an impression of a certain emotion whether true or feigned; therefore, the term "emotive,"

---

[3] Martin Joos, "Description of language design," *Journal of the Acoustical Society of America* 22 (1950), pp. 701–708.

launched and advocated by Marty[4] has proved to be preferable to "emotional." The purely emotive stratum in language is presented by interjections. They differ from the means of referential language both by their sound pattern (peculiar sound sequences or even sounds elsewhere unusual) and by their syntactic role (they are not components but equivalents of sentences). *"Tut! Tut!* said McGinty"*: the complete utterance of Conan Doyle's character consists of two suction clicks. The emotive function, laid bare in the interjections, flavors to some extent all our utterances, on their phonic, grammatical, and lexical level. If we analyze language from the standpoint of the information it carries, we cannot restrict the notion of information to the cognitive aspect of language. A man, using expressive features to indicate his angry or ironic attitude, conveys ostensible information, and evidently this verbal behavior cannot be likened to such nonsemiotic, nutritive activities as "eating grapefruit" (despite Chatman's bold simile). The difference between [big] and the emphatic prolongation of the vowel [bi:g] is a conventional, coded linguistic feature like the difference between the short and long vowel in such Czech pairs as [vi] 'you' and [vi:] 'knows,' but in the latter pair the differential information is phonemic and in the former emotive. As long as we are interested in phonemic invariants, the English /i/ and /i:/ appear to be mere variants of one and the same phoneme, but if we are concerned with emotive units, the relation between the invariant and variants is reversed: length and shortness are invariants implemented by variable phonemes. Saporta's surmise that emotive difference is a nonlinguistic feature, "attributable to the delivery of the message and not to the message," arbitrarily reduces the informational capacity of messages.

A former actor of Stanislavskij's Moscow Theater told me how at his audition he was asked by the famous director to make forty different messages from the phrase *Segodnja večerom* 'This evening,' by diversifying its expressive tint. He made a list of some forty emotional situations, then emitted the given phrase in accordance with each of these situations, which his audience had to recognize only from the changes in the sound shape of the same two words. For our research work in the description any analysis or contemporary Standard Russian (under the auspices of the Rockefeller Foundation) this actor was asked to repeat Stanislavskij's test. He wrote down some fifty situations framing the same elliptic sentence and made of it fifty corresponding messages for a tape record. Most of the messages were correctly and circumstantially decoded by Moscovite listeners. May I add that all such emotive cues easily undergo linguistic analysis.

---

[4] Anton Marty, *Untersuchungen zur Grundlegung der allgemeinen Grammatik und Sprachphilosophie*, Vol. 1 (Halle, 1908).

Orientation toward the ADDRESSEE, the CONATIVE function, finds its purest grammatical expression in the vocative and imperative, which syntactically, morphologically, and often even phonemically deviate from other nominal and verbal categories. The imperative sentences cardinally differ from declarative sentences: the latter are and the former are not liable to a truth test. When in O'Neill's play *The Fountain*, Nano, "(in a fierce tone of command)," says "Drink!"—the imperative cannot be challenged by the question "is it true or not?" which may be, however, perfectly well asked after such sentences as "one drank," "one will drink," "one would drink." In contradistinction to the imperative sentences, the declarative sentences are convertible into interrogative sentences: "did one drink?" "will one drink?" "would one drink?"

The traditional model of language as elucidated particularly by Bühler[5] was confined to these three function—emotive, conative, and referential—and the three apexes of this model—the first person of the addresser, the second person of the addressee, and the "third person," properly—someone or something spoken of. Certain additional verbal functions can be easily inferred from this triadic model. Thus the magic, incantatory function is chiefly some kind of conversion of an absent or inanimate "third person" into an addressee of a conative message. "May this sty dry up, *tfu, tfu, tfu, tfu*" (Lithuanien spell)[6]. "Water, queen river, daybreak! Send grief beyond the blue sea, to the sea-bottom, like a gray stone never to rise from the sea-bottom, may grief never come to burden the light heart of God's servant, may grief be removed and sink away." (North Russian incantation)[7]. "Sun, stand thou still upon Gibeon; and thou, Moon, in the valley of Aj-a-lon. And the sun stood still, and the moon stayed..." (Josh. 10.12). We observe, however, three further constitutive factors of verbal communication and three corresponding functions of language.

There are messages primarily serving to establish, to prolong, or to discontinue communication, to check whether the channel works ("Hello, do you hear me?"), to attract the attention of the interlocutor or to confirm his continued attention ("Are you listening?" or in Shakespearean diction, "Lend me your ears!"—and on the other end of the wire "Um-hum!") This set for CONTACT, or in Malinowski's terms PHATIC function[8], may be displayed by a profuse exchange of ritualized formulas, by entire dialogues with the mere purport of prolonging communication. Dorothy Parker caught eloquent examples: "'Well!' the

---

[5] Karl Bühler, "Die Axiomatik der Sprachwissenschaft," *Kant-Studien* 38 (1933), pp. 19–90.

[6] V. T. Mansikka, *Litauische Zaubersprüche*. *Folklore Fellows Communications* 87 (1929), p. 69.

[7] Pavel Nikolaevich Rybnikov, *Pesni*, Vol. 3 (Moscow, 1910), pp. 217 ff.

[8] Bonislaw Malinowski, "The problem of meaning in primitive languages," in C.K. Ogden and I.A. Richards, *The meaning of meaning* (New York, 1953), pp. 296–336.

young man said. 'Well!' she said. 'Well, here we are,' he said. 'Here we are,' she said, 'Aren't we?' 'I should say we were,' he said, 'Eeyop! Here we are.' 'Well!' she said. 'Well!' he said, 'well.'" The endeavor to start and sustain communication is typical of talking birds; thus the phatic function of language is the only one they share with human beings. It is also the first verbal function acquired by infants; they are prone to communicate before being able to send or receive informative communication.

A distinction has been made in modern logic between two levels of language, "object language" speaking of objects and "metalanguage" speaking of language. But metalanguage is not only a necessary scientific tool utilized by logiciens and linguists; it plays also an important role in our everyday language. Like Molière's Jourdain who used prose without knowing it, we practice metalanguage without realizing the metalingual character of our operations. Whenever the addresser and/or the addressee need to check up whether they use the same code, speech is focused on the CODE: it performs a METALINGUAL (i.e., glossing) function "I don't follow you—what do you mean?" asks the addressee, or in Shakespearean diction, "What is't thou say'st?" And the addresser in anticipation of such recapturing questions inquires: "Do you know what I mean?" Imagine such an exasperating dialogue: "The sophomore was plucked." "But what is *plucked?*" "*Plucked* means the same as *plunked.*" "*And flunked?*" "*To be flunked* is *to fail in an exam.*" "And what is *sophomore?*" persists the interrogator innocent of school vocabulary. "A *sophomore* is (or means) a *second-year student.*" All these equational sentences convey information merely about the lexical code of English; their function is strictly metalingual. Any process of language learning, in particular child acquisition of the mother tongue, makes wide use of such metalingual operations; and aphasia may often be defined as a loss of ability for metalingual operations.

We have brought up all the six factors involved in verbal communication except the message itself. The set *(Einstellung)* toward the MESSAGE as such, focus on the message for its own sake, is the POETIC function of language. This function cannot be productively studied out of touch with the general problems of language, and, on the other hand, the scrutiny of language requires a thorough consideration of its poetic function. Any attempt to reduce the sphere of poetic function to poetry or to confine poetry to poetic function would be a delusive oversimplification. Poetic function is not the sole function of verbal art but only its dominant, determining function, whereas in all other verbal activities it acts as a subsidiary, accessory constituent. This function, by promoting the palpability of signs, deepens the fundamental dichotomy of signs and objects. Hence, when dealing with poetic function, linguistics cannot limit itself to the field of poetry.

"Why do you always say *Joan and Margery,* yet never *Margery and Joan?* Do you prefer Joan to her twin sister?" "Not at all, it just sounds smoother." In a sequence of two coordinate names, as far as no rank problems interfere, the precedence of the shorter name suits the speaker, unaccountably for him, as a well-ordered shape of the message.

A girl used to talk about "the horrible Harry." "Why horrible?" "Because I hate him." "But why not *dreadful, terrible, frightful, disgusting?*" "I don 't know why, but *horrible* fits him better." Without realizing it, she clung to the poetic device of paronomasia.

The political slogan "I like Ike" /ay layk ayk/, succinctly structured, consists of three monosyllables and counts three diphthongs /ay/, each of them symmetrically followed by one consonantal phoneme, /..I..k..k/. The make-up of the three words presents a variation: no consonantal phonemes in the first word, two around the diphthong in the second, and one final consonant in the third. A similar dominant nucleus layl was noticed by Hymes in some of the sonnets of Keats. Both cola of the trisyllabic formula "I like / Ike" rhyme with each other, and the second of the two rhyming words is fully included in the first one (echo rhyme), /ay/-/ayk/, a paronomastic image of a feeling which totally envelops its object. Both cola alliterate with each other, and the first of the two alliterating words is included in the second: /ay/-/ayk/, a paronomastic image of the loving subject enveloped by the beloved object. The secondary, poetic function of this electional catch phrase reinforces its impressiveness and efficacy.

As we said, the linguistic study of the poetic function must overstep, the limits of poetry, and, on the other hand, the linguistic scrutiny of poetry cannot limit itself to the poetic function. The particularities of diverse poetic genres imply a differently ranked participation of the other verbal functions along with the dominant poetic function. Epic poetry, focused on the third person, strongly involves the referential function of language; the lyric, oriented toward the first person, is intimately linked with the emotive function; poetry of the second person is imbued with the conative function and is either supplicatory or exhortative, depending on whether the first person is subordinated to the second one or the second to the first.

Now that our cursory description of the six basic functions of verbal communication is more or less complete, we may complement our scheme of the fundamental factors by a corresponding scheme of the functions:

REFERENTIAL

EMOTIVE	POETIC	CONATIVE
	PHATIC	

METALINGUAL

What is the empirical linguistic criterion of the poetic function? In particular, what is the indispensable feature inherent in any piece of poetry? To answer this question we must recall the two basic modes of arrangement used in verbal behavior, *selection* and *combination*. If "child" is the topic of the message, the speaker selects one among the extant, more or less similar, nouns like child, kid, youngster, tot, all of them equivalent in a certain respect, and then, to comment on this topic, he may select one of the semantically cognate verbs—sleeps, dozes, nods, naps. Both chosen words combine in the speech chain. The selection is produced on the base of equivalence, similarity and dissimilarity, synonymity and antonymity, while the combination, the build up of the sequence, is based on contiguity. *The poetic function projects the principle of equivalence from the axis of selection into the axis of combination.* Equivalence is promoted to the constitutive device of the sequence. In poetry one syllable is equalized with any other syllable of the same sequence; word stress is assumed to equal word stress, as unstress equals unstress; prosodic long is matched with long, and short with short; word boundary equals word boundary, no boundary equals no boundary; syntactic pause equals syntactic pause, no pause equals no pause. Syllables are converted into units of measure, and so are morae or stresses.

It may be objected that metalanguage also makes a sequential use of equivalent units when combining synonymic expressions into an equational sentence: A = A *("Mare is the female of the horse")*. Poetry and metalanguage, however, are in diametrical opposition to each other: in metalanguage the sequence is used to build an equation, whereas in poetry the equation is used to build a sequence.

In poetry, and to a certain extent in latent manifestations of poetic function, sequences delimited by word boundaries become commensurable whether they are sensed as isochronic or graded. "Joan and Margery" showed us the poetic principle of syllable gradation, the same principle which in the closes of Serbian folk epics has been raised to a compulsory law[9]. Without its two dactylic words the combination "innocent bystander" would hardly have become a hackneyed phrase. The symmetry of three disyllabic verbs with an identical initial consonant and identical final vowel added splendor to the laconic victory message of Caesar: *"Veni, vidi, vici."*

---

[9] *Cf.* Tomislav Maretic, "Metrika narodnih naših pjesama," *Rad Yugoslavenske Akademije* (Zagreb, 1907), pp. 168 and 170.

7

The Semiology of Language

Émile Benveniste[1]

> *Semiology will have much to accomplish if*
> *it does nothing else but discover its own*
> *boundaries.*
> Ferdinand de Saussure[2]

Since the time when those two antithetical geniuses, Peirce and Saussure, almost simultaneously,[3] in total ignorance of one another, conceived of the possibility of a science of signs and worked at establishing it, an important problem has arisen which has not as yet found a precise formulation. In the midst of the confusion that reigns in this field, this problem has not even been clearly stated. What is the place of language among the systems of signs?

Peirce devoted his entire life to the further elaboration of concepts based on the term *semiotic*, returning to the designation Σημειωτική, which John Locke had applied to a science of signs and significations derived from logic, which was itself conceived of as a science of language. The enormous quantity of his notes bears witness to an obstinate effort to analyze logical, mathematical, physical, and even psychological and religious notions within the framework of semiotics. This study, pursued throughout his life, involved an increasingly complex apparatus of definitions aimed at distributing all of reality, the conceptual, and the experiential into various categories of signs. In order to construct this 'universal algebra of relations',[4] Peirce proposed a tripartite division of signs into *icons, indices,* and *symbols*: today this is nearly all we retain of the immense logical superstructure underlying this division.

As for language, Peirce made no precise or specific formulations. For him, language was both everywhere and nowhere at all. He was never concerned with the way language functioned, if he even paid attention to it. Language for him was reduced to its components, words,

---

[1] Emile Benveniste, "The Semiology of Language," *Semiotica* 1 (1969): 1–12 and 127–135.

[2] Handwritten note (Saussure 1957: 19).

[3] Charles Sanders Peirce (1839–1914); Ferdinand de Saussure (1857–1913)

[4] "My universel algebra of relations, with the subjacent indices ε andπ, is susceptible of being enlarged so as to comprise everything and so, still better, thouglh not to ideal perfection, is the system of existential graphs" (Peirce 1958: 389).

which are certainly signs. Yet, they are not derived from a distinct category, or even from a constant type. Words belong, for the most part, to the category of "symbols": certain ones, for example, demonstrative pronouns, are 'indices', and therefore are classified with their corresponding gestures, the gesture of pointing, for example. Consequently, Peirce did not recognize the fact that such a gesture is universally understood, whereas the demonstrative is part of a special system of oral signs, language, and of a particular linguistic system, the idiom. Moreover, in Peirce's terms the same word can appear as several varieties of "signs," such as the *qualisign*, the *sinsign*, or the *legisign*.[5] We do not see, therefore, the operative utility of similar distinctions, nor to what extent they would help the linguist construct a semiology of language as a system. The difficulty that prevents any specific application of Peirce's concepts (except for the well-known but much too general tripartite framework is that the sign is definitively posited as the base of the entire universe, and functions simultaneously as the principle of definition for each element and as the principle of explanation for the entire ensemble, be it abstract or concrete. Man himself is a sign; his thought is a sign;[6] his every emotion is a sign.[7] But finally, since these signs are all signs for each other, for what could they be a sign that is not a sign itself? Where could we find a fixed point to anchor the first signifying relationship? The semiotic edifice that Peirce constructs is not self-inclusive in its own definition. In order to keep the notion of sign from disappearing completely amidst his proliferation *ad infinitum*, we must recognize a difference, somewhere in this universe, between sign and signified. Therefore, each sign must be included and articulated within a system of signs. Therein lies the condition for *significance*. It then follows, to counter Peirce, that all signs cannot function identically, nor belong to one system alone. We have to establish several systems

---

[5] "As it is in itself, a sign is either of the nature of an appearance, when I call it a QUAL-ISIGN; or secondly, it is an individuel object or event, when I call it a SINSIGN (the syllable *sin* being the first syllable of *semer, simul, singular*, etc.); or thirdly, it is of the nature of a general type, when I call it a LEGISIGN. As we use the term 'word' in most cases, saying that 'the' is one 'word' and 'an' is a second 'word,' a 'word' is a legisign. But when we say of a page in a book that it has 250 'words'upon it, of which twenty are 'the's', the 'word' is a legisign. A sinsign so embodying a legisign, I term a 'replica'of the legisign" (1958: 391).

[6] ". . . the word or sign which man uses is man himself. For, as the fact that every thought is a sign, taken in conjunction with the fact that life is a train of thought, proves that man is a sign; so that every thought is an EXTERNAL sign that proves that man is an external sign" (Peirce 1958: 71).

[7] "Everything in which we take the least interest creates in us its particular emotion, however slight this emotion may be. This emotion is a sign and a predicate of the thing" (Peirce 1958: 67).

of signs, and among these systems, make explicit the relationships of difference and analogy.

It is here that Saussure presents himself directly as the exact opposite of Peirce, in methodology as well as in practice. In Saussure's work, reflection proceeds from language and adopts language as its exclusive object. Language is considered in itself. Linguistics has a threefold task: (1) to describe all known languages synchronically and diachronically; (2) to extract the general laws at work in languages; and (3) to delimit and define itself (1966: 6).

Under its external rational appearance, the peculiarity that this program conceals passes unnoticed; yet, this peculiarity is precisely its force and audacity. Hence, the third aim of linguistics: to define itself by itself. This task, if we are willing to understand it fully, absorbs the two others, and in a sense eliminates them. How will linguistics be able to set its own boundaries and define itself by itself, if not by delimiting and defining its very own object, language? But in such a case, can it accomplish the first two tasks that it must undertake, i.e., the description and history of language? How would linguistics be able "to determine the forces that are permanently and universally at work in all languages, and to deduce the general laws to which all specific historical phenomena can be deduced" (1966: 6), if we have not begun by defining the powers and resources of linguistics (that is to say, the hold it has on language, and consequently, the nature and characteristics peculiar to this entity called language)? Everything is dependent upon this requirement, and the linguist cannot deem any one of these tasks distinct from the others, nor fulfill any one of them, if he is not first aware of the singular nature of language with respect to all other objects of science. This insight contains the basic condition preliminary to all other active and cognitive linguistic proceedings. Far from being located on the same plane as the other two tasks, and thus implying their completion, this third task, "to delimit and define itself" (1966: 6), forces linguistics to postpone the fulfillment of the other two until it has discovered its own limits and definition as a science. Herein lies the great innovation of Saussure's program. Reference to his *Course* readily confirms that for Saussure a linguistic science is possible only on the condition that it ultimately find itself through the discovery of its own object.

Everything then proceeds from the question: "What is both the integral and concrete object of linguistics?" (1966: 7). Saussure's first step aims at destroying all previous responses to this question. "From whatever direction we approach the question, nowhere do we find the integral object of linguistics" (1966: 9). The field thus cleared, Saussure posits his first methodological requirement: language (*la langue*) must be separated from human speech (*le langage*). The essential concepts furtively slip into the following few lines:

> Taken as a whole, speech is many-sided and heterogeneous: strad-
> dling several areas simultaneously—physical, physiological, and
> psychological—it belongs both to the individual and to society;
> we cannot put it into any category of human facts, for we cannot
> discover its unity.
>   Language, on the contrary, is a self-contained whole and a
> principle of classification. As soon as we give language first place
> among the facts of speech, we introduce a natural order into a
> mass that lends itself to no other classification. (1966: 9)

Saussure's chief concern is the discovery of the principle of unity
dominating the multiplicity of forms under which languages appear.
This principle alone allows us to classify linguistic facts among human
activities. The reduction of human speech to language satisfies this double condition: it allows us to propose language as a unifying principle,
and in the same stroke, establishes a place for language among human
activities. In formulating the principle of unity and the principle of classification Saussure presents the two concepts which, in turn, introduce
semiology. Both principles are necessary to establish linguistics as a science. We could not conceive of a science uncertain of its object, undefined in terms of its relevance. This goes well beyond a concern for
rigor; it proceeds from the very rules specific to the totality of human
acts.

Here again, no one has sufficiently emphasized the originality of
Saussure's procedure. It is not a question of deciding whether or not linguistics is closer to psychology or sociology, not of finding a place for it
in the midst of existing disciplines. The problem is presented on another level, and in terms that create their own concepts. Linguistics is part
of a science that does not yet exist, a science that has as its subject other
systems of the same order in the totality of human activities: *semiology,*
Saussure states and situates this relationship thusly:

> Language is a system of signs that expresses ideas, and is there-
> fore comparable to a system of writing, the alphabet of
> deaf-mutes, symbolic rites, polite formulas, military signals, etc.
> But it is the most important of these systems.
>   *A science that studies the life of signs within society* is conceiv-
> able; it would be a part of social psychology and consequently of
> general psychology; I shall call it semiology (from Greek sēmeîon
> sign). Semiology would show what constitutes signs, what laws
> govern them. Since the science does not yet exist, no one can say
> what it would be; but it has a right to existence, a place staked out
> in advance. Linguistics is only a part of the general science of
> semiology; the laws discovered by semiology will be applicable to

linguistics, and the latter will circumscribe a well-defined area within the mass of anthropological facts.

To determine the exact place of semiology is the task of the psychologist[8] The task of the linguist is to find out what makes language a special system within the mass of semiological data. This issue will be taken up later, here I wish merely to call attention to one thing: if I have succeeded in assigning linguistics a place among the sciences, it is because I have related it to semiology. (1966: 16)

The basics of the long commentary that this page demands are included in the discussion that we broach further on. In order to emphasize them, we shall consider only the primordial characteristics of semiology as Saussure perceives it, and furthermore, as he recognized it long before alluding to it in his teachings.[9]

Language, in all its aspects, appears as a duality: a social institution, set to work by the individual; continuous discourse, composed of fixed units. Language is independent of the phonoacoustic mechanism of speech: it consists of a "system of signs in which the only essentiel thing is the union of meanings and sound images, and in which both parts of the sign are psychological" (1966: 15). Where is language to find its unity and its functional principle? In its semiotic character. In that way it defines *its* own nature, and also integrates itself into a set of systems, all having the same characteristics.

For Saussure, in contrast to Peirce, the sign is a linguistic concept which extends more widely to certain orders of anthropological and social data. Thereby its domain is circumscribed. But besides language, this domain includes systems homologous to it. Saussure refers to several. The latter all have the characteristic of being systems of *signs*. Language "is the most important of these systems" (1966: 16). The most important in relation to what? Is it simply because language has more importance in social life than any other system? There is nothing which allows us to determine this.

Saussure's thought, most affirmative about the relationship of language to systems of signs, is less clear on the relationship of linguistics to semiology, the science of the systems of signs. The future of linguistics will be in its incorporation into semiology, which in turn will form "a part of social psychology and consequently of general psychology" (1966: 16). But we must wait for the establishment of semiology, "a *science that studies the life of signs within society*," in order to learn "what constitutes signs, what laws govern them" (1966: 16). Saussure, there-

---

[8] Here Saussure refers to Naville (1888: 104).

[9] This idea and the term are already found in a handwritten note in Saussure's 1846 manuscript, published in Godel (1957: 46 and cf. 37).

fore, defers the task of defining the sign itself to this future science. Nevertheless, he elaborates, for linguistics, the instrument of its own semiology, the linguistic sign: "To me, the language problem is mainly semiological, and all developments derive their significance from that important fact" (1966: 17).

This principle, that the linguistic sign is 'arbitrary' placed at the center of linguistics, connects linguistics to semiology. In a general manner, the principal object of semiology will be "the whole group of systems grounded on the arbitrariness of the sign" (1966: 68). Consequently, in the totality of systems of expression, preeminence belongs to language.

> Signs that are wholly arbitrary realize better than the others the ideal of the semiological process; this is why language, the most complex and universal of all systems of expression, is also the most characteristic; in this sense linguistics could become the master-pattern for all branches of semiology although language is only one particular semiological system (1966: 68).

In this way, while clearly formulating the idea that linguistics has a necessary relationship to semiology, Saussure refrains from defining the nature of that relationship, except by means of the principle of the "arbitrary nature of the sign," which would govern the totality of systems of expression, and above all, language. Semiology, as a science of signs, remains latent in Saussure's work as a prospect which in its most precise features models itself on linguistics.

Saussure limits himself to rapidly citing several systems which, along with language, are included under semiology; he far from exhausts the list, since he puts forth no delimiting criteria: "a system of writing, the alphabet of deaf-mutes, symbolic rites, polite formulas, military signals, etc." (1966: 16). Elsewhere he speaks of considering rites, customs, etc., as signs (1966: 17).

Taking up this important problem at the point where Saussure left off, we would like to insist first upon the necessity of establishing a preliminary classification if we are to advance the analysis and consolidate the bases of semiology at all.

We will say nothing about writing here, saving this difficult problem for special examination. Are symbolic rites and rules of etiquette autonomous systems? Can we really put them on the same level as language? They only occur in a semiological relationship through the intermediary of a discourse: the "myth," which accompanies the "rite"; the "protocol" which governs the rules of etiquette. These signs, if they are to be established as a system, presuppose the existence of language, which produces and interprets them. They are therefore of a distinct order in a hierarchy yet to be defined. We already suspect that, no less than the systems of signs, the *relationships* between these systems will constitute the subject of semiology.

It is finally time to forsake generalities and tackle the central problem of semiology, the status of language among the systems of signs. We cannot guarantee anything in this theory as long as we lack a clear idea of the sign's concept and worth within those groups where it is already accessible to study. We believe this examination should begin with nonlinguistic systems.

The role of the sign is to represent, to take the place of something else while alluding to it by virtue of a substitute. A more precise definition, one which would distinguish several varieties of signs specifically, presupposes a reflection upon the principle of a science of signs, of a semiology, and an effort to elaborate it. The smallest attention to our behavior, to the conditions of intellectual and social life, of our dealings with others, of the relationship between production and exchange, shows us that we are utilizing several systems of signs concurrently at every moment: first, the signs of language, which are those that we acquire the earliest, with the beginning of conscious life; graphic signs; the signs of politeness, of gratitude, and of persuasion in all their varieties and hierarchies; the signs regulating vehicular movement; the "external signs" indicating social conditions; "monetary signs," values and indices of economic life; cult signs, rites, and beliefs, and the signs of art in all its varieties (music, images, figurative reproductions). In short and without going beyond empiric verification, it is clear that our whole life is caught up in networks of signs that condition us to the point where we do not know how to omit a single one without endangering the equilibrium between society and individual. These signs seem to engender themselves and multiply by virtue of some internal necessity, apparently responding as well to a necessity within our mental organization. What principle can be introduced into the numerous and diverse ways in which signs arrange themselves in configurations that will order these relationships and delimit their sets?

The common characteristic of all these systems and the criterion for their inclusion in semiology is their signifying property, or *meaning*, and their composition into units of meaning, or *signs*. We have come to the point where we must describe their distinctive characteristics.

A semiological system is characterized by: (1) its mode of operation (2) the domain of its validity; (3) the nature and number of its signs; and (4) its type of operation.

Each one of these features entails a certain number of variations.

The *mode of operation* is the manner in which the system acts, more particularly the sense (sight, hearing, etc.) to which it is directed.

The *domain of validity* is that area in which the system imposes itself and must be recognized or obeyed.

The *nature* and *number of signs* are a function of the aforesaid conditions.

The *type of operation* is the relationship that unites the signs and confers their distinguishing function upon them.

Let us put this definition to the test against an elementary system, the system of traffic signal lights: Its mode of operation is visual, generally diurnal, on a clear day; its domain of validity is vehicular traffic on highways; its signs are constituted by the chromatic opposition green/red (sometimes with an intermediary phase of simple transition, yellow), i.e., it is a binary system; its type of operation is a relationship of alternation (never of simultaneity), green/red signifying road open/road closed, or under its prescriptive form, stop/go.

This system is capable of expansion or transference, but only under one of its four conditions, the domain of validity. We can apply it to fluvial navigation, to channel buoy markers, or to aviation runways, provided that we keep the same chromatic opposition, with the same signification. The nature of the signs can only be modified temporarily, and for reasons of expediency.[10]

The traits subsumed under this definition form two groups: the first two, relative to the mode of operation and to the domain of validity, provide the external empirical conditions of the system; the last two, relative to signs and to their type of operation, indicate their internal semiotic conditions. The first two allow certain variations or accommodations; the other two do not. This structure delineates a canonical model for the binary system, which we recognize, for example, in voting customs—using a black or white ball, standing or being seated, etc.—and in all the circumstances where the alternative could be (but is not) stated in linguistic terms such as: yes/no.

From now on, we are able to extract two principles which pertain to the relationships between semiotic systems.

The first principle can be stated as the *principle of nonredundancy* between systems. Semiotic systems are nor "synonymous"; we are not able to say "the same thing" with spoken words that we can with music, as they are systems with different bases.

In other words, two semiotic systems of different types cannot be mutually interchangeable. In the example cited, speech and music have as a common trait the production of sounds and the fact that they appeal to hearing; but this relationship does not prevail, in view of the difference in nature between their respective units and their types of operation, as we shall show further on.

---

[10] Material impediments (fog) can require additional methods, auditory signals instead of visuel ones, for example, but these temporary expedients do not change the normal conditions.

Non redundancy in the universe of sign systems occurs as a result of the nonconvertibility of systems with different bases. Man does not have several distinct systems at his disposal for the *same* signifying relationship.

On the other hand, the written alphabet and the Braille alphabet, or Morse code, or the deaf-mute alphabet are mutually interchangeable, all being systems based on the alphabetic principle: one letter, one sound.

A second principle follows from and completes the preceding one.

Two systems can have the same sign in common without being, as a result, synonymous or redundant; that is to say, the functional difference of a sign alone matters, not its substantial identity. The red in the binary system of highway traffic signals has nothing in common with the red of the French tricolor flag, nor does the white of that flag have anything to do with the white worn for mourning in China. The value of a sign is defined only in the system which incorporates it. There is no sign that bridges several systems, that is transsystemic.

Are these systems, then, just so many closed worlds, having nothing between them except a relationship of coexistence, itself perhaps fortuitous? We have to draw up new methodological requirements. The relationship laid down between semiotic systems must itself be semiotic in nature. It is determined first of all by the same cultural background which in some way produces and nurtures all systems in its particular group. Therein, again, lies an external link which does not necessarily imply a coherent relationship between individual systems. There is a second condition: Can it be determined whether a given semiotic system can interpret itself by itself, or must it receive its interpretation from another system? The semiotic relationship between systems is expressed, then, as the relationship between *interpreting system* and *interpreted system*. It is this unit of sound; but it only assumes this value within the scale, which fixes the paradigm of notes. Is this a semiotic unit? We can discern that it is in its own order, since it determines the oppositions. But then it has no relationship with the semiotics of the linguistic sign, and, in fact, it is not convertible into units of language, at whatever level this may occur.

The following analogy, at the same time, discloses a profound difference. Music is a system which functions on two axes: a simultaneous and a sequential axis. We might think of a homology with the function of language along its paradigmaric and syntagmatic axes. However, the axis of simultaneity in music contradicts the very principle of the paradigm in language, which is the principle of selection, excluding all intrasegmental simultaneity; and the sequential axis in music does not coincide with the syntagmatic axis of language either, since the musical sequence is compatible with the simultaneity of sounds, and is not subjected to any restriction of liaison (syncopation) or of exclusion with regard to any sound or group of sounds.

In this way it can be seen that the musical combination derived from harmony and counterpoint has no equivalent in language, where paradigms as often as syntagme are subjected to specific arrangements: rules of consistency, of selectivity, of recurrence, etc., upon which depend frequency and statistical predictability on the one hand, and the possibility of constructing intelligible statements on the other. This difference does not depend on a special musical system or on a chosen sound scale: the twelve-tone serial scale is as rigorously bound here as the diatonic scale.

We can say, on the whole, if music is considered as a language, it has syntactic features, but not semiotic features. This difference delineates in advance a positive necessary feature of linguistic semiology that we should keep in mind.

Let us now go on to another field, that of the so-called plastic arts, an enormous area, where we will limit ourselves to pursuing some similarity or opposition capable of elucidating the semiology of language. Here from the very first we run up against a difficulty in principle: is there something common at the base of all these arts, aside from the vague notion of the 'plastic'? Can we find in each or in only one of them a formal entity which we may call the *unit* of the system under consideration? But what can be the unit in painting or drawing? Is it shape, line, color? Formulated in this fashion, is the question still meaningful?

At this point we can state the minimal conditions for comparison between systems of different orders. Every semiotic system based on signs must necessarily include (1) a finite repertory of *signs*, (2) and rules of order governing its *figures*, (3) existing independently of the nature and number of the *discourses* that the system allows to be produced. None of the plastic arts considered in its totality seems to reproduce such a model. At the most, we might be able to find some approximation of it in the work of a particular artist. However, it would no longer be a matter of constant general conditions, but of individual characteristics, and this again would lead us astray from language.

The notion of unit is central to the problems which concern us[11] and no serious theory can be formulated without considering the question,

---

[11] Personally speaking, it seems hardly useful or even possible to burden these pages with a discussion of previous theories. The informed reader will see, in particuler, what separates us from Louis Hjelmslev on an essentiel point. He defines *semiotics* as "a hierarchy, any of whose components admits of a further analysis into classes defined by mutual relations, so that any of these classes admits of an analysis into derivates defined by mutual mutation" (1963: 106). Such a definition will only be admissible if we totally adhere to the principles of glossematics. Th considerations of the same author (1963: 109) on the place of language in semiotic structures, on the limit between the

since every signifying system must be defined by its mode of signification. Consequently, such a system must designate the units it brings
into play in order to produce meaning and to specify the nature of the
meaning produced.

Two questions then emerge: (1) Can we reduce all semiotic systems
to units? (2) In the systems in which they exist, are these units signs?

The unit and the sign remain as distinct features. The sign is necessarily a unit, but the unit may not be a sign. We are assured of at least
one thing: language is composed of units, and these units are signs.
What about other semiological systems?

First we shall consider the functioning of the so-called artistic systems, those of image and sound, while deliberately ignoring their aes-
thetic function. Musical language is composed of diversely articulated
sound combinations and sequences; the elementary unit, the sound, is
not a sign; each sound is identifiable in the scalar structure upon which
it depends; none is endowed with meaning in itself. This is a typical
example of units which are not signs, which do not designate, because
they are merely the degrees of a scale whose range has been arbitrarily
set. We have here a principle of selection: The systems based upon units
are divided between systems of signifying units and systems of non signifying units. Language is in the first category, and music in the second.[12]

In the figurative arts (painting, design, and sculpture), which have
fixed or mobile images, it is the existence of units which comes under
discussion. What would their nature be? If it is a matter of colors, we
recognize that they can be divided into a scale whose principal degrees
are identifiable by name. They are designated, they do not designate;
they neither refer to anything, nor suggest anything in an univocal way.

---

semiotic and the nonsemiotic, reflect a completely temporary and still imprecise position. We can only approve the invitation to study the diverse semiotic disciplines from
a similar point of view:

it seems fruitful and necessary to establish a common point of view for a large number
of disciplines, from the study of literature, art, and music, and general history, all the
way to logistics and mathematics, so that from this common point of view these sciences are concentrated around a linguistically defined setting of problems (1963: 108).

However, this vast program remains a mere wish so long as we have not elaborated the
theoretical bases for a comparison among the systems. That is what we are attempting
to do here. More recently, Charles Morris (1964: 62) restricts himself to noting that for a
number of linguists whose names he cites, linguistics is a part of semiotics, but he does
not define the situation of language in this relationship..

12 Roland Harweg (1968: 273) verifies that "the sign theoretic approach is inadequate for
the study of music, for the only thing it can provide with regard to it are negative statements—'negative' taken in a logical, not in an evaluative sense. All it can state may be
comprised in the statement that music is NOT a significational-representational institution as is language." This verification, however, lacks the support of theoretical formulation. The problem which we are discussing is precisely that of the intersemiotic validity of the notion of "sign."

The artist chooses them, blends them, and arranges them on the canvas according to his taste; finally, it is in composition alone that, technically speaking, they assume a "signification" through selection and arrangement. Thus the artist creates his own semiotics; he sets up his own oppositions in features which he renders significant in their order. Therefore, he does not acquire a repertory of signs, recognized as such, nor does he establish one. Color, the material, comprises an unlimited variety of gradations in shade, of which none is equivalent to the linguistic sign.

With regard to the figurative arts, they are already derived from another level, that of representation, where feature, color, and movement combine to form a whole governed by its own necessities. In this case, they are separate systems of great complexity, in which the definition of the sign can only be precisely stated after the development of this still vague study of semiology.

The signifying relationships of any artistic language are to be found within the compositions that make us aware of it. Art is nothing more than a specific work of art in which the artist freely sets up contrasts and values over which he assumes supreme authority. He answers to no one, nor must he eliminate contradictions. He must merely express a vision, to which the entire composition bears witness, and of which it becomes a manifestation, according to conscious or unconscious criteria.

We can thus distinguish the systems in which meaning is imparted by the author to the composition from those in which meaning is expressed by the initial elements in an isolated state, independently of the interrelationships which they may undergo. In the former, meaning emerges from the relationships forming a closed world; in the latter it is inherent in the signs themselves. Therefore, the meaning of art may never be reduced to a convention accepted by two partners.[13] New terms must always be found, since they are unlimited in number and unpredictable in nature; thus they must be redevised for each work and, in short, prove unsuitable as an institution. On the other hand, the meaning of language is meaning itself, establishing the possibility of all exchange and of all communication, and thus of all culture.

---

[13] Mieczyslaw Wallis (1964, 1966) makes useful observations on iconic signs, especially in medieval art, where he discerns a "vocabulary," and rules of "syntax." Surely, we can recognize in medieval sculpture a certain iconic repertory which corresponds to certain religious themes, to certain theological or moral teachings. But these are conventional messages, produced in an equally conventional topology where figures occupy symbolic places consistent with familiar representations. In addition, the figurative scenes are the iconic transposition of narratives or of parables; they reproduce an initial verbalization. The real semiological problem, which to our knowledge has not yet been formulated would be to investigate *how* this transposition of a verbal statement into an iconic representation is carried out, what are the possible correspondences from one system to another and in what measure this confrontation could be pursued up to the ascertainment of the correspondences between distinct *signs*.

It is still permissible, taking into account certain metaphors, to compare the execution of a musical composition to the production of a linguistic statement; we can speak about a musical "discourse," analyzed into phrases separated by "pauses," or by "silences," set off by recognizable "motifs." We might also look for morphological and syntactical principles in the figurative arts.[14] One thing at least is certain: no semiology of sound, color, or image can be formulated or expressed in sounds, colors, or images. Every semiology of a nonlinguistic system must use language as an intermediary, and thus can only exist in and through the semiology of language. Whether language serves here as an instrument rather than as an object of analysis does not alter this situation which governs all semiotic relationships; language is the interpreting system of all other systems, linguistic and nonlinguistic.

At this point we must specify the nature and the feasibility of relationships among semiotic systems. We propose three kinds of relationships.

(1) One system can generate another system. Ordinary language generates logical and mathematical formalization; ordinary writing generates stenographic writing; the normal alphabet generates the Braille alphabet. this *generative relationship* is useful between two distinct, contemporaneous systems, of the same kind, where the second one is constructed from the first one and fulfills a specific function. We should carefully distinguish this generative relationship from the derivative relationship, which supposes evolution and historical transition. Between hieroglylphic writing and demotic writing there is derivation, not generation. The history of writing systems provides many examples of derivation.

(2) The second kind of relationship is the *relationship of homology*, which establishes a correlation between the parts of two semiotic systems. In contrast to the preceding relationship, it is not explicitly stated, but is set up by virtue of the connections we find or establish between two distinct systems. The kind of homology may vary: intuitive or rational, substantial or structural, conceptual or poetic. "Les parfums, les couleurs, les sons se répondent." ["Fragrances, colors, and sounds mutually respond."] These "correspondences" are unique to Baudelaire; they organize his poetic universe and the imagery which reflects it. Of a more intellectual nature is the homology that Panofsky sees between Gothic architecture and scholastic thought.[15] The homology

---

[14] The possibility of extending semiological categories to pictorial techniques, and particularly to films, is discussed in an instructive manner by Christian Metz (1968). J. L. Scheffer (1969) inaugurales a semiological "reading" of painting and proposes an analysis of it similar to that of a "text." This research already shows an awakening of an original reflection on the fields and categories of nonlinguistic semiology.

[15] *Cf*. Panofsky (1957: 104 ff.). In his translation of Erwin Panofsky's *Gothic Architecture and Scholasticism*, Pierre Bourdieu cites the homologies indicated by R. Marichal between writing and Gothic architecture (Panofsky 1967:152).

between writing and ritual gesture in China has also been pointed out. Two linguistic structures of different makeup can reveal partial or extended homologies. All depends upon the way in which we lay down the two systems, the parameters which we use, and the fields in which we perform. According to the situation, the homology established will serve as a uniting principle between two fields and will be limited to this functional role, or it will create new kinds of semiotic values. Nothing assures the validity of this relationship in advance, nothing limits the extent of it.

(3) We will term the third relationship between semiotic systems a *relationship of interpretance*. We designate the relationship established between an interpreting system and an interpreted system in this way. From the standpoint of language it is the fundamental relationship, the one which divides the systems into articulate systems, because they exhibit their own semiotics, and articulated systems, whose semiotics appears only through the grid of another mode of expression. Thus we can introduce and justify the principle that language is in the interpreting system (interpretant) of all other semiotic systems. No other system has at its disposal a "language" by which it can categorize and interpret itself according to its semiotic distinctions, while language can, in principle, categorize and interpret everything, including itself.

We see here how the semiological relationship is distinguished from every other, especially from the sociological. If, for example, we question ourselves on the respective status of language and of society— a topic of interminable debate—and also on their mode of mutual dependency, the sociologist and probably anyone else who perceives the question in dimensional terms will notice that language functions within the society that encompasses it; from thence, it is relatively easy to determine that society is the whole, and language, one of its parts. However, consideration from a semiological perspective reverses this relationship, because language alone permits society to exist. Language forms that which holds men together, the basis of all relationships, which in turn establish society. We could say, then, that it is language which contains society.[16] In this way the *interpretance* relationship, which is semiotic, moves in an opposite direction to that of inclusion, a nesting relationship, which is sociological. While the former relationship makes language and society mutually dependent according to their capacity of semiotization, the latter, if we objectify the external dependencies, reifies language and society in a similar manner.

Thereupon we may verify a criterion we indicated above, when, in order to determine the relationships between semiotic systems, we proposed that these relationships ought to be themselves semiotic in

---

[16] We treat this relationship in more detail elsewhere (see Benveniste 1974: 91–102).

nature. The irreversible relationship of *interpretance*, which includes other systems in language, satisfies this condition.

Language provides us with the only model of a system that is at the same time semiotic in its formal structure and in its functioning:

(1) it manifests itself by a statement making reference to a given situation; to speak is always to speak about;

(2) it consists formally of distinct units, each of which is a sign;

(3) it is produced and accepted with the same values of reference by all members of a community;

(4) it is the only actualization of intersubjective communication.

For these reasons, language is the preeminent semiotic organization. It explains the function of a sign, and it alone offers an exemplary formula of the sign. Thus language alone can—and, in fact, does—confer on other groups the rank of signifying system by acquainting them with the relationship of the sign. There is then a *semiotic modeling* which language practices and whose principle we cannot expect to find anywhere else than in language. The nature of language, its representative function, its dynamic power, and its relational role make of it the great semiotic matrix, the modeling structure from which other structures reproduce its features and its mode of action.

To what may we attribute this property? Can we discern why language is the interpreting system of every signifying system? Is it simply because language is the most common system, the one which has the largest field, the greatest frequency of use and—in practice—the greatest effectiveness? On the contrary, this privileged position of language in the pragmatic order of things is a consequence, not a cause, of its preeminence as a signifying system, and only a semiological principle can explain this preeminence. We will discover it by becoming aware of the fact that language signifies in a specific way which belongs to it alone, in a way that no other system copies. It is invested with *double meaning*. In this aspect it is appropriately a model without parallel. Language combines two distinct modes of meaning, which we designate on the one hand as the *semiotic* mode, and on the other, the *semantic* mode.[17]

Semiotics designates the mode of signification proper to the linguistic *sign* that establishes it as a unit. We can, for purposes of analy-

---

[17] This distinction was proposed for the first time at the inaugural session of the 13th Congress of Societies for the Investigation of the Philosophy of the French Language, held in Geneva, 3 September 1966. The fruit of this analysis appears as "The levels of linguistic analysis" (Benveniste 1971: 85–100). In order to better emphasize the distinction, we would have preferred to choose terms less alike than *semiotics* and *semantics*, since both assume a technical meaning here. It was necessary, however, that both evoke the notion of *sema* to which both are effectively, although differently, connected. This terminological question should not inconvenience those who are willing to consider the entire perspective of our analysis.

sis, consider separately the two surfaces of the sign, but with respect to its signification, it is a unit; it remains a unit. The only question to which a sign gives rise, if it is to be recognized as such, is that of its existence, and the latter is answered by yes or no: *tree—song—to wash,—nerve—yellow—on*, and not **tro—*rong—*dawsh—*lerve—*sellow—*ton*. Further, we compare the sign in order to define it, either to signifiers which are partially alike: saber:sober, or saber:sable, or saber:taber; or to neighboring things signified: saber:gun, or saber:epee. All semiotic research; in the strictest sense, consists of the identification of units, the description of characteristic features, and the discovery of the increasingly fine criteria of their distinctiveness. In this way each sign asserts its own meaning still more clearly in the midst of a constellation or among an ensemble of signs. Taken in itself, the sign is pure identity itself, totally foreign to all other signs, the signifying foundation of language, the material necessity for statement. It exists when it is recognized as signifier by all members of a linguistic community, and when it calls forth for each individual roughly the same associations and oppositions. Such is the province and the criterion of semiotics.

With the semantic, we enter into the specific mode of meaning which is generated by *discourse*. The problems raised here are a function of language as producer of messages. However, the message is not reduced to a series of separately identifiable units; it is not the sum of many signs that produces meaning; on the contrary, it is meaning *(l'intenté)*, globally conceived, that is actualized and divided into specific signs, the *words*. In the second place, semantics takes over the majority of referents, while semiotics is in principle cut off and independent of all reference. Semantic order becomes identified with the world of enunciation and with the universe of discourse.

Whether or not it is a question of two distinct orders of ideas and of two conceptual universes, we can still demonstrate this distinction through the difference in criteria of validity required by each. Semiotics (the sign) must be *recognized;* semantics (the discourse) must be *understood*. The difference between recognition and comprehension refers to two distinct faculties of the mind: that of discerning the identity between the previous and the present, and that of discerning, on the other hand, the meaning of a new enunciation. In the pathological forms of language, these two powers are frequently dissociated.

Language is the only system whose meaning is articulated this way in two dimensions. The other systems have a unidimensional meaning; either semiotics (gestures of politeness, *mudras}* without semantics; or semantics (artistic expressions) without semiotics. It is the prerogative of language to comprise simultaneously the meaning of signs and the meaning of enunciation. Therein originates its major strength, that of creating a second level of enunciation, where it becomes possible to retain meaningful remarks about meaning. Through this metalinguistic faculty we discover the origin of the interpreting relationship through which language embraces all other systems.

When Saussure defined language as a system of signs, he laid the foundation for linguistic semiology. But we now see that if the sign corresponds well to the signifying units of language, we cannot set it up as a unique principle of language in its discursive operation. Saussure was not unaware of the sentence, but obviously it created a serious obstacle for him and it was relegated to 'speech' (cf. Saussure [1966: 106, 124–128] and Godel [1966: 490 ff.]), solving nothing; we must know precisely if and how we can proceed from the sign to 'speech'. In reality the world of the sign is closed. From the sign to the sentence there is no transition, either by syntagmatization or otherwise. A hiatus separates them. Consequently, we must admit that language comprises two separate domains, each of which requires its own conceptual apparatus. For the one which we call semiotics, Saussure's theory of the linguistic sign will serve as a basis for research. The semantic domain, on the other hand, should be recognized as separate. It will require a new conceptual and definitional apparatus.

The semiology of language has been obstructed, paradoxically, by the same instrument which created it, the sign. We cannot brush aside the idea of the linguistic sign without omitting the most important characteristic of language; nor can we extend it to discourse as a whole without contradicting its definition as a minimal unit.

In conclusion, we must go beyond Saussure's concern for the sign as a unique principle, on which depend both the structure and the function of language.

This transcendence is achieved through two channels: in intralinguistic analysis, through the opening of a new dimension of meaning, that of discourse (which we call semantic), henceforth distinct from that which is connected to the sign (which we call semiotic); and in the translinguistic analysis of texts and other manifestations through the elaboration of a metasemantics founded on the semantics of enunciation.

The instruments and methodology of this "second generation" semiology shall in turn contribute to the development of other branches of general semiology.

References

Benveniste, Émile. 1971. *Problems in General Linguistics,* translated by Mary Elizabeth Meek. Coral Gables, Fla.: University of Miami Press.

——. 1974. *Problèmes de linguistique générale.* Paris: Gallimard.

Godel, Robert. 1957. *Les Sources manuscrites du* Cours de linguistique générale *de F. de Saussure.* Geneva: Droz.

——. 1966. "Current trends in linguistics." *Theoretical Foundations.*

Harweg, Roland. 1968. "Language and music, an immanent sign theoretic approach." *Foundations of Language* 4.

Hjelmslev, Louis. 1963. *Prolegomena to a Theory of Language,* translated by Francis Whitfield. Madison: University *of* Wisconsin Press.

Metz, Christian. 1968. *Essais sur la signification au cinéma.* Paris: Klincksieck.

Morris, Charles. 1964. *Signification and Significance.* Cambridge, Mass.: MIT Press.

Naville, Adrien. 1888. *De la classification des sciences.* Geneva: H. Georg Bale.

Panofsky, Erwin. 1957. *Gothic Architecture and Scholasticism.* London: Meridian

——. 1967. *Architecture gothique et pensée scolastique,* translated by Pierre Bourdieu. Paris: Minuit.

Peirce, Charles S. 1958. *Selected Writings,* edited by Philip Wiener. New York: Dover.

de Saussure. Ferdinand. 1966. *Course in General Linguistics,* translated by Wade Baskin. New York: McGraw-Hill.

——. 1957. *Les Cahiers F. De Saussure,* 15.

Sheffer, Jean Louis. 1969. *Scénographie d'un tableau.* Paris: Klincksieck.

Wallis, Mieczyslaw. 1964. "Medieval art as a language." *Actes du 5e Congrès International d'Esthétique,* Amsterdam.

——.1966. "La Notion du champ sémantique et son application à la théorie de l'art." *Sciences de l'art,* special issue.

8

Sign Function

Louis Hjelmslev[1]

That a language is a system of signs seems *a priori* an evident and fundamental proposition, which linguistic theory will have to take into account at an early stage. Linguistic theory must be able to tell us what meaning can be attributed to this proposition, and especially to the word *sign*. For the present we shall have to be content with the vague conception bequeathed by tradition. According to this conception a "sign" (or, as we shall say, in anticipation of a terminological refinement to be introduced later a *sign-expression*) is characterized first and foremost by being a sign *for* something else—a peculiarity that is likely to arouse our interest, since this seems to indicate that a "sign" is defined by a function. A "sign" functions designates, denotes; a "sign," in contradistinction to a non-sign is the bearer of a meaning.

We shall content ourself with this provisional conception and try on the basis of it to decide to what extent the proposition can be correct that a language is a system of "signs."

In its first stages, a certain tentative textual analysis might seem to give full support to this proposition. The entities commonly referred to as sentences, clauses, and words seem to fulfill the stated conditions: they are bearers of meanings, thus "signs," and the inventories established by an analysis following such traditional lines would lead us to recognize a sign system behind the sign process. Here as elsewhere it will be of interest to try to carry out the analysis as far as possible, in order to test for an exhaustive and maximally simple description. Words are not the ultimate, irreducible signs, as the centering of conventional linguistics around the word might lead us to think. Words can be analyzed into parts which, like words, are themselves bearers of meaning: roots, derivational elements, inflexional elements. Some languages go further in this respect than others. The Latin ending *-ibus* cannot be resolved into signs of smaller extension, but is in itself a simple sign that bears both case meaning and number meaning; the Hungarian ending for the dative plural in a word like *magyaroknak* (from *magyar* 'Hungarian') is a composite sign consisting of one sign *-ak*, bearing plural meaning, and another sign *-nak*, bearing dative meaning. Such an

[1] Louis Hjelmslev, *Prolegomena to a Theory of language* trans. F. Whitfield (Madison: University of Wisconsin Press, 1963), pp. 43–49. Reprinted by permission of publisher.

analysis is not affected by the existence of languages without derivational and inflexional elements, or by the fact that even in languages
that have such elements words may occur consisting of a root alone.
Once we have made the general observation that an entity can sometimes be of the same extension as an entity of a higher degree, and in
that case will have to be transferred unanalyzed from operation to operation, this fact can no longer cause us difficulties. The analysis has, precisely for this reason, the same general form in this as in all other cases,
and can be continued until it can be considered exhausted. When, for
example, the analysis of an English word like *in-act-iv-ate-s* is carried
through in this way it can be shown to contain five distinguishable entities which each bear meaning and which are consequently five signs.

In suggesting so far-reaching an analysis on a conventional basis we
should perhaps draw attention to the fact that the "meaning" which
each such minimal entity can be said to bear must be understood as
being a purely contextual meaning. None of the minimal entities, nor
the roots have such an "independent" existence that they can be
assigned a lexical meaning. But from the basic point of view we have
assumed the continued analysis on the basis of functions in the text
there exist no other perceivable meanings than contextual meanings:
any entity and thus also any sign, is defined relatively, not absolutely,
and only by its place in the context. From this point of view it is meaningless to distinguish between meanings that appear only in the context
and meanings that might be assumed to have an independent existence,
or with the old Chinese grammarians between "empty" and "full"
words. The so-called lexical meanings in certain signs are nothing but
artificially isolated contextual meanings, or artificial paraphrases of
them. In absolute isolation no sign has any meaning; any sign-meaning
arises in a context, by which we mean a situational context or explicit
context, it matters not which, since in an unlimited or productive text (a
living language) we can always transform a situational into an explicit
context. Thus we must not imagine, for example, that a substantive is
more meaningful than a preposition, or a word more meaningful than
a preposition, or a word more meaningful than a derivational or inflexional ending. When comparing one entity with another we may speak
not merely of a difference in meaning but also of different kinds of
meaning, but concerning all such entities we may speak of meaning
with precisely the same relative right. This is not changed by the fact
that meaning in the traditional sense is a vague concept that we shall
not retain in the long run without closer analysis.

But when we attempt to analyze sign-expressions in the manner
suggested, inductive experience shows that in all hitherto observed languages there comes a stage in the analysis of the expression when the
entities yielded can no longer be said to be bearers of meaning and thus

no longer are sign-expressions. Syllables and phonemes are not sign expressions, but only parts of sign-expressions. That a sign-expression, for example a word or an ending, can consist of one syllable and can consist of one phoneme does not mean that the syllable is a sign-expression or that the phoneme is a sign-expression. From one point of view the *s* in *in-act-iv-ate-s* is a sign-expression, from another point of view a phoneme. The two points of view lead to the recognition of two different objects. We can very well preserve the formulation the sign-expression *s* includes one, and only one, phoneme, but this is not the same as identifying the sign-expression with that phoneme; the phoneme enters into other combinations where it is not a sign-expression (e.g., in the word *sell*).

Such considerations lead us to abandon the attempt to analyze into "signs," and we are led to recognize that a description in accordance with our principles must analyze content and expression separately, with each of the two analyzes eventually yielding a restricted number of entities, which are not necessarily susceptible of one-to-one matching with entities in the opposite plane.

The relative economy between inventory lists for signs and for non signs corresponds entirely to what is presumably the aim of language. A language is be its aim first and foremost a sign system; in order to be fully adequate it must always be ready to form new signs, new words or new roots. But, with all its limitless abundance, in order to be fully adequate, a language must likewise be easy to manage, practical in acquisition and use. Under the requirement of an unrestricted number of signs, this can be achieved by all the signs being constructed of non-signs whose number is restricted, and, preferably, severely restricted. Such non-signs as enter into a sign system as parts of signs we shall here call *figurae*; this is a purely operative term, introduced simply for convenience. Thus, a language is so ordered that with the help of a handful of figurae and through ever new arrangements of them a legion of signs can be constructed. If a language were not so ordered it would be a tool unusable for its purpose. We thus have every reason to suppose that in this feature the construction of the sign from a restricted number of figurae—we have found an essential basic feature in the structure of any language.

Languages, then, cannot be described as pure sign systems. By the aim usually attributed to them they are first and foremost sign systems; but by their internal structure they are first and foremost something different, namely systems of figurae that can be used to construct signs. The definition of a language as a sign system has thus shown itself, on closer analysis, to be unsatisfactory. It concerns only the external functions of a language, its relation to the non-linguistic factors that surround it, but not its proper, internal functions.

Expression and Content

Up to this point we have intentionally adhered to the old tradition according to which a sign is first and foremost a sign *for* something. In this we are certainly in agreement with the popular conception and, moreover, with a conception widely held by epistemologists and logicians. But it remains for us to show that their conception is linguistically untenable, and here we are in agreement with recent linguistic thinking.

While, according to the first view, the sign is an *expression* that points to a *content* outside the sign itself, according to the second view (which is put forth in particular by Saussure and, following him, by Weisgerber) the sign is an entity generated by the connexion between an expression and a content.

Which of these views shall be preferred is a question of appropriateness. In order to answer this question we shall for the moment avoid speaking about signs, which are precisely what we shall attempt to define. Instead, we shall speak of something whose existence we think we have established, namely the *sign function*, posited between two entities, and *expression* and a *content*. On this basis we shall be able to determine whether it is appropriate to consider the sign function as an external or an internal function of the entity that we shall call a *sign*.

We have here introduced *expression* and *content* as designations of the functives that contract the function in question, the sign function. This is a purely operative definition and a formal one in the sense that, in this context, no other meaning shall be attached to the terms *expressions* and *content*.

There will always be solidarity between a function and (the class of) its functives: a function is inconceivable without its terminals, and the terminals are only end points for the function and are thus inconceivable without it. If one and the same entity contracts different functions in turn, and thus might apparently be said to be selected by them, it is a matter, in each case, not of one and same functive, but of different functives, different objects, depending on the point of view that is assumed, i.e., depending on the function from which the view is taken. This does not prevent us from speaking of the "same" entity from other points of view, for example from a consideration of the functions that enter into it (are contracted by its components) and establish it. If several sets of functives contract one and the same function, this means that there is solidarity between the function and the whole class of these functives, and that consequently each individual functive selects the function.

Thus there is also solidarity between the sign function and its two functives, expression and content. There will never be a sign function without the simultaneous presence of both these functives; and an expression and its content, or a content and its expression, will never appear together without the sign function's also being present between them.

The sign function is in itself a solidarity. Expression and content are solidary—they necessarily presuppose each other. An expression is expression only by virtue of being an expression of a content, and a content is content only by virtue of being a content of an expression. Therefore except by an artificial isolation there can be no content without an expression, or expressionless content; neither can there be an expression without a content, or content-less expression. If we think without speaking, the thought is not a linguistic content and not a functive for a sign function. If we speak without thinking, and in the form of series of sounds to which no content can be attached by any listener, such speech is an abracadabra, not a linguistic expression and not a functive for a sign function. Of course, lack of content must not be confused with lack of meaning: an expression may very well have a content which from some point of view (for example, that of normative logic or physicalism) may be charaterized as meaningless, but it is a content.

9
Structural Analysis

Claude Lévi-Strauss[1]

Linguistics occupies a special place among the social sciences, to whose ranks it unquestionably belongs. It is not merely a social science like the others, but, rather, the one in which by far the greatest progress has been made. It is probably the only one which can truly claim to be a science and which has achieved both the formulation of an empirical method and an understanding of the nature of the data submitted to its analysis. This privileged position carries with it several obligations. The linguist will often find scientists from related but different disciplines drawing inspiration from his example and trying to follow his lead. *Noblesse oblige.* A linguistic journal like *Word* cannot confine itself to the illustration of strictly linguistic theories and points of view. It must also welcome psychologists, sociologists, and anthropologists eager to learn from modern linguistics the road which leads to the empirical knowledge of social phenomena. As Marcel Mauss wrote already forty years ago: "Sociology would certainly have progressed much further if it had everywhere followed the lead of the linguists...."[2] The close methodological analogy which exists between the two disciplines imposes a special obligation of collaboration upon them.

Ever since the work of Schrader[3] it has been unnecessary to demonstrate the assistance which linguistics can render to the anthropologist in the study of kinship. It was a linguist and a philologist (Schrader and Rose)[4] who showed the improbability of the hypothesis of matrilineal survivals in the family in antiquity, to which so many anthropologists still clung at that time. The linguist provides the anthropologist with etymologies which permit him to establish between certain kinship terms relationships that were not immediately apparent. The anthropologist, on the other hand, can bring to the attention of the linguist

---

[1] Claude Lévi-Strauss, *Structural Anthropology* (New York: Basic Books, 1963).Permission by The Perseus Books Group.

[2] Marcel Mauss, "Rapports réels et pratiques de la psychologie et de la sociologie," *Journal de Psychologie Normale et Pathologique* (1924); reprinted in *Sociologie et Anthropologie* (Paris 1951), p. 299.

[3] O. Schrader, *Prehistoric Antiquities of the Aryan Peoples,* trans. F. B. Jevons (London: 1890), Chapter XII, Part 4.

[4] *Ibid.* See also H. J. Rose, "On the Alleged Evidence for Mother-Right in Early Greece," *Folklore,* XXII (1911), and the more recent studies by George Thomson, which support the hypothesis of matrilineal survivals.

customs, prescriptions, and prohibitions that help him to understand the persistence of certain features of language or the instability of terms or groups of terms. At a meeting of the Linguistic Circle of New York, Julien Bonfante once illustrated this point of view by reviewing the etymology of the word for uncle in several Romance languages. The Greek Θεῖος corresponds in Italian, Spanish, and Portuguese to *zio* and *tio*; and he added that in certain regions of Italy the uncle is called *barba*. The "beard," the "divine" uncle—what a wealth of suggestions for the anthropologist! The investigations of the late A. M. Hocart into the religious character of the avuncular relationship and the "theft of the sacrifice" by the maternal kinsmen immediately come to mind.[5] Whatever interpretation is given to the data collected by Hocart (and his own interpretation is not entirely satisfactory), there is no doubt that the linguist contributes to the solution of the problem by revealing the tenacious survival in contemporary vocabulary of relationships which have long since disappeared. At the same time, the anthropologist explains to the linguist the bases of etymology and confirms its validity. Paul K. Benedict, in examining, as a linguist, the kinship systems of Southeast Asia, was able to make an important contribution to the anthropology of the family in that area.[6]

But linguists and anthropologists follow their own paths independently. They halt, no doubt, from time to time to communicate to one another certain of their findings; these findings, however, derive from different operations, and no effort is made to enable one group to benefit from the technical and methodological advances of the other. This attitude might have been justified in the era when linguistic research leaned most heavily on historical analysis. In relation to the anthropological research conducted during the same period, the difference was one of degree rather than of kind. The linguists employed a more rigorous method, and their findings were established on more solid grounds; the sociologists could follow their example in "renouncing consideration of the spatial distribution of contemporary types as a basis for their classifications."[7] But, after all, anthropology and sociology were looking to linguistics only for insights; nothing foretold a revelation.[8]

---

[5] A.M. Hocart, "Chieftainship and the Sister's Son in the Pacific," *American Anthropologist*, n.s., XVII (1915); "The Uterine Nephew," *Man*, XXIII, No. 4 (1923); "The Cousin in Verdic Ritual," *Indian Antiquary*, LIV (1925); etc.

[6] Paul K. Benedict, "Tibetan and Chinese Kinship Terms," *Harvard Journal of Asiatic Studies*, VI (1942); "Studies in Thai Kinship Terminology," *Journal of the American Oriental Society*, LXIII (1943).

[7] L. Brunschvicg, *Le Progrès de la conscience dans la philosophie occidentale* (Paris: 1927), II, p. 562.

[8] Between 1900 and 1920 Ferdinand de Saussure and Antoine Meillet, the founders of modern linguistics, placed themselves determinedly under the wing of the anthropolo-

The advent of structural linguistics completely changed this situation. Not only did it renew linguistic perspectives; a transformation of this magnitude is not limited to a single discipline. Structural linguistics will certainly play the same renovating role with respect to the social sciences that nuclear physics, for example, has played for the physical sciences. In what does this revolution consist, as we try to assess its broadest implications? N. Troubetzkoy, the illustrious founder of structural linguistics, himself furnished the answer to this question. In one programmatic statment,[9] he reduced the structural method to four basic operations. First, structural linguistics shifts from the study of *conscious* linguistic phenomena to study of their *unconscious* infrastructure; second, it does not treat *terms* as independent entities, taking instead as its basis of analysis the *relations* between terms; third, it introduces the concept of *system:* "Modern phonemics does not merely proclaim that phonemes are always part of a system; it *shows* concrete phonemic systems and elucidates their structure"[10]; finally, structural linguistics aims at discovering *general laws,* either by induction "or . . . by logical deduction, which would give them an absolute character."[11]

Thus, for the first time, a social science is able to formulate necessary relationships. This is the meaning of Troubetzkoy's last point, while the preceding rules show how linguistics must proceed in order to attain this end. It is not for us to show that Troubetzkoy's claims are justified. The vast majority of modern linguists seem sufficiently agreed on this point. But when an event of this importance takes place in one of the sciences of man, it is not only permissible for, but required of, representatives of related disciplines immediately to examine its consequences and its possible application to phenomena of another order.

New perspectives then open up. We are no longer dealing with an occasional collaboration where the linguist and the anthropologist, each working by himself, occasionally communicate those findings which each thinks may interest the other. In the study of kinship problems (and, no doubt, the study of other problems as well), the anthropologist finds himself in a situation which formally resembles that of the structural linguist. Like phonemes, kinship terms are elements of meaning; like phonemes, they acquire meaning only if they are integrated into systems. "Kinship systems," like "phonemic systems," are built by the mind on the level of unconscious thought. Finally, the recurrence of kinship patterns, marriage rules, similar prescribed attitudes between cer-

---

gists. Not until the 1920s did Marcel Mauss begin—to borrow a phrase from economics—to reverse this tendency.

[9] N. Troubetzkoy, "La Phonologie actuelle," in *Psychologie du language* (Paris: 1933).

[10] *Ibid.,* p. 243.

[11] *Loc. cit.*

tain types of relatives, and so forth, in scattered regions of the globe and in fundamentally different societies, leads us to believe that, in the case of kinship as well as linguistics, the observable phenomena result from the action of laws which are general but implicit. The problem can therefore be formulated as follows: Although they belong to *another order of reality,* kinship phenomena are *of the same type* as linguistic phenomena. Can the anthropologist, using a method analogous *in form* (if not in content) to the method used in structural linguistics, achieve the same kind of progress in his own science as that which has taken place in linguistics?

We shall be even more strongly inclined to follow his part after an additional observation has been made. The study of kinship problems is today broached in the same terms and seems to be in the throes of the same difficulties as was linguistics on the eve of the structuralist revolution. There is a striking analogy between certain attempts by Rivers and the old linguistics, which sought its explanatory principles first of all in history. In both cases, it is solely (or almost solely) diachronic analysis which must account for synchronic phenomena. Troubetzkoy, comparing structural linguistics and the old linguistics, defines structural linguistics as a "systematic structuralism and universalism," which he contrasts with the individualism and "atomism" of former schools. And when he considers diachronic analysis, his perspective is a profoundly modified one: "The evolution of a phonemic system at any given moment is directed by the *tendency toward a goal....* This evolution thus has a direction, an internal logic, which historical phonemics is called upon to elucidate."[12] The "individualistic" and "atomistic" interpretation, founded exclusively on historical contingency, which is criticized by Troubetzkoy and Jakobson, is actually the same as that which is generally applied to kinship prolems.[13] Each detail of terminology and each special marriage rule is associated with a specific custom as either its consequence or its survival. We thus meet with a chaos of discontinuity. No one asks how kinship systems, regarded as synchronic wholes, could be the arbitrary product of a convergence of several heterogeneous institutions (most of which are hypothetical), yet nevertheless function with some sort of regularity and effectiveness.[14]

However, a preliminary difficulty impedes the transposition of the phonemic method to the anthropological study of primitive peoples.

[12] *Ibid.,* p. 245; Roman Jakobson, "Principien der historischen Phonologie," *Travaux du Cercle linguistique de Prague, IV* (1931); and also Jakobson, "Remarques sur l'évolution phonologique du russe," *ibid.,* 11 (1929).

[13] W. H. R. Rivers, *The History of Melanesian Society* (London: 1914), *passim; Social Organization,* ed. W. J. Perry (London: 1924), Chapter IV.

[14] In the same vein, see Sol Tax, "Some Problems of Social Organization," in Fred Eggan (ed.), *Social Anthropology of North American Tribes* (Chicago: 1937).

The superficial analogy between phonemic systems and kinship systems is so strong that it immediately sets us on the wrong track. It is incorrect to equate kinship terms and linguistic phonemes from the viewpoint of their formal treatment. We know that to obtain a structural law the linguist analyzes phonemes into "distinctive features," which he can then group into one or several "pairs of oppositions."[15] Following an analogous method, the anthropologist might be tempted to break down analytically the kinship terms of any given system into their components. In our own kinship system, for instance, the term *father* has positive connotations with respect to sex, relative age, and generation; but it has a zero value on the dimension of collaterality, and it cannot express an affinal relationship. Thus, for each system, one might ask what relationships are expressed and, for each term of the system, what connotation—positive or negative—it carries regarding each of the following relationships: generation, collaterality, sex, relative age, affinity, etc. It is at this "microsociological" level that one might hope to discover the most general structural laws, just as the linguist discovers his at the infra-phonemic level or the physicist at the infra-molecular or atomic level. One might interpret the interesting attempt of Davis and Warner in these terms.[16]

But a threefold objection immediately arises. A truly scientific analysis must be real, simplifying, and explanatory. Thus the distinctive features which are the product of phonemic analysis have an objective existence from three points of view: psychological, physiological, and even physical; they are fewer in number than the phonemes which result from their combination; and, finally, they allow us to understand and reconstruct the system. Nothing of the kind would emerge from the preceding hypothesis. The treatment of kinship terms which we have just sketched is analytical in appearance only; for, actually, the result is more abstract than the principle; instead of moving toward the concrete, one moves away from it, and the definitive system—if system there is—is only conceptual. Secondly, Davis and Warner's experiment proves that the system achieved through this procedure is infinitely more complex and more difficult to interpret than the empirical data.[17] Finally, the hypothesis has no explanatory value; that is, it does not lead

---

[15] Roman Jakobson, "Observations sur le classement phonologique des consonnes," *Proceedings of the Third International Congress of Phonetic Sciences* (Ghellt: 1938).

[16] K. Davis and W. L. Warner, "Structural Analysis of Kinship," *America Anthropologist*, n.s., XXXVII (1935).

[17] Thus at the end of the analysis carried out by these authors, the term *husband* is replaced by the formula:

$$C^{2a} / 2d / {}^{0} S \: U^{1a \: 8} / \: Ego \: (Ibid.)$$

There are now available two works which employ a much more refined logical apparatus and offer greater interest in terms both of method and of results. See F. G. Louns-

to an understanding of the nature of the system and still less to a reconstruction of its origins.

What is the reason for this failure? A too literal adherence to linguistic method actually betrays its very essence. Kinship terms not only have a sociological existence; they are also elements of speech. In our haste to apply the methods of linguistic analysis, we must not forget that, as a part of vocabulary, kinship terms must be treated with linguistic methods in direct and not analogous fashion. Linguistics teaches us precisely that structural analysis cannot be applied to words directly, but only to words previously broken down into phonemes. *There are no necessary relationships at the vocabulary level.*[18] This applies to all vocabulary elements, including kinship terms. Since this applies to linguistics, it ought to apply *ipso facto* to the sociology of language. An attempt like the one whose possibility we are now discussing would thus consist in extending the method of structural linguistics while ignoring its basic requirements. Kroeber prophetically foresaw this difficulty in an article written many years ago[19] And if, at that time, he concluded that a structural analysis of kinship terminology was impossible, we must remember that linguistics itself was then restricted to phonetic, psychological, and historical analysis. While it is true that the social sciences must share the limitations of linguistics, they can also benefit from its progress.

Nor should we overlook the profound differences between the phonemic chart of a language and the chart of kinship terms of a society. In the first instance there can be no question as to function; we all know that language serves as a means of communication. On the other hand, what the linguist did not know and what structural linguistics alone has allowed him to discover is the way in which language achieves this end. The function was obvious; the system remained unknown. In this respect, the anthropologist finds himself in the opposite situation. We know, since the work of Lewis H. Morgan, that kinship terms constitute systems; on the other hand, we still do not know their function. The misinterpretation of this initial situation reduces most structural analyses of kinship systems to pure tautologies. They demonstrate the obvious and neglect the unknown.

This does not mean that we must abandon hope of introducing order and discovering meaning in kinship nomenclature. But we should at least recognize the special problems raised by the sociology of

bury, "A Semantic Analysis of the Pawnee Kinship Usage," *Language*, XXXII, No. I(1956), and W. H. Goodenough, "The Componential Analysis of Kinship," ibid.

[18] As will be seen in Chapter V [not included in this selection], I have now refined this formulation.

[19] A. L. Kroeber, "Classificatory Systems of Relationship," *Journal of the Royal Anthropological Institute, XXXIX* (1909).

vocabulary and the ambiguous character of the relations between its methods and those of linguistics. For this reason it would be preferable to limit the discussion to a case where the analogy can be clearly established. Fortunately, we have just such a case available.

What is generally called a "kinship system" comprises two quite different orders of reality. First, there are terms through which various kinds of family relationships are expressed. But kinship is not expressed solely through nomenclature. The individuals or classes of individuals who employ these terms feel (or do not feel, as the case may be) bound by prescribed behavior in their relations with one another, such as respect or familiarity, rights or obligations, and affection or hostility. Thus, along with what we propose to call the *system of terminology* (which, strictly speaking, constitutes the vocabulary system), there is another system, both psychological and social in nature, which we shall call the *system of attitudes*. Although it is true (as we have shown above) that the study of systems of terminology places us in a situation analogous, but opposite, to the situation in which we are dealing with phonemic systems, this difficulty is "inversed," as it were, when we examine systems of attitudes. We can guess at the role played by systems of attitudes, that is, to insure group cohesion and equilibrium, but we do not understand the nature of the interconnections between the various attitudes, nor do we perceive their necessity.[20] In other words, as in the case of language, we know their function, but the system is unknown.

Thus we find a profound difference between the *system* of *terminology* and the *system* of *attitudes*, and we have to disagree with A. R. Radcliffe Brown if he really believed, as has been said of him, that attitudes are nothing but the expression or transposition of terms on the affective level.[21] The last few years have provided numerous examples of groups whose chart of kinship terms does not accurately reflect family attitudes, and vice versa.[22] It would be incorrect to assume that the kinship system constitutes the principal means of regulating interpersonal relationships in all societies. Even in societies where the kinship system does function as such, it does not fulfill that role everywhere to the same extent. Furthermore, it is always necessary to distinguish between

---

[20] We must except the remarkable work of W. L. Warner, "Morphology and Functions of the Australian Murngin Type of Kinship," *American Anthropologist*, n.s., XXXII–XXXIII (1930–1931), in which his analysis of the system of attitudes, although fundamentally debatable, nevertheless initiates a new phase in the study of problems of kinship.

[21] A. R. Radcliffe-Brown, "Kinship Terminology in California," *American Anthropologist*, n.s., XXXVII (1935); "The Study of Kinship Systems," *Journal of the Royal Anthropological Institute*, LXXI (1941).

[22] M. E. Opler, "Apache Data Concerning the Relationship of Kinship Terminology to Social Classification," *American Anthropologist*, n.s., XXXIX (1937); A. M. Halpern, "Yuma Kinship Terms," *American Anthropologist*, n.s., XLIV (1942).

two types of attitudes: first, the diffuse, uncrystallized, and non-institutionalized attitudes, which we may consider as the reflection or transposition of the terminology on the psychological level; and second, along with, or in addition to, the preceding ones, those attitudes which are stylized, prescribed, and sanctioned by taboos or privileges and expressed through a fixed ritual. These attitudes, far from automatically reflecting the nomenclature, often appear as secondary elaborations, which serve to resolve the contradictions and overcome the deficiencies inherent in the terminological system. This synthetic character is strikingly apparent among the Wik Munkan of Australia. In this group, joking privileges sanction a contradiction between the kinship relations which link two unmarried men and the theoretical relationship which must be assumed to exist between them in order to account for their later marriages to two women who do not stand themselves in the corresponding relationship.[23] There is a contradiction between two possible systems of nomenclature, and the emphasis placed on attitudes represents an attempt to integrate or transcend this contradiction. We can easily agree with Radcliffe-Brown and assert the existence of "real relations of interdependence between the terminology and the rest of the system."[24] Some of his critics made the mistake of inferring, from the absence of a rigorous parallelism between attitudes and nomenclature, that the two systems were mutually independent. But this relationship of interdependence does not imply a one-to-one correlation. The system of attitudes constitutes, rather, a dynamic integration of the system of terminology.

Granted the hypothesis (to which we whole-heartedly subscribe) of a functional relationship between the two systems, we are nevertheless entitled, for methodological reasons, to treat independently the problems pertaining to each system. This is what we propose to do here for a problem which is rightly considered the point of departure for any theory of attitudes—that of the maternal uncle. We shall attempt to show how a formal transposition of the method of structural linguistics allows us to shed new light upon this problem. Because the relationship between nephew and maternal uncle appears to have been the focus of significant elaboration in a great many primitive societies, anthropologists have devoted special attention to it. It is not enough to note the frequency of this theme; we must also account for it.

Let us briefly review the principal stages in the development of this

[23] D. F. Thomson, "The Joking Relationship and Organized Obscenity in North Queensland," *American Anthropologist*, n.s., XXXVII (1935).

[24] Radcliffe-Brown, "The Study of Kinship Systems," p. 8. This later formulation seems to us more satisfactory than his 1935 statement that attitudes present "a fairly high degree of correlation with the terminological classification" (*American Anthropologist*, n.s., XXXVII [1935], p. 53).

problem. During the entire nineteenth century and until the writings of Sydney Hartland,[25] the importance of the mother's brother was interpreted as a survival of matrilineal descent. This interpretation was based purely on speculation, and, indeed, it was highly improbable in the light of European examples. Furthermore, Rivers' attempt[26] to explain the importance of the mother's brother in southern India as a residue of cross-cousin marriage led to particularly deplorable results. Rivers himself was forced to recognize that this interpretation could not account for all aspects of the problem. He resigned himself to the hypothesis that *several* heterogeneous customs which have since disappeared (cross-cousin marriage being only one of them) were needed to explain the existence of a *single* institution.[27] Thus, atomism and mechanism triumphed. It was Lowie's crucial article on the matrilineal complex[28] which opened what we should like to call the "modern phase" of the problem of the avunculate. Lowie showed that the correlation drawn or postulated between the prominent position of the maternal uncle and matrilineal descent cannot withstand rigorous analysis. In fact, the avunculate is found associated with patrilineal, as well as matrilineal, descent. The role of the maternal uncle cannot be explained as either a consequence or a survival of matrilineal kinship; it is only a specific application "of a very general tendency to associate definite social relations with definite forms of kinship regardless of maternal or paternal side." In accordance with this principle, introduced for the first time by Lowie in 1919, there exists a general tendency to *qualify attitudes,* which constitutes the only empirical foundation for a theory of kinship systems. But, at the same time, Lowie left certain questions unanswered. What exactly do we call an avunculate? Do we not merge different customs and attitudes under this single term? And, if it is true that there is a tendency to qualify all attitudes, why are only certain attitudes associated with the avuncular relationship, rather than just any possible attitudes, depending upon the group considered?

A few further remarks here may underline the striking analogy between the development of this problem and certain stages in the evolution of linguistic theory. The variety of possible attitudes in the area of interpersonal relationships is almost unlimited; the same holds true for the variety of sounds which can be articulated by the vocal appara-

[25] Sydney Hartland, "Matrilineal Kinship and the Question of its Priority," *Memoirs of the American Anthropological Association,* No. 4 (1917).

[26] W. H. R. Rivers, "The Marriage of Cousins in India," *Journal of the Royal Asiatic Society* (July, 1907).

[27] *Ibid.,* p. 624.

[28] R. H. Lowie, "The Matrilineal Complex," *University of California Publications in American Archaeology and Ethnology,* XVI, No. 2 (1919).

tus—and which are actually produced during the first months of human life. Each language, however, retains only a very small number among all the possible sounds, and in this respect linguistics raises two questions: Why are certain sounds selected? What relationships exist between one or several of the sounds chosen and all the others.[29] Our sketch of the historical development of the avuncular problem is at precisely the same stage. Like language, the social group has a great wealth of psycho physiological material at its disposal. Like language too, it retains only certain elements, at least some of which remain the same throughout the most varied cults and are combined into structures which are always diversified. Thus we may wonder about the reason for this choice and the laws of combination.

For insight into the specific problem of the avunculate we should turn to Radcliffe-Brown. His well-known article on the maternal uncle in South Africa[30] was the first attempt to grasp and analyze the modalities of what we might call the "general principle of attitude qualification." We shall briefly review the fundamental ideas of that now-classic study.

According to Radcliffe-Brown, the term *avunculate* covers two antithetical systems of attitudes. In one case, the maternal uncle represents family authority; he is feared and obeyed, and possesses certain rights over his nephew. In the other case, the nephew holds privileges of familiarity in relation to his uncle and can treat him more or less as his victim. Second, there is a correlation between the boy's attitude toward his maternal uncle and his attitude toward his father. We find the two systems of attitudes in both cases, but they are inversely correlated. In groups where familiarity characterizes the relationship between father and son, the relationship between maternal uncle and nephew is one of respect; and where the father stands as the austere representative of family authority, it is the uncle who is treated with familiarity. Thus the two sets of attitudes constitute (as the structural linguist would say) two pairs of oppositions. Radcliffe-Brown concluded his article by proposing the following interpretation: In the final analysis, it is descent that determines the choice of oppositions. In patrilineal societies, where the father and the father's descent group represent traditional authority, the maternal uncle is considered a "male mother." He is generally treated in the same fashion, and sometimes even called by the same name, as the mother. In matrilineal societies, the opposite occurs. Here, authority is vested in the maternal uncle, while relationships of tenderness and familiarity revolve about the father and his descent group.

---

[29] Roman Jakobson, *Kindersprache, Aphasie und allgemeine Lautgesetze* (Uppsala: 1941).

[30] A. R. Radcliffe-Brown, "The Mother's Brother in South Africa," *South African Journal of Science*, XXI (1924).

It would indeed be difficult to exaggerate the importance of Radcliffe Brown's contribution, which was the first attempt at synthesis on an empirical basis following Lowie's authoritative and merciless criticism of evolutionist metaphysics. To say that this effort did not entirely succeed does not in any way diminish the homage due this great British anthropologist; but we should certainly recognize that Radcliffe-Brown's article leaves unanswered some fundamental questions. First, the avunculate does not occur in all matrilineal or all patrilineal systems, and we find it present in some systems which are neither matrilineal or patrilineal.[31] Further, the avuncular relationship is not limited to two terms, but presupposes four, namely, brother, sister, brother-in-law, and nephew. An interpretation such as Radcliffe-Brown's arbitrarily isolates particular elements of global structure which must be treated as a whole. A few simple examples will illustrate this twofold difficulty.

The social organization of the Trobriand Islanders of Melanesia is characterized by matrilineal descent, free and familiar relations between father and son, and a marked antagonism between maternal uncle and nephew.[32] On the other hand, the patrilineal Cherkess of the Caucasus place the hostility between father and son, while the maternal uncle assists his nephew and gives him a horse when he marries.[33] Up to this point we are still within the limits of Radcliffe-Brown's scheme. But let us consider the other family relationships involved. Malinowski showed that in the Trobriands husband and wife live in an atmosphere of tender intimacy and that their relationship is characterized by reciprocity. The relations between brother and sister, on the other hand, are dominated by an extremely rigid taboo. Let us now compare the situation in the Caucasus. There, it is the brother-sister relationship which is tender—to such an extent that among the Pschav an only daughter "adopts" a "brother" who will play the customary brother's role as her chaste bed companion.[34] But the relationship between spouses is entirely different. A Cherkess will not appear in public with his wife and visits her only in secret. According to Malinowski, there is no greater insult in the Trobriands than to tell a man that he resembles his sister. In the Caucasus there is an analogous prohibition: It is forbidden to ask a man about his wife's health.

---

[31] As among the Mundugomor of New Guinea, where the relationship between maternal uncle and nephew is always familiar, although descent is alternately patrilineal or matrilineal. See Margaret Mead, *Sex and Temperament in Three Primitive Societies* (New York: 1935), pp. 176–185.

[32] B. Malinowski, *The Sexual Life of Savages in Northwestern Melanesia* (London: 1929), 2 vols.

[33] Dubois de Monpereux (1839), cited in M. Kovalevski, "La Famille matriarcale au Caucase," *L'Anthropologie*, IV (1893).

[34] *Ibid.*

When we consider societies of the Cherkess and Trobriand types it is not enough to study the correlation of attitudes between *father / son* and *uncle / sister's son*. This correlation is only one aspect of a global system containing four types of relationships which are organically linked, namely: *brother / sister, husband / wife, father / son,* and *mother's brothers / sister's son*. The two groups in our example illustrate a law which can be formulated as follows: In both groups, the relation between maternal uncle and nephew is to the relation between brother and sister as the relation between father and son is to that between husband and wife. Thus if we know one pair of relations, it is always possible to infer the other.

Let us now examine some other cases. On Tonga, in Polynesia, descent is patrilineal, as among the Cherkess. Relations between husband and wife appear to be public and harmonious. Domestic quarrels are rare, and although the wife is often of superior rank, the husband "... is nevertheless of higher authority in all domestic matters, and no woman entertains the least idea of rebelling against that authority."[35] At the same time there is great freedom between nephew and maternal uncle. The nephew is *fahu,* or above the law, in relation to his uncle, toward whom extreme familiarity is permitted. This freedom strongly contrasts with the father-son relationship. The father is *tapu;* the son cannot touch his father's head or hair; he cannot touch him while he eats, sleep in his bed or on his pillow, share his food or drink, or play with his possessions. However, the strongest *tapu* of all is the one between brother and sister, who must never be together under the same roof.

Although they are also patrilineal and patrilocal, the natives of Lake Kutubu in New Guinea offer an example of the opposite type of structure. F. E. Williams writes: "I have never seen such a close and apparently affectionate association between father and son...."[36] Relations between husband and wife are characterized by the very low status ascribed to women and "the marked separation of masculine and feminine interests...."[37] The women, according to Williams, "are expected to work hard for their masters ... they occasionally protest, and protest may be met with a beating."[38] The wife can always call upon her brother for protection against her husband, and it is with him that she seeks refuge. As for the relationship between nephew and maternal uncle, it is "... best summed up in the word respect' ... tinged with appre-

---

[35] E. W. Gifford, "Tonga Society," *Bernice P. Bishop Museum Bulletin,* No. 61 (Honolulu: 1929), pp. 16–22.

[36] F. E. Williams, "Group Sentiment and Primitive Justice," *American Anthropologist,* n.s., XLIII, No. 4, Part I (1941), p. 523.

[37] F. E. Williams, "Natives of Lake Kurubu, Papua," *Oceania,* XI (1940–1941), p. 266.

[38] *Ibid.,* p. 268.

hensiveness,"[39] for the maternal uncle has the power to curse his nephew and inflict serious illness upon him (just as among the Kipsigi of Africa).

Although patrilineal, the society described by Williams is structurally of the same type as that of the Siuai of Bougainville, who have matrilineal descent. Between brother and sister there is "... friendly interaction and mutual generosity...."[40] As regards the father-son relationship, Oliver writes, "... I could discover little evidence that the word 'father' evokes images of hostility or stern authority or awed respect."[41] But the relationship between the nephew and his mother's brother "appears to range between stern discipline and genial mutual dependence...." However, "... most of the informants agreed that all boys stand in some awe of their mother's brothers, and are more likely to obey them than their own fathers...."[42] Between husband and wife harmonious understanding is rare: "... there are few young wives who remain altogether faithful ... most young husbands are continually suspicious and often give vent to jealous anger ... marriages involve a number of adjustments, some of them apparently difficult...."[43]

The same picture, but sharper still, characterizes the Dobuans, who are matrilineal and neighbors of the equally matrilineal Trobrianders, while their structure is very different. Dobuan marriages are unstable, adultery is widespread, and husband and wife constantly fear death induced by their spouse's witchcraft. Actually, Fortune's remark, "It is a most serious insult to refer to a woman's witchcraft so that her husband will hear of it"[44] appears to be a variant of the Trobriand and Caucasian taboos cited above.

In Dobu, the mother's brother is held to be the harshest of all the relatives. "The mother's brother may beat children long after their parents have ceased to do so," and they are forbidden to utter his name. There is a tender relationship with the "navel," the mother's sister's husband, who is the father's double, rather than with the father himself. Nevertheless, the father is considered "less harsh" than the mother's brother and will always seek, contrary to the laws of inheritance, to favor his son at the expense of his uterine nephew. And, finally, "the strongest of all social bonds" is the one between brother and sister.[45]

---

[39] *Ibid.*, p. 280. See also *Oceania*, XII (1941–1942).

[40] Douglas L. Oliver, *A Solomon Island Society: Kinship and Leadership among the Sinai of Bougainville* (Cambridge, Mass.: 1955), p. 255.

[41] *Ibid.*, p. 251.

[42] *Ibid.*, p. 257.

[43] *Ibid.*, pp. 168–9.

[44] R. F. Fortune, *The Sorcerers of Dobu* (New York: 1932), p. 45.

[45] *Ibid.*, pp. 8, 10, 62–4.

What can we conclude from these examples? The correlation between types of descent and forms of avunculate does not exhaust the problem. Different forms of avunculate can coexist with the same type of descent, whether patrilineal or matrilineal. But we constantly find the same fundamental relationship between the four pairs of oppositions required to construct the system. This will emerge more clearly from the diagrams which illustrate our examples. The sign + indicates free and familiar relations, and the sign – stands for relations characterized by hostility, antagonism, or reserve (Figure 1). This is an oversimplification, but we can tentatively make use of it. We shall describe some of the indispensable refinements farther on.

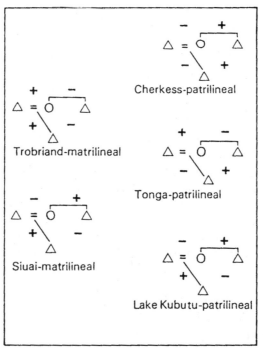

Figure 1

The synchronic law of correlation thus suggested may be validated diachronically. If we summarize, after Howard, the evolution of family relationships during the Middle Ages, we find approximately this pattern: The brother's authority over his sister wanes, and that of the prospective husband increases. Simultaneously, the bond between father and son is weakened and that between maternal uncle and nephew is reinforced.[46]

[46] G. E. Howard, A *History of Matrimonial Institutions*, 3 vols. (Chicago: 1904).

This evolution seems to be confirmed by the documents gathered by Léon Gautier, for in the "conservative" texts (Raoul de Cambrai, Geste des Loherains, etc.),[47] the positive relationship is established chiefly between father and son and is only gradually displaced toward the maternal uncle and nephew.[48]

Thus we see[49] that in order to understand the avunculate we must treat it as one relationship within a system, while the system itself must be considered as a whole in order to grasp its structure. This structure rests upon four terms (brother, sister, father, and son), which are linked by two pairs of correlative oppositions in such a way that in each of the two generations there is always a positive relationship and a negative one. Now, what is the nature of this structure, and what is its function? The answer is as follows: This structure is the most elementary form of kinship that can exist. It is, properly speaking, *the unit of kinship.*

One may give a logical argument to support this statement. In order for a kinship structure to exist, three types of family relations must always be present: a relation of consanguinity, a relation of affinity, and a relation of descent—in other words, a relation between siblings, a relation between spouses, and a relation between parent and child. It is evident that the structure given here satisfies this threefold requirement, in accordance with the scientific principle of parsimony. But these considerations are abstract, and we can present a more direct proof for our thesis.

The primitive and irreducible character of the basic unit of kinship, as we have defined it, is actually a direct result of the universal presence of an incest taboo. This is really saying that in human society a man must obtain a woman from another man who gives him a daughter or a sister. Thus we do not need to explain how the maternal uncle emerged in the kinship structure: He does not emerge—he is present initially. Indeed, the presence of the maternal uncle is a necessary precondition for the structure to exist. The error of traditional anthropology, like that of traditional linguistics, was to consider the terms, and not the relations between the terms.

Before proceeding further, let us briefly answer some objections which might be raised. First, if the relationship between "brothers-in-law" is the necessary axis around which the kinship structure is built,

[47] *Translator's note:* The "Chansons de Geste," which survive in manuscript versions of the twelfth to the fifteenth century, are considered to be remodelings of much earlier originals, dating back to the age of Charlemagne. These poems of heroic and often legendary exploits also constitute a source of information on the family life of that period.

[48] Léon Gautier, *La Chevalerie* (Paris: 1890). See also: F. B. Gummere, "The Sister's Son," in *An English Miscellany Presented to Dr. Furnivall* (London: 1901); W. O. Farnsworth, *Uncle and Nephew in the Old French Chanson de Geste* (New York: 1913).

[49] The preceding paragraphs were written in 1957 and substituted for the original text, in response to the judicious remark by my colleague Luc de Heusch of the Université Libre of Brussels that one of my examples was incorrect. I take this opportunity to thank him.

why need we bring in the child of the marriage when considering the elementary structure? Of course the child here may be either born or yet unborn. But, granting this, we must understand that the child is indispensable in validating the dynamic and teleological character of the initial step, which establishes kinship on the basis of and through marriage. Kinship is not a static phenomenon: it exists only in self-perpetuation. Here we are not thinking of the desire to perpetuate the race, but rather of the fact that in most kinship systems the initial disequilibrium produced in one generation between the group that gives the woman and the group that receives her can be stabilized only by counter-prestations in following generations. Thus, even the most elementary kinship structure exists both synchronically and diachronically.

Second, could we not conceive of a symmetrical structure, equally simple, where the sexes would be reversed? Such a structure would involve a sister, her brother, brother's wife, and brother's daughter. This is certainly a theoretical possibility. But it is immediately eliminated on empirical "rounds. In human society, it is the men who exchange the women, and not vice versa. It remains for further research to determine whether certain cultures have not tended to create a kind of fictitious image of this symmetrical structure. Such cases would surely be uncommon.

We come now to a more serious objection. Possibly we have only inverted the problem. Traditional anthropologists painstakingly endeavored to explain the origin of the avunculate, and we have brushed aside that research by treating the mother's brother not as an extrinsic element, but as an immediate *given* of the simplest family structure. How is it then that we do not find the avunculate at all times and in all places? For although the avunculate has a wide distribution, it is by no means universal. It would be futile to explain the instances where it is present and then fail to explain its absence in other instances.

Let us point out, first, that the kinship system does not have the same importance in all cultures. For some cultures it provides the active principle regulating all or most of the social relationships. In other groups, as in our own society, this function is either absent altogether or greatly reduced. In still others, as in the societies of the Plains Indians, it is only partially fulfilled. The kinship system is a language; but it is not a universal language, and a society may prefer other modes of expression and action. From the viewpoint of the anthropologist this means that in dealing with a specific culture we must always ask a preliminary question: Is the system systematic? Such a question, which seems absurd at first, is absurd only in relation to language; for language is the semantic system par excellence; it cannot but signify, and exists only through signification. On the contrary, this question must be rigorously examined as we move from the study of language to the consideration of other systems which also claim to have semantic functions, but whose fulfillment remains partial, fragmentary, or subjective, like, for example, social organization, art, and so forth.

Furthermore, we have interpreted the avunculate as a characteristic trait of elementary structure. This elementary structure, which is the product of defined relations involving four terms, is, in our view, the true *atom of kinship*.[50] Nothing can be conceived or given beyond the fundamental requirements of its structure, and, in addition, it is the sole building block of more complex systems. For there are more complex systems; or, more accurately speaking, all kinship systems are constructed on the basis of this elementary structure, expanded or developed through the integration of new elements. Thus we must entertain two hypotheses: first, one in which the kinship system under consideration operates through the simple juxtaposition of elementary structures, and where the avuncular relationship therefore remains constantly apparent; second, a hypothesis in which the building blocks of the system are already of a more complex order. In the latter case, the avuncular relationship, while present, may be submerged within a differentiated context. For instance, we can conceive of a system whose point of departure lies in the elementary structure but which adds, at the right of the maternal uncle, his wife, and, at the left of the father, first the father's sister and then her husband. We could easily demonstrate that a development of this order leads to a parallel splitting in the following generation. The child must then be distinguished according to sex—a boy or a girl, linked by a relation which is symmetrical and inverse to the terms occupying the other peripheral positions in the structure (for example, the dominant position of the father's sister in Polynesia, the South African *nhlampsa*, and inheritance by the mother's brother's wife). In this type of structure the avuncular relationship continues to prevail, but it is no longer the predominant one. In structures of still greater complexity, the avunculate may be obliterated or may merge with other relationships. But precisely because it is part of the elementary structure, the avuncular relationship re-emerges unmistakably and tends to become reinforced each time the system under consideration reaches a crisis—either because it is undergoing rapid transformation (as on the Northwest Coast), or because it is a focus of contact and conflict between radically different cultures (as in Fiji and southern India), or, finally, because it is in the throes of a mortal crisis (as was Europe in the Middle Ages).

We must also add that the positive and negative symbols which we have employed in the above diagrams represent an oversimplification, useful only as a part of the demonstration. Actually, the system of basic attitudes comprises at least four terms: an attitude of affection, tenderness, and spontaneity; an attitude which results from the reciprocal exchange of prestations and counter-prestations; and, in addition to these bilateral relationships, two unilateral relationships, one which corresponds to the attitude of the creditor, the other to that of the debtor. In other words there are: mutuality (=), reciprocity (+), rights (+), and obligations (−). These four fundamental attitudes are represented in their reciprocal relationships in Figure 2.

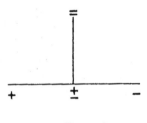

Figure 2

In many systems the relationship between two individuals is often expressed not by a single attitude, but by several attitudes which together form, as it were, a "bundle" of attitudes (as in the Trobriands, where we find both mutuality *and* reciprocity between husband and wife. There is an additional reason behind the difficulty in uncovering the basic structure.

We have tried to show the extent to which the preceding analysis is indebted to outstanding contemporary exponents of the sociology of primitive peoples. We must stress, however, that in its most fundamental principle this analysis departs from their teachings. Let us cite as an example Radcliffe-Brown:

> The unit of structure from which a kinship is built up is the group which I call an "elementary family," consisting of a man and his wife and their child or children.... The existence of the elementary family creates three special kinds of social relationship, that between parent and child, that between children of the same parents (siblings), and that between husband and wife as parents of the same child or children.... The three relationships that exist within the elementary family constitute what I call the first order. Relationships of the second order are those which depend on the connection of two elementary families through a common member, and are such as father's father, mother's brother, wife's sister, and so on. In the third order are such as father's brother's son and mother's brother's wife. Thus we can trace, if we have genealogical information, relationships of the fourth, fifth or nth order.[51]

[51] A. R. Radcliffe-Brown, "The Study of Kinship Systems." p. 2.

The idea expressed in the above passage, that the biological family constitutes the point of departure from which all societies elaborate their kinship systems, has not been voiced solely by Radcliffe-Brown. There is scarcely an idea which would today elicit greater consensus. Nor is there one more dangerous, in our opinion. Of course, the biological family is ubiquitous in human society. But what confers upon kinship its sociocultural character is not what it retains from nature, but, rather, the essential way in which it diverges from nature. A kinship system does not consist in the objective ties of descent or consanguinity between individuals. It exists only in human consciousness; it is an arbitrary system of representations, not the spontaneous development of a real situation. This certainly does not mean that the real situation is automatically contradicted, or that it is to be simply ignored. Radcliffe-Brown has shown, in studies that are now classic, that even systems which are classes, take biological parenthood carefully into account. But while this observation is irrefutable, still the fact (in our view decisive) remains that, in human society, kinship is allowed to establish and perpetuate itself only through specific forms of marriage. In other words, the relationships which Radcliffe-Brown calls "relationships of the first order" are a function of, and depend upon, those which he considers secondary and derived. The essence of human kinship is to require the establishment of relations among what Radcliffe-Brown calls "elementary families." Thus, it is not the families (isolated terms) which are truly "elementary," but, rather, the relations between those terms. No other interpretation can account for the universality of the incest taboo; and the avuncular relationship, in its most general form, is nothing but a corollary, now covert, now explicit, of this taboo.

Because they are symbolic systems, kinship systems offer the anthropologist a rich field, where his efforts can almost (and we emphasize the "almost") converge with those of the most highly developed of the social sciences, namely, linguistics. But to achieve this convergence, from which it is hoped a better understanding of man will result, we must never lose sight of the fact that, in both anthropological and linguistic research, we are dealing strictly with symbolism. And although it may be legitimate or even inevitable to fall back upon a naturalistic interpretation in order to understand the emergence of symbolic thinking, once the latter is given, the nature of the explanation must change as radically as the newly appeared phenomenon differs from those which have preceded and prepared it. Hence, any concession to naturalism might jeopardize the immense progress already made in linguistics, which is also beginning to characterize the study of family structure, and might drive the sociology of the family toward a sterile empiricism, devoid of inspiration.

10
Signs and Human Behavior

Charles Morris[1]

There is wide disagreement as to when something is a sign. Some persons would unhesitatingly say that brushing is a sign, others would not. There are mechanical dogs which will come out of their kennels if one claps one's hands loudly in their presence. Is such clapping a sign? Are clothes signs of the personality of those who wear them? Is music a sign of anything? Is a word such as 'Go!' a sign in the same sense as is a green light on a street intersection? Are punctuation marks signs? Are dreams signs? Is the Parthenon a sign of Greek culture? Disagreements are widespread; they show that the term 'sign' is both vague and ambiguous.

This disagreement extends to many other terms which are commonly used in describing sign-processes. The terms 'express', 'understand', 'refer', 'meaning' would provide many instances. So would 'communication' and 'language'. Do animals communicate? If so, do they have a language? Or do only men have language? Yes, run some answers; no, run others. We find the same diversity of replies if we ask whether thought or mind or consciousness is involved in a sign-process; whether a poem "refers" to what it "expresses"; whether men can signify what cannot be experienced; whether mathematical terms signify anything; whether language signs are preceded genetically by non-language signs; whether the elements in an undeciphered "dead" language are signs.

In the face of such disagreements, it is not easy to find a starting point. If we are to seek for a formulation of the word 'sign' in biological terms, the task is to isolate some distinctive kind of behavior which agrees fairly well with frequent usages of the term 'sign'. Since usage of the term is, however, not consistent, it cannot be demanded that the chosen behavioral formulation agree with all the various usages which are actually current. At some point the semiotician must say: "Henceforth we will recognize that anything which fulfills certain conditions is a sign. These conditions are selected in the light of current usages of the term 'sign', but they may not fit in with all such usages. They do not therefore claim to be a statement of the way the term 'sign' is always used, but a statement of the conditions under which we will henceforth

---

[1] Charles Morris, *Signs, Language and Behavior* (New York: Braziller, 1946), pp. 3–11.

admit within semiotic that something is a sign."

Then from such a starting point a behavioral theory of signs will build up step by step a set of terms to talk about signs (taking account of current distinctions but attempting to reduce for scientific purposes their vagueness and ambiguity), and will endeavor to explain and predict sign phenomena on the basis of the general principles of behavior which underlie all behavior, and hence sign-behavior. The aim is to take account of the distinctions and analyses which former investigators have made, but to ground these results whenever possible upon general behavior theory. In the nature of the case such a scientific semiotic will often deviate from current terminology, and can only be developed slowly and laboriously. It will often seem pedantic and less illuminating for many purposes than less scientific approaches—which therefore are to be encouraged in the light of the many problems and purposes which a treatment of signs aims to fulfill. It is not to be expected that all discussions of literary, religious, and logical signs can be translated at once with profit into a behavioral formulation. The present approach does not therefore wish to exclude other approaches to semiotic. But it does proceed upon the belief that basic progress in this complex field rests finally upon the development of a genuine science of signs, and that this development can be most profitably carried on by a biological orientation which places signs within the context of behavior.

Preliminary Isolation of Sign Behavior

We shall begin by taking two examples of behavior to which the term 'sign' is often applied both in common usage and in the writings of semioticians. Then a superficial analysis of these examples will disclose the features which a more technical formulation of the nature of a sign must embody. If both situations reveal certain common elements, then both may be called sign-behavior; the differences in the two situations would then suggest differences between kinds of signs. If analysis shows too great differences, then the alternative would be to choose different terms to describe the two situations, and to adopt a narrower definition of 'sign': in either case we would then be in a position to consider whether any additional phenomena are to be called signs, that is, whether the characterization of signs based upon the two examples in question is to be held as a basis for determining when something is a sign or whether it is to be expanded to include situations of a widely different sort.

The first example is drawn from experiments on dogs. If a hungry dog that goes to a certain place to obtain food when the food is seen or smelled, is trained in a certain way, it will learn to go to this place for food when a buzzer is sounded even though the food is not observed. In this case the dog is attentive to the buzzer but does not normally go to the buzzer itself; and if the food is not made available until some time after the buzzer has sounded, the dog may not go to the place in question until the time interval has elapsed. Many persons would say in such a situation that the buzzer sound is to the dog a sign of food at the given place, and in particular, a non-language sign. If we abstract from the experimenter and his purposes in this example, and consider only the dog, the example approximates what have often been called "natural signs," as when a dark cloud is a sign of rain. It is in this way that we wish the experiment to be considered.

The second example is drawn from human behavior. A person on the way to a certain town is driving along a road; he is stopped by another person who says that the road is blocked some distance away by a landslide. The person who hears the sounds which are uttered does not continue to the point in question, but turns off on a side-road and takes another route to his destination. It would be commonly said that the sounds made by the one person and heard by the other (and indeed by the utterer also) were signs to both of them of the obstacle on the road, and in particular were language signs, even though the actual responses of the two persons are very different.

Common to these two situations is the fact that both the dog and the person addressed behave in a way which satisfies a need—hunger in the one case, arrival at a certain town in the other. In each case the organisms have various ways of attaining their goals: when food is smelled the dog reacts differently than when the buzzer is sounded; when the obstacle is encountered the man reacts differently than when spoken to at a distance from the obstacle. Further, the buzzer is not responded to as food nor the spoken words as an obstacle; the dog may wait awhile before going for food and the man may continue to drive for a time down the blocked road before turning off to another road. And yet in some sense both the buzzer and the words control or direct the course of behavior toward a goal in a way similar to (though not identical with) the control which would be exercised by the food or the obstacle if these were present as stimuli: the buzzer determines the dog's behavior to be that of seeking food in a certain place at a certain time; the words determine the man's behavior to be that of getting to a certain town by avoiding a certain obstacle at a given place on a given road. The buzzer and the words are in some sense "substitutes" in the control of behavior for the control over behavior which would be exercised by what they signify if this was itself observed. The differences between non-language and language signs remain for subsequent discussion.

It is clear at once that the formulation of 'sign' frequent in early behavior theory is too simple: namely, it cannot be simply said that a sign is a substitute stimulus which calls out to itself the same response which would have been called out be something else had it been present. For the response to food is to food itself, while the response to the buzzer is not to it as if it were food; and the actual response to the situation in which the sign appears may be greatly different from the response to a situation where what is signified, and not the sign, is present. The dog, for instance, may salivate when the buzzer is sounded but it cannot actually eat unless food is present; the man may feel anxiety when he is addressed, but his turning off the road before reaching the obstacle is a very different response from that which he would make if he had gone directly to the place of blockage itself (and even more different from the behavior of the person who told him of the obstacle).

Nor can the difficulties in the earlier attempts to identify signs with any and all substitute stimuli be avoided by attempting to say that whatever influences a response with respect to what is not at the moment a stimulus is a sign. For example, a drug will influence the way an organism will respond to stimuli which later affect it, and yet it would be too great a departure from common usage to call such a drug a sign.

The difficulties in these formulations may perhaps be avoided if, as our examples suggest, signs are identified within goal-seeking behavior. So in the light of our analysis of what the two examples chosen as a point of reference have in common (and neglecting for the time being their differences) we arrive at the following preliminary formulation of at least one set of conditions under which something may be called a sign: *If something, A, controls behavior towards a goal in a way similar to (but not necessarily identical with) the way something else, B, would control behavior with respect to that goal in a situation in which it were observed, then A is a sign.*

The buzzer and the spoken sounds are then signs of food and obstacle because they control the course of behavior with respect to the goals of getting food and getting to a certain place in a way similar to the control which food and obstacle would exercice if they were observed. Whatever exercices this type of control in goal-seeking behavior is a sign. And goal seeking behavior in which signs exercise control may be called *sign-behavior.*

Toward Precision in the Identification of Sign-Behavior

For many purposes the preceding account of a sign is adequate; it at least suggests a behavioral way of formulating what is commonly meant in saying that a sign "stands for" or "represents" something other than itself. But for more strictly scientific purposes a more exact formulation is required in order to clarify the notions of similarity of behavior and goal seeking behavior. We might at this point simply leave it to the scientists in their field to state further refinements, and indeed anything we add is in the nature of the case tentative. But since our concern is to push semiotic as rapidly as possible in the direction of a natural science, the following suggestions are made.

Implicit in the preceding account are four concepts which need further clarifications: preparatory-stimulus, disposition to respond, response-sequence, and behavior-family. When these notions are elucidated a more precise statement of a set of conditions sufficient for something be called a sign can be given.

A *preparatory-stimulus* is any stimulus which influences a response to some other stimulus. Thus it has been found by O. H. Mowrer that the magnitude of the jump of a rat to a shock stimulus is increased if a tone sound before the shock stimulus is encountered. Such a stimulus differs from other stimuli, say the shock, in that as a preparatory-stimulus it influences a response to something other than itself rather than causing a response to itself (it may of course also cause a response to itself, that is, not be merely or solely a preparatory-stimulus). By a *stimulus* is meant, following Clark L. Hull, any physical energy which acts upon a receptor of a living organism; the source of this energy will be called the *stimulus-object*. By a *response* is meant any action of a muscle or gland; hence there are reactions of an organism which are not necessarily responses. A preparatory-stimulus affects or causes a reaction in an organism, but, as Mowrer makes clear, it need not call out a response to itself, but only to some other stimulus. In the account toward which we are moving it is not held that all preparatory-stimuli are signs, but only that preparatory-stimuli which meet certain additional requirements are signs. That a preparatory-stimulus need not when presented call out a response makes intelligible the fact that a command to turn right at a certain place may produce at the time of utterance no overt, or as for as we know, "implicit" response of turning right, and yet may determine that the person commanded turns right when he reaches the place in question. A preparatory stimulus does however cause some reaction in an organism, affects it in some way, and this leads to the introduction of the term 'disposition to respond'.

A *disposition to respond* to something in a certain way is a state of an organism at a given time which is such that under certain additional conditions the response in question takes place. These additional conditions may be very complex. An animal disposed to go to a certain place to obtain food may not go there even if food is observed—he may not be willing or able to swim across an intervening water barrier or to move if certain other animals are present as stimulus-objects. The complex of conditions also includes other states of the organism. The person commanded to turn at a certain corner may not turn even when the corner is reached: as he walked to the corner he may have come to believe that his informant was deliberately trying to misdirect him, so that confidence in one's informant may be at times a necessary condition for making a response to which one is disposed because of signs.

There may be dispositions to respond which are not caused by preparatory-stimuli, but every preparatory-stimulus causes a disposition to respond in a certain way to something else. Logically, therefore, 'disposition to respond' is the more basic notion, and a preparatory-stimulus is a stimulus which causes a disposition to respond in a certain way to something else. And since not all preparatory-stimuli would normally be called signs, and not all dispositions to response which are caused by preparatory-stimuli are relevant to the delimitation of sign-processes, additional criteria are involved; and to be in accord with our own preliminary formulation of sign-behavior, these criteria must introduce the notion of behavior toward a goal.

A response-sequence is any sequence of consecutive responses whose first member is initiated by a stimulus-object and whose last member is a response to this stimulus-object as a goal-object, that is, to an object which partially or completely removes the state of the organism (the "need") which motivates the sequence of responses. Thus the series of responses of a hungry dog which sees a rabbit, runs after it, kills it, and so obtains food is a response-sequence. For the sight of the rabbit starts a series of responses to the rabbit in terms of which the rabbit is finally obtained as food. The intervening responses in the sequence can occur only if the environment provides the necessary stimuli for their release and such sources of stimuli may be called *supporting stimulus-objects.* The terrain over which the dog runs in this case provides the support necessary for the responses of following the rabbit and tracking it down, while the rabbit provides the stimuli initiating and terminating the series of responses.

A behavior-family is any set of response-sequences which are initiated by similar stimulus-objects and which terminate in these objects as similar goal-objects for similar needs. Hence all the response-sequences which start from rabbits and eventuate in securing rabbits as food would constitute the rabbit-food behavior-family. A behavior-family may in an extreme case have only one member; no limit is set to the number of possible members. Behavior-families have various degrees of inclusiveness. All the objects which a dog eats would, for instance, determine an extensive "object-food" behavior-family which would include the rabbit-food behavior-family as a subordinate behavior-family.

In these terms it is possible to formulate more precisely a set of conditions sufficient for something to be a sign: *If anything, A, is a preparatory-stimulus which in the absence of stimulus-objects initiating response-*

sequences of a certain behavior-family causes a disposition in some organism to respond under certain condition by response-sequences of this behavior-family, then A is a sign.

According to these conditions, the buzzer is a sign to the dog since it disposes the animal to seek food in a certain place in the absence of direct stimulation from food objects at this place, and similarly, the spoken words are signs to the driver since they dispose him to response-sequences of avoiding an obstacle at a certain point on a certain road although the obstacle is not itself at the time of hearing the sounds a stimulus-object.

The merit of this formulation is that it does not require that the dog or the driver respond to the sign itself, the sign serving merely as a preparatory-stimulus for response to something else. Nor does it require that the dog or the driver finally respond overtly as they would if food or an obstacle had been stimulus-objects; it merely requires that if the animal makes the response-sequences which it is disposed to make when certain additional conditions are met (conditions of need and of supporting stimulus-objects) these response-sequences will be of the same behavior-family as those which the food or obstacle would have initiated. In this way the difficulties which earlier behavioral formulations of signs encountered are avoided. And yet objective behavioral criteria are furnished for determining whether something is or is not a sign. It is further believed that these criteria do not deviate from those which underlie certain common usages of the term 'sign'.

11
Language vs. Speech

Roland Barthes[1]

In Saussure: The (dichotomic) concept of *language/speech* is central in Saussure and was certainly a great novelty in relation to earlier linguistics which sought to find the causes of historical changes in the evolution of pronunciation, spontaneous associations and the working of analogy, and was therefore a linguistics of the individual act. In working out this famous dichotomy, Saussure started from the "multiform and heterogeneous" nature of language, which appears at first sight as an unclassifiable reality the unity of which cannot be brought to light, since it partakes at the same time of the physical, the physiological, the mental, the individual and the social. Now this disorder disappears if, from the heterogeneous whole, is extracted a purely social object, the systematized set of conventions necessary to communication, indifferent to the *material* of the signals which compose it, and which is a *language (langue)*; as opposed to which *speech (parole)* covers the purely individual part of language (phonation, application of the rules and contingent combinations of signs).

The language (langue): A *language* is therefore, so to speak, language minus speech: it is at the same time a social institution and a system of values. As a social institution, it is by no means an act, and it is not subject to any premediation. It is the social part of language, the individual cannot by himself either create or modify it; it is essentially a collective contract which one must accept in its entirety if one wishes to communicate. Moreover, this social product is autonomous, like a game with its own rules, for it can be handled only after a period of learning. As a system of values, a language is made of a certain number of elements, each one of which is at the same time the equivalent of a given quantity of things and a term of a larger function, in which are found, in a differential order, other correlative values: from the point of view of the language the sign is like a coin which has the value of a certain amount of goods which it allows one to buy, but also has value in relation to other coins, in a greater or lesser degree. The institutional and the systematic aspect are of course connected: it is because a language is a system of contractual values (in part arbitrary, or more exactly, unmotivated) that

---

[1] Roland Barthes *Elements of Semiology,* trans. A. Lavers and C. Smith (New York: Hill and Wang, 1968), pp. 13–17, 25–30.

it resists the modifications coming from a single individual, and is consequently a social institution.

Speech (parole): In contrast to the language, which is both institution and system, *speech is* essentially an individual act of selection and actualization; it is made in the first place of the "combination thanks to which the speaking subject can use the code of the language with a view to expressing his personal thought" (this extended speech could be called *discourse),* and secondly by the "psycho-physical mechanisms which allow him to exteriorize these combinations." It is certain that phonation for instance, cannot be confused with the language; neither the institution not the system are altered if the individual who resorts to them speaks loudly or softly, with slow or rapid delivery, etc. The combinative aspect of speech is of course of capital importance, for it implies that speech is constituted by the recurrence of identical signs: it is because signs are repeated in successive discourses and within one and the same discourse (although they are combined in accordance with infinite diversity of various people's speech) that each sign becomes an element of language; and it is because speech is essentially a combinative activity that it corresponds to an individual act and not to a pure creation.

The dialectics of language and speech: Language and speech: each of these two terms of course achieves its full definition only in the dialectical process which unites one to the other: there is no language without speech, and no speech outside language: it is in this exchange that the real linguistic praxis is situated, as Merleau-Ponty has pointed out. And V. Brondal writes, "A language is a purely abstract entity, a norm which stands above individuals, a set of essential types, which speech actualizes in an infinite variety of ways." Language and speech are therefore in a relation of reciprocal comprehensiveness. On the one hand, the language is "the treasure deposited by the practice of speech, in the subject belonging to the same community" and since it is a collective summa of individual imprints, it must remain incomplete at the level of each isolated individual: a language does not exist perfectly except in the "speaking mass"; one cannot handle speech except by drawing on the language. But conversely, a language is possible only starting from speech: historically, speech phenomena always precede language phenomena (it is speech which makes language evolve), and genetically, a language is constituted in the individual through his learning from the environmental speech (one does not teach grammar and vocabulary which are, broadly speaking, the language to babies). To sum, a language is at the same time the product and the instrument of speech: their relationship is therefore a genuinely dialectical one. It will be noticed (an important fact when we come to semiological prospects) that there could not possibly be (at least according to Saussure) a linguistics of speech, since any speech, as soon as it is grasped as a process of communication, is *already* part of the language: the latter only can be the object of a science. This disposes of two questions at the outset: it is useless to wonder whether speech must be studied *before* the language: the opposite is impossible: one can only study speech straight away inasmuch as it reflects the language (inasmuch as it is "glottic"). It is just as useless to wonder *at the outset* how to separate the language from speech: this is no preliminary operation, but on the contrary the very essence of linguistic and later semiological investigation: to separate the language from the speech means *ipso facto* constituting the problematics of the meaning.

It can be seen from these brief indications how rich in extra- or metalinguistic developments the notion *language/speech* is. We shall therefore postulate that there exists a general category *language/speech*, which embraces all the systems of signs; since there are no better ones, we shall keep the terms *language* and *speech*, even when they are applied to communications whose substance is not verbal.

The garment system: We saw that the separation between the language and speech represented the essential feature of linguistic analysis; it would therefore be futile to propose to apply this separation straight-away to systems of objects, images or behavior patterns which have not yet been studied from a semantic point of view. We can merely, in the case of some of these hypothetical systems, foresee that certain classes of facts will belong to the category of the language and others to that of speech, and make it immediately clear that in the course of its application to semiology, Saussure's distinction is likely to undergo modifications which it will be precisely our task to note.

Let us take the garment system for instance; it is probably necessary to subdivide it into three different systems, according to which substance is used for communication.

In clothes as *written* about, that is to say described in a fashion magazine by means of articulated language, there is practically no "speech": the garment which is described never corresponds to an individual handling of the rules of fashion, it is a systematized set of signs and rules: it is a language in its pure state. According to the Saussurean schema, a language without speech would be impossible; what makes the fact acceptable here is, on the one hand, that the language of fashion does not emanate from the "speaking mass" but from a group which makes the decisions and deliberately elaborates the code, and on the other hand that the abstraction inherent in any language is here materialized as written language: fashion clothes (as written about) are the language at the level of vestimentary communication and speech at the level of verbal communication.

In clothes as photographed (if we suppose, to simplify matters, that there is not duplication by verbal description), the language still issues from the fashion group, but it is no longer given in a wholly abstract form, for a photographed garment is always worn by an individual woman. What is given by the fashion photograph is a semi-formalized state of the garment system: for on the one hand, the language of fashion must here be inferred from a pseudo-real garment, and on the other, the wearer of the garment (the photographed model) is, so to speak, a normative individual, chosen for her canonic generality, and who consequently represents a "speech" which is fixed and devoid of all combinative freedom.

Finally in clothes as *worn* (or real clothes), as Trubetzkoy had suggested, we again find the classic distinction between language and speech. The language, in the garment system, is made i) by the oppositions of pieces, parts of garment and "details," the variation of which entails a change in meaning (to wear a beret or a bowler hat does not have the same meaning); ii) by the rules which govern the association of the pieces among themselves, either on the length of the body or in depth. Speech, in the garment system, comprises all the phenomena of anomic fabrication (few are still left in our society) or of individual ways of wearing (size of the garment, degree of cleanliness or wear, personal quirks, free association of pieces). As for the dialectic which unites here costume (the language) and clothing (speech), it does not resemble that of verbal language; true clothing always draws on costume (except in the case of eccentricity which, by the way, also has its signs), but costume, at least today, *precedes* clothing, since it comes from the ready-made industry, that is, from a minority group (although more anonymous than that of Haute Couture).

The food system: Let us now take another signifying system: food. We shall find there without difficulty Saussure's distinction. The alimentary language is made of i) rules of exclusion (alimentary taboos); ii) signifying oppositions of units, the type of which remains to be determined (for instance the type of *savoury/sweet);* iii) rules of association, either simultaneous (at the level of a dish) or successive (at the level of a menu); iv) rituels of use which function, perhaps as a kind of alimentary *rhetoric.* As for alimentary "speech," which is very rich, it comprises all the personal (or family) variations of preparation and association (one might consider cookery within one family, which is subject to a number of habits as an idiolect). The *menu,* for instance, illustrates very well this relationship between the language and speech: any menu is concocted with reference to a structure (which is both national—or regional—and social); but this structure is filled differently according to the days and the users, just as a linguistic "form" is filled by the free variations and combinations which a speaker needs for a particular message. The relationship between the language and speech would here be fairly similar to that which is found in verbal language: broadly, it is usage, that is to say, a sort of sedimentation of many people's speech, which makes up the alimentary language; however, phenomena of individual innovation can acquire an institutional value within it. What is missing, in any case, contrary to what happened in the garment system, is the action of a deciding group; the alimentary language is evolved only from a broadly collective usage, or from a purely individual speech.

The car system, the furniture system: To bring to a close, somewhat arbitrarily, this question of the prospects opened up by the *language/ speech* distinction, we shall mention a few more suggestions concerning two systems of objects, very different, it is true, but which have in common a dependence in each case on a deciding and manufacturing group: cars and furniture.

In the car system, the language is made up by a whole set of forms and details, the structure of which is established differentially by comparing the prototypes to each other (independently of the number of their "copies"); the scope of "speech" is very narrow because, for a given status of buyer, freedom in choosing a model is very restricted: it can involve only two or three models, and within each model, color and fittings. But perhaps we should here exchange the notion of cars as *object* for that of cars as sociological facts; we would then find in the *driving* of cars the variations in usage of the object which usually make up the plane of speech. For the user cannot in this instance have a direct action on the model and combine its units; his freedom of interpretation is found in the usage developed in time and within which "forms" issuing from the language must, in order to become actual, be relayed by certain practices.

Finally, the last system about which we should like to say a word, that of furniture, is also a semantic object: the "language" is formed both by the oppositions of functionally identical pieces (two types of wardrobe, two types of bed, etc.), each of which, according to its "style," refers to a different meaning, and by the rules of association of the different units at the level of a room ("furnishing"); the "speech" is here formed either by the insignificant variations which the user can introduce into one unit (by tinkering with one element, for instance), or by freedom in associating pieces of furniture together.

12
Nonverbal Communication

Thomas A. Sebeok[1]

All known living organisms communicate exclusively by nonverbal means, with the sole exception of some members of the species *Homo sapiens*, who are capable of communicating, simultaneously or in turn, by both nonverbal and verbal means.

The expression "by verbal means" is equivalent to some such expression as "by means of speech," or "by means of script," or "by means of a sign language" (e.g., for use in a deaf group), that are, each, manifestations of any prerequisite natural language with which human beings are singularly endowed. However, not all humans are literate or can even speak: infants normally do develop a capacity for speaking, but only gradually; some adults never acquire speech; and others lose speech as a result of some trauma (e.g., a stroke) or in consequence of aging. Such conditions notwithstanding, humans lacking a capacity to verbalize—speak, write, or sign—can, as a rule, continue to communicate nonverbally.

A terminological note might be in order at the outset. The word "language" is sometimes used in common parlance in an inappropriate way to designate a certain nonverbal communicative device. Such may be confusing in this context where, if at all, "language" should be used only in a technical sense, in application to humans. Metaphorical uses such as "body language," "the language of flowers," "the language of bees," "ape language," or the like, are to be avoided.

Nonverbal communication takes place within an organism or between two or more organisms. Within an organism, participators in communicative acts may involve—as message sources or destinations or both—on rising integration levels, cellular organelles, cells, tissue, organs, and organ systems. In addition, basic features of the whole biological organization, conducted nonverbally in the *milieu intérieur*, include protein synthesis, metabolism, hormone activity, transmission of nervous impulses, and so forth. Communication on this level is usually studied (among other sciences) by subdomains of biosemiotics labeled protosemiotics, microsemiotics, cytosemiotics, or, comprehensively, endosemiotics.

[1] Thomas A. Sebeok, *Nonverbal Communication* (Toronto: Program in Semiotics and Communication Theory, 1999). Reprinted by permission of MIT Press.

Internal communication takes place by means of chemical, thermal, mechanical, and electrical sign operations, or *semiosis,* consisting of unimaginably busy trafficking. Take as an example a single human body, which consists of some 25 trillion cells, or about 2000 times the number of living earthlings, and consider further that these cells have direct or indirect connections with one another through messages delivered by signs in diverse modalities. The sheer density of such transactions is staggering. Only a minuscule fraction is known to us, let alone understood. Interior messages include information about the significance of one somatic scheme for all of the others, for each over-all control grid (such as the immune system), and for the entire integrative regulatory circuitry, especially the brain.

The earliest forms of interorganismic communication in our biosphere are found in prokaryotes—that is, mostly one-celled creatures lacking a nucleus. These are commonly called bacteria. In the last two decades, bacterial associations have come to be viewed as being of three sorts: localized teams; a single global superorganism; and in interactions with eukaryotes (which are familiar life forms composed of cells having a membrane-bounded nucleus, notably animals and plants, but also several others). Localized teams of great complexity exist everywhere on earth: there are intestinal bacteria, dental plaque bacteria, bacterial mats, and others. There is of course a very large bacterial population in both soils and in the sludge at the bottom of bodies of waters. Such teams busily draw upon information fitting particular sets of circumstances, especially as regards the exchange of genetic information. A distinguished bacteriologist has noted that, in this way, a local bacterial team can adopt sophisticated communicative survival strategies, that is, it can function for a certain period of time as a single multicellular organism.

Importantly, all bacteria, worldwide, have the potential to act in concert, that is, in the manner of a boundless planetary aggregation, as a sort of vast biological communications network—an Internet, if you like. This ensemble has been characterized as a superorganism, possessing more basic information than the brain of any mammal, and whose myriad parts are capable of shifting and sharing information to accommodate to any and all circumstances.

The bacterial superorganism created environmental conditions conducive to the evolution of an entirely different life form: the eukaryotes. Bacteria exploited the eukaryotes as habitats as well as used them for vehicles to advance their own further dispersal. Indeed, eukaryotes evolved in consequence of a succession of intimate intracellular associations among prokaryotes. Biologists call such associations symbioses, but as these crucially entail diverse nonverbal communicative processes, they might more generally be characterized as forms of biological *semioses*. Biosemioses between bacterial entities started more than a thousand million years ago and are thus at the root of all communication.

Both in form and as to variety of their communicative transactions, animals are the most diverse of living creatures. Estimates of the number of animal species range from about three million up to more than thirty million species. Since the behavior of every species differs from every other—most of which are in any case scarcely fathomed—it will be evident that only a few general observations about these can be made here.

Animals communicate through different channels or combinations of media. Any form of energy propagation can, in fact, be exploited for purposes of message transmission. The convoluted ramifications of these can only be hinted at here. Take acoustic events as one set of illustrations of this. Since sound emission and sound reception are so ubiquitous in human communication, it may come as something of a surprise how rare sound is in the wider scheme of biological existence. In fact, the great majority of animals is both deaf and dumb. True hearing and functional sound-production is prevalent—although by no means universal—only among the two most advanced phyla: the invertebrate Arthropods and the vertebrate Chordates (to which we also belong). Among the former, the insects far outnumber the rest of the animal kingdom. Sound is most widespread in the Orthoptera among these, including grasshoppers, especially the katydids, mantises, and cockroaches, and the cicadas of the order of Homoptera. Possessing the most complex of arthropodan sound-producing mechanisms, they also have well-developed hearing organs on the forepart of their abdomen. The Coleoptera, or beetles, contain quite a number of noisy forms. By contrast, sound-use is rather rare among the Arachnids, which include ticks, mites, scorpions, and spiders.

As we move on to the vertebrates, it becomes useful to distinguish not only nonverbal from verbal but also nonvocal from vocal communication, and to introduce yet further discriminations with the advent of tools The vocal mechanism that works by means of a current of air passing over the cords, setting them into vibration, seems to be confined to ourselves and, with distinctions, to our nearest relatives, the other mammals, the birds (endowed with a syrinx), the reptiles, and the amphibians; although some fish do use wind instruments as well, they do so without the reed constituted by our vocal cords. So far as we know, no true vocal performances are found outside the land vertebrates or their marine descendants (such as whales).

Humans communicate via many channels, only one of which is the acoustic. Acoustic communication among us may be *both* verbal *and* vocal, such as of course very commonly as we speak. But so-called alternative sign languages developed by emitters/receivers to be employed on special occasions or during times when speech is not permitted or is rendered difficult by special circumstances are, though generally verbal, not vocal. In this category are included North and South American Indian sign languages, Australian aboriginal sign languages, monastic communication systems actualized under a religious ban of silence, certain occupational or performance sign languages as in pantomime theater or some varieties of ballet. Unvoiced signing may also be freely chosen in preference to speech when secrecy is wanted, for instance, when a baseball catcher prefers to keep the batter ignorant of the next type of pitch to be made; or if a criminal attempts to keep certain messages from witnesses. More complex sign languages used for secrecy are those employed by religious cults or secret societies where ritual codes are meant to manipulate problematic social relationships between "insiders" vs. "outsiders."

Acoustic communication in humans may, moreover, be somatic or artifactual. This is well illustrated by contrasting humming or so-called "whistle talk," produced by the body alone, with "drum signaling," which requires some sort of percussion instrument (or at least a tree-trunk). Sometimes nonverbal acoustic messages—with or without speech—are conveyed at a remove, from behind masks, through inanimate figures, such as puppets or marionettes, or through other performing objects. Again, acoustic somatic communication might be vocal, like a fearsome shriek, or non-vocal, like snapping one's fingers to summon a waiter. Furthermore, in humans, nonverbal communication in the acoustic mode, in all known communities, has been artfully elaborated into a large variety of musical realizations. These might be accompanied by a verbal text (as in a song), or crooned without lyrics, or be produced by all sorts of musical instruments, or be embedded in an enormously complex, multi-dimensional work of art, like an opera. Thus while the overture to Mozart's *Don Giovanni* is a pure sonata-allegro, the enchanting duet between the Don and Zerlina, "Là ci darem la mano," (Act I, Scene 7) immediately following *a secco* (i.e. purely verbal) recitative, gives way to a melody solo then voices intertwining, climaxing in a gesture of physical touching and, dancelike (i.e. 6/8 meter) skipping off-stage arm in arm ("Andiam, andiam mio bene"...). An opera being the supremely syncretic art form, Mozart's musical code, with Lorenzo da Ponte's libretto, is in this scene supported by a host of additional nonverbal artistic codes, such as mime, scenery, setting, costuming, and lighting, among others (as, elsewhere in the same opera, dancing, the culinary art, and even statuary).

Perhaps somewhat less complicated but comparably fused artistic structures include sound films. These usually partake of at least four codes: one visual, three auditory, including speech, music, and sound effects. Circus acrobatic performances, which are realized through at least five codes: the performer's dynamic behavior, his social behavior, his costume and other accessories, the verbal accompaniment, and the musical accompaniment furnish still another blended artistic achievement. The dazzling complexity of the messages generated by theater events (Hamlet's "...suit the action to the word, the word to the action" providing but a modest start) can only be hinted at here.

Another interesting sort of nonverbal communication takes place during conducting, which can be defined as involving the elicitation from an orchestra with the most appropriate minimum choreographic gestures a maximum of acoustical results. In a public setting, the conductor connects not just with the members of the orchestra but also with the audience attending the concert. The gestures shaped by his entire upper body equipment—including hands, arms, shoulders, head, eyes—are decoded by the onlookers through the visual channel, transformed by the players into sound, which is then fed back to the audience. (Operatic conductors often mouth the lyrics.) And, as the eminent pianist Charles Rosen recently wrote: "For all of us, music is bodily gesture as well as sound, and its primitive connection with dance is never entirely distilled away."

The functional advantages or disadvantages of the different channels of communication have never been fully analyzed, but certain statements can be made about acoustic communication in these respects which, other things being equal, apply to animals including man. A clear disadvantage, in contrast for instance to molecular traces such as pheromones, or chemical messengers, which tend to persist over time is the short-lived character of sound. To counteract this transience, humans eventually had recourse to writing and, more recently, introduced all sorts of sound recording devices. This apparent defect may be outweighed by several advantages sound has over other media. For one thing, sound is independent of light and therefore can be used day or night. For another, it fills the entire space around the source. Accordingly, it does not require a straight line of connection with the destination. Too, it involves a minuscule expenditure of energy. In most animals, solely the body produces sound—ordinarily, no tool is requisite. In the case of humans, it can also be modulated to vary from intimate whisper to long distance shouting.

In summarizing what is known of the acoustic behavior of vertebrates, we can only scratch the surface here. Among fish, as in the insects, sound-production seems to occur but sporadically. Almost all are in the Teleosts, and their methods are, Huxley tells us, of three distinct kinds: by stridulation of one hard part against another (grinding their teeth, for instance); by expulsion of gas (a sort of breathing sound); or by vibrating their gas bladder. Some fish hiss like a cat, some growl, some grunt like a pig, others croak, snore, or croon, some bellow, purr,

178 Thomas A. Sebeok

buzz, or whistle, one even vibrates like a drum. And of course fish can hear (although their auditory powers vary considerably).

Most amphibians cannot hear and seldom produce any sound other than a weak squeak, but frogs and toads are quite noisy in highly diverse ways. Reptiles can in general hear better; yet few produce sounds (though crocodiles roar and grunt).

Birds signify by sounds, given and received, but, more comprehensively, by so-called *displays*—stereotyped motor patterns involved in communication—which also include visual movements and posturing. Birds produce a huge variety of vocalizations, ranging from short, monosyllabic calls, to long, complicated sequences, their songs. Some birds can more or less faithfully reproduce, that is to say, "parrot," noises of their environment, imitating those of other species, notably even speech-sounds. The communication systems of birds, which have been well studied for many centuries, are so heterogeneous that they cannot be dealt with here adequately. The same must be said of their multifarious, often dazzling, visible displays—stereotyped motor patterns—including their sometimes spectacular plumage, (e.g., in peacocks or birds of paradise) and their constructs (as in bower-birds).

Mammals have elaborate auditory organs and rely on the sense of hearing more than do members of any other group, but they also, like many birds, communicate, if sporadically, by non-vocal methods as well. A familiar example of this is the drumming behavior in the gorilla, produced by clenched fists beating on the chest. Echolocation refers to the phenomenon where the emitter and receiver of a train of sounds is the same individual; this is found in bats as well as marine mammals, such as certain species of whales and dolphins. (The capability of blind people to navigate by echolocation has not been proved.) Some vertebrates like rats, mice, gerbils, and hamsters communicate in a range inaudible to normal human hearing, by ultrasonic calls. (Analogously, the most effective color for the social bees seems to be ultraviolet, a spectrum beyond unaided human vision.)

All carnivores (cats, dogs, hyenas, etc.) as well as all primates more or less vigorously vocalize, including man's closest relatives, the apes. But the characteristic performances of these creatures are both so rich and varied—ranging from the relatively silent orangutans to the remarkably diverse "singing" gibbons—that describing these would demand a book-length treatment. Instead of attempting to even sketch these here, it's worth emphasizing that apes do *not* communicate verbally in the wild and that, furthermore, even the most strenuous undertakings to inculcate any manifestation of any natural language in captive apes—contrary to insistent claims made in the media—have uniformly failed.

Attempts to teach language-like skills to apes or to any other animals (such as captive marine mammals or pet birds) have been extensively criticized on the grounds that the Clever Hans effect, or fallacy, might have been at work. Since this phenomenon has profound implications for (among other possible dyads) man-animal communications of all sorts, some account seems in order here. In brief, a stallion named Hans, in Berlin at the turn of the century, was reputed to be able to do arithmetic and perform comparably impressive verbal feats, responding nonverbally to spoken or written questions put to him by tapping out the correct answers his foot. Ingenious tests eventually proved that the horse was in fact reacting to nonverbal cues unwittingly given off by the questioner. Ever since that demonstration of how unintended cueing can affect an experiment on animal behavior, alert and responsible scientists tried to exclude the sometimes highly subtle perseverance of the effect.

It later turned out that there are two variants of the Clever Hans fallacy: those based on self-deception, indulged in by Hans's owner/trainer and other interrogators; and those performances—with "wonder horses," "talking dogs," "learned" pigs or geese—based on deliberate trickery, performed by stage magicians and common con "artists" (portrayed over many centuries). Deceptive nonverbal signaling pervades the world of animals and men. In animals, basic shapes of unwitting deception are known as *mimicry*.

This is usually taken to include the emulation of dangerous models by innocuous mimics in terms of visible or auditory signals, or distasteful scents, in order to fool predators. In humans, deceptive communications in daily life has been studied by psychologists; and on the stage by professional magicians. Various body parts may be mendaciously entailed, singly or in combination: gaze, pupil dilation, tears, winks, facial expression, smile or frown, gesture, posture, voice, etc.

A consideration of mainly acoustic events thus far should by no means be taken for neglect of other channels in which nonverbal messages can be encoded, among them chemical optical, tactile, electric, thermal, or others. The chemical channel antedates all the others in evolution and is omnipresent in all organisms. Bacterial communication is exclusively chemical.

Plants interact with other plants via the chemical channel, and with animals (especially insects, but humans as well), in addition to the usual contact channels, by optical means. While the intricacies of plant communication (technically known as *phytosemiosis*) can not be further explored here, mention should at least be made of two related fields of interest: the pleasant minor semiotic artifice of floral arrangements; and the vast domain of gardens as major nonverbal semiosic constructs. Formal gardens, landscape gardens, vegetable gardens, water gardens, coral gardens, Zen gardens are all remarkable nonverbal contrivances, which are variously cultivated from Malinowski's Trobriands to traditional Japanese *kare sansui* (dry garden), to Islamic lands, China, and, notably so, in France and Britain

Smell (olfaction, odor, scent, aroma) is used for purposes of communication crucially, say, by sharks and hedgehogs, social insects as bees, termites, and ants, and such social mammals as wolves and lions. It is less important in birds and primates, which rely largely on sight. In modern societies, smell has been roundly commercialized in the olfactory management of food and toiletry commodities, concerned with repulsive body odor and tobacco products. Perfumes are often associated with love and sexual potency.

The body by itself can be a prime tool for communication, verbal as well as nonverbal. Thus, in animals, it is well-known that dogs and cats display their bodies in acts of submission and intimidation, as famously pictured in Charles Darwin's book on *The Expression of the Emotions,* in Figs. 5–8 (dogs) and Figs. 9-10 (cats). There are many striking illustrations in Desmond Morris's field guide and in the photos assembled by Weldon Kees of how the human frame is brought into habitual play. Professional wrestling is   popular entertainment masquerading as a sport featuring two or a group of writhing bodies, groaning and grunting, pretending in a quasi-morality play to vie for victory of good vs. evil; the players obviously interacting with one another, but, more subtlety, communicating with a live audience. Performances like this differ from legitimate bouts like boxing and collegiate wrestling, or sports like tennis matches, and group events, such as soccer or cricket, in that the outcome of the contest is hardly in suspense.

Dance is one sophisticated art form that can express human thought and feeling through the instrumentality of the body in many genres and in many cultures. One of these is Western ballet, which intermingles with sequences of hand and limb gestural exchanges and flowing body movements and a host of such other nonverbal protocols that echo one another, like music, costumes, lighting, masks, scenery, wigs, etc. Dance and music usually accompany pantomime or dumb shows. Silent clowns or mimes supplement their body movements by suitable make-up and costuming.

Facial expressions, pouting, the curled lip, a raised eyebrow, crying, flaring nostrils, constitute a powerful, universal communication system, solo or in concert. Eye work, including gaze and mutual gaze, can be particularly powerful in understanding a range of quotidian vertebrate as well as human social behavior. Although the pupil response has been observed since antiquity, in the last couple of decades it has matured into a broad area of research called *pupillometry*. Among circus animal trainers it has long been an unarticulated rule to carefully watch the pupil movements of their charges, for instance tigers, to ascertain their mood alteration. Bears, to the contrary, are reported to be "unpredictable," hence dangerous precisely because they lack the pupil display as well as owing to their inelastic muzzle which thus cannot "telegraph" an imminent attack. In interpersonal relationships between human couples a dilation in pupil size acts in effect as an unwitting message transmitted to the other person (or an object) of an intense often sexually toned interest.

Many voluminous dictionaries, glossaries, manuals, and sourcebooks exist to explicate and illustrate the design and meaning of brands, emblems, insignia, signals, symbols, and other signs (in the literal, tangible sense), including speech-fixing signs such as script and punctuation, numerical signs, phonetic symbols, signatures, trademarks, logos, watermarks, heraldic devices, astrological signs, signs of alchemy, cabalistic and magical signs, talismans, technical and scientific signs (as in chemistry), pictograms, and other such imagery, many of them used extensively in advertising. Regulatory signs (NO SMOKING), direction signs deployed at airports (PASSPORT CONTROL, MEN, WOMEN) or in hospitals (PEDIATRICS), international road signs (NO PASSING) are commonly supplemented by icons under the pressure of the need for communication across language barriers, certain physical impairments, or comparable handicaps.

The labyrinthine ramifications of optical communication in the world of animals and for humanity are boundless and need to be dealt with separately. Such sciences as astronomy and the visual arts since prehistoric times naturally and mainly unfold in the optical channel. Alterations of the human body and its physical appearance, from nonpermanent, such as body painting, or theatrical make-up, or routine hair service, to quasi-permanent metamorphoses, by dint of procedures as body sculpture: e.g., the past Chinese "lotus foot" or Western "tightlacing" customs; infibulation, cicatrization, or tattooing; and, more generally, plastic surgery, all convey messages—frequently, as reconstruction, cosmetic in intent, in female breast size—by nonverbal means. The art of mummy painting in Roman Egypt was intended to furnish surrogates for the head by which to facilitate silent communication of a deceased individual during his or her passage to the afterlife.

An intriguing variety of nonverbal human communicative-behavior-at-a-remove features a bizarre form of barter known since Herodotus, modern instances of which are still reported, labeled by ethnographers "silent trade." None of the common direct channels are usually involved, only the abstract idea of *exchange*. What happens is something like this: one party to a commercial transaction leaves goods at a prearranged place, then withdraws to a hidden vantage point to watch unobserved—or more likely not. The other party then appears and inspects the left commodity. If satisfied by the find, it leaves a comparable amount of some other articles of trade.

The study of spatial and temporal bodily arrangements (sometimes called *proxemics*) in personal rapport, the proper dimensions of a cage in the zoo or of a prison cell, the layout of offices, classrooms, hospital wards, exhibitions in museums and galleries, and a myriad other architectural designs—involve the axiology of volume and duration. A map is a graphic representation of a milieu, containing both pictorial or iconic and non-pictorial or symbolic elements, ranging from a few simple configurations to highly complex blueprints or other diagrams and mathematical equations. All maps are also indexical. They range from the local, such as the well-known multicolored representation of the London underground, to the intergalactic metal plaque on Pioneer 10 spacecraft speeding its way out of our solar system. All organisms communicate by use of models (*umwelts*, or self-worlds, each according to it species-specific sense organs), from the simplest representations of maneuvers of approach and withdrawal to the most sophisticated cosmic theories of Newton and Einstein. It would be well to recall that Einstein originally constructed his model of the universe out of nonverbal signs, "of visual and some of muscular type." As he wrote to a colleague in 1945: "The words or the language, as they are written or spoken, do not seem to play any role in my mechanism of thought. The psychical entities which seem to serve as elements in thought are certain signs and more or less clear images which can be 'voluntarily' reproduced and combined." Later, "only in a secondary stage," after long and hard labor to transmute his nonverbal construct into "conventional words and other signs," was he able to communicate it to others.

Appendix A

A Lexicon of Commonly-Used Terms in Semiotics

A

abduction process by which a new concept is formed on the basis of an existing concept that is perceived as having something in common with it (the theory of the atom as a miniature solar system)

abstract concept a mental form whose external referent cannot be demonstrated or observed directly (*love, hope, justice, democracy*, etc.)

actant a unit of narration that recurs in all kinds of stories (a hero, an opponent, etc.)

adaptor bodily movement indicating or satisfying some emotional state or need (scratching one's head when puzzled, rubbing one's forehead when worried)

addressee the receiver of a message; the individual(s) to whom a message is directed

addresser the sender of a message; the creator of message

aesthesia the experience of meaningful sensation; in art appreciation it refers to the fact that our senses and feelings are stimulated holistically by art works

aesthetics the study of beauty and meaning in art and of the psychological responses to it

affect displays hand movements and facial expressions communicating emotional meaning

alliteration the repetition of the initial consonant sounds or clusters of words (*slipping, sliding, slinking*, etc.)

allusion indirect reference to a theme, plot, character, idea, etc. in a conversation, play, narrative, discourse, etc. (*Without naming names, the chairperson criticized the troublemakers*)

alphabet system of characters (marks, figures, letters, symbols, etc.) for representing speech sounds (a, b, c, etc.)

analogy structural relation whereby a form replaces another that is similar in form, function, or use (a Roman numeral with a digit from our decimal system)

anthroposemiosis semiosis in humans

anthroposemiotics the study of semiosis, and representation in humans

anticlimax	rhetorical technique by which ideas are sequenced in abruptly diminishing importance, generally for satirical effect (*After you scale Mt. Everest, then try climbing up that hill*)
antinomy	contradiction or inconsistency between two apparently reasonable principles, or between conclusions drawn from them (*In this case, what is good is really bad!*)
antinovel	fictional narrative characterized by the absence of the traditional elements of the novel, such as a coherent plot structure, a consistent point of view, realistic portrayals of character, etc.
antithesis	rhetorical technique by which two words, phrases, clauses, or sentences are opposed in meaning in such a way as to give emphasis to contrasting ideas (*You are going, I am staying*)
antonomasia	use of an epithet or title in place of a name; use of a well-known personage to describe someone (referring to a philanderer as a *Don Juan*)
antonymy	relation by which different words, phrases, sentences, etc. stand in a discernible oppositeness of meaning to each other (*light and dark*)
apostrophe	rhetorical technique by which an actor turns from the audience, or a writer from his or her readers, to address a person who usually is absent or deceased, an inanimate object, or an abstract idea (*Oh Fate, why do you pursue me so relentlessly?*)
arbitrariness	with that the relation between a form and its meaning or referent (a word and its meaning) is, in most cases, purely arbitrary and/or conventional
archetype	an original model or type after which other similar things are patterned; any unconscious image that manifests itself in dreams, myths, art forms, and performances across cultures
argument	in Peircean theory, the interpretant of a legisign (i.e. how we interpret symbols); a type of reasoning that unfolds when propositions about something are made
artifact	an object produced or shaped by human craft, especially a tool, a weapon, or an ornament of archaeological or historical interest
artifactual media	media such as books, paintings, sculptures, letters, etc. made by human beings in order to transmit messages

B

binary opposition	minimal difference between two forms (*pin* vs. *bin*)
biosemiotics	branch of semiotics aiming to study semiosis in all life forms

C

cacophony	use of harsh, jarring sounds to create a dissonant effect (*glitch* for *error*)
catachresis	obscure use of a word or phrase for rhetorical effect; improper use of a word or phrase (the misuse of *blatant* to mean *flagrant*)
channel	the physical means by which a signal or message is transmitted
character	person portrayed in an artistic piece, such as a drama or novel
chiasmus	structural inversion of the second of two parallel phrases or clauses (*She went to London; to Rome went he*)
cliché	trite or overused expression or idea (*All's well that end's well*)
climax	rhetorical technique by which ideas are sequenced in abruptly increasing importance, from the least to the most forcible (*Sarah starts by giggling, then she goes on to chuckle loudly, and ends up laughing raucously*)
closed text	text with a singular or fairly limited range of meaning (e.g. a map)
code	the system that organizes specific kinds of signs, determining how they relate to each other and how they can be used to represent things (the alphabet, language, gesture, clothing style, etc.)
communication	capacity to participate with other organisms in the reception and processing of specific kinds of signals; the production and exchange of messages and meanings
competence	abstract knowledge of language
conativity	the effect of a message on the addressee
conceit	elaborate, often extravagant, metaphor or simile that makes an association between things that are normally perceived to be totally dissimilar (*My life is a wart*)
concept	a connection made by the human mind (within cultural contexts); a mental image of something
conceptual metaphor	a generalized metaphorical formula that defines a specific abstraction (*Love is a sweetness experience*)
concrete concept	a mental image whose external referent is demonstrable and observable in a direct way
connotation	the extended or secondary meaning of a sign; the symbolic or mythic meaning of a certain signifier (word, image, etc.)
connotation	the extended, historical, and implicative meanings of a sign (the meanings of lion as "courage," "royalty," etc.)

connotatum	the actual unit of connotative meaning of a sign
contact	the physical channel employed in communication and the psychological connections between addresser and addressee
context	the situation (physical, social, psychological, historical) in which signs are produced and messages generated, shaping how they are interpreted

D

decoding	the process of deciphering the message in a text in terms of the specific code used (In order to decode the meaning of the numeral *10* one must know from which code it was made. If it was constructed from the code of decimal numbers, then it stands for the number "ten;" if it was constructed from the code of binary numbers, then it stands for the number "two")
deconstruction	method of literary analysis originated by Jacques Derrida (1930—) in the mid-20th century, based on his view that, by the very nature of language and literary usage, no text can have a fixed, central meaning
deduction	reasoning and concept-formation which unfolds by the application of a general concept or line of reasoning to a specific occurrence (If A is greater than B, and B greater than C, then it can be deduced that A is greater than C)
deixis	the process of referring to beings, objects, and events in time, space or relation to each other
denotation	the intentional meaning of a sign
denotatum	the actual unit of denotative meaning of a sign
diachronicity	change in a form over time
diachrony	the study of change in signs and codes over time
dicisign	in Peircean theory the term refers to the meanings elicited by such indexical signs as the words *here, there,* etc.
displacement	the ability of the human mind to conjure up the things to which signs refer even though these might not be physically present for the senses to perceive
distinctive feature	minimal element that makes up a form and which singularly or in combination with other distinctive features serves to differentiate its meaning from other forms (e.g. *sip* is distinguished from *zip* by a distinctive feature in the initial consonant, namely the vibration of the vocal cords in the case of *z* and its absence in the case of *s*)
duality of patterning	feature of language whereby vocal sounds have no intrinsic meaning in themselves but combine in differ-

ent ways to form elements that do convey meanings (The sound /p/, articulated in isolation, has no meaning. However, when combined with other sounds in certain patterned ways, it becomes an ingredient in the make-up of meaningful words: *pin, ploy, print*, etc.)

E

emblem	gesture that directly translates words or phrases (the *Okay* sign and the *Come here* sign); a symbol that stands for an entire referential domain (the *cross* representing Christianity)
emotive function	the addresser's emotional intent in communicating something
encoding	the process of putting together a message in terms of a specific code (The quantity "two" can be encoded with the symbol 2 in terms of the code of decimal numerals or with the symbol 10 in terms of the code of binary numerals)
entropy	term referring to anything that is unpredictable in a message or text; measure of the information content of a message derived as a factor of its uncertainty or unexpectedness
environmentalism	view of human mental functioning and development emphasizing the role of upbringing
eponym	name of a city, country, era, institution, or other place or thing derived from the name of a person (*Rome* was derived from the mythic name *Romulus*)
ethnography	comparative study of cultures based on field work and observation within the cultures themselves
etymology	the study of the origin and evolution of verbal signs
euphemism	rhetorical technique by which a term or phrase that has coarse, sordid, or other unpleasant associations is replaced by one that is perceived to be more delicate or inoffensive (*number two* for *defecation*)
exclamation	rhetorical technique by which a sudden outcry expressing strong emotion, such as fright, grief, or hatred, is interpolated into a text (*Wow! Curses!*)

F

feedback	information, signals, cues issuing from the receiver of a message as detected by the sender, thus allowing him or her to adjust the message to make it clearer, more meaningful, more effective

188 Paul Perron & Marcel Danesi

feminist semiotics	important movement within semiotics devoted to showing how sign systems and social power structures coalesce to define gender categories
fetish	an object that is believed to have magical or spiritual powers, or which can cause sexual arousal
fiction	a literary work whose content is produced by the imagination and is not necessarily based on fact
firstness	in Peircean theory the first level of meaning derived from bodily and sensory processes
form	a mental image, or an external representation of something

G

genre	works of literature, art, etc. classified together according to subject, theme, or style
gesticulant	the gesture accompanying speech
gesture	use of the hands, the arms, and to a lesser extent, the head, to make bodily forms of all kinds
glossematics	approach in semiotics and linguistics initiated by Louis Hjelmslev (1899-1965) and Hans Jørgen Uldall (1907—1957) which formalizes the basic binary notions of structuralism: denotation vs. connotation, paradigm vs. syntagm, etc.
grammar	system of rules that characterize any code (especially language)
grammatology	study of language from the perspective developed by Jacques Derrida (1930—) whereby oral speech is seen as a derivative of writing, and not the other way around, as linguists have traditionally maintained. Derrida formulated grammatological theory on the basis of archeological evidence, which suggested to him that pictographic language was the precursor of vocalized language.
ground	the meaning of a metaphor (*Life is a stage*)

H

haptics	the study of touching patterns during social interaction
hermeneutics	the study and interpretation of texts
homonymy	verbal coincidence by which two or more words with distinct meanings, are pronounced and/or spelled in the same way (*bore* vs. *boar*)
hyperbole	rhetorical exaggeration for effect (*He's stronger than an ox*)

hypertext	electronic text that provides links between key elements, allowing the user to move through information non-sequentially (navigating among the links to the word "language" in an article might lead the user to the *International Phonetic Alphabet,* the science of linguistics, samples of the world's languages, etc.)
hypoicon	Peirce's term for an icon that is shaped by cultural convention but which can nonetheless be figured out by those who are not members of the culture
hyponymy	semantic relation whereby one concept embraces another

I

icon	a sign that represents a referent by resemblance or simulation; sign form that simulates its referent (what it stands for) in some way; a sign that has a direct (nonarbitrary) connection to a referent (a word such as *plop* standing for a dropping sound)
iconicity	the process of representing referents with iconic forms
ideographic writing	type of writing system in which a character, known as an ideograph, may bear some resemblance to its referent, but is also in part a symbolic signifier (the use of a moon figure to refer to the night)
image schema	mental impression of a recurring structure of, or in, our perceptual interactions, bodily experiences, and cognitive operations that portray locations, movements, shapes, etc. (impression of orientation, containment, etc.)
index	a sign that represents a referent existentially; i.e. it indicates that it is located somewhere or is related to something else in some way; sign form which establishes a contiguity with its referent (pointing it out, showing its relation to other things, etc.)
indexicality	the process of representing referents with indexical signs
induction	process of deriving a concept from particular facts or instances (If one were to measure the three angles of, say, 100 *specific* triangles (of varying shapes and sizes), one would get the same total (1800) each time. This would then lead one to *induce* that the sum of the three angles of *any* triangle is the same)
innatism	view of human mental functioning and development emphasizing the role of Nature
Innenwelt	the world of internal experiences of a species
interpretant	the process by which a sign is adapted to personal and social experiences

interpretation	process of deciphering what a sign or text means
intertext	the allusion of a text to some other text
intertextuality	texts implicit in one text (e.g. the presence of Biblical stories and characters in such novels as *The Pilgrim's Progress*); the allusion within a text to some other text that the interpreter/receiver would have access to or knowledge of
irony	the use of signs to express something different from and often opposite to their literal meaning (*Beautiful day today, isn't it?*) uttered when the temperature is well below zero centigrade and a frigid snow storm is taking place)

K

kinesics	the study of bodily semiosis

L

langue	term used by Saussure to refer to the largely unconscious knowledge that speakers of a language share about what is appropriate in that language
legisign	in Peircean theory, a sign that designates something by pure convention (a whistle blown by a referee at a football match means stop play)
lexical field	a set of lexical items (words) related to each other by some characteristic (*weather vocabulary, geometrical terms,* etc.)
linguistic competence	term designating the innate, often unconscious knowledge that allows people to produce and understand sentences, many of which they have never heard before
linguistic performance	term used to designate the use of a language in actual situations of speech
litotes	understatement for effect, especially by negation of the contrary (*This is no small problem*)
logographic writing	highly symbolic writing system in which a character, known as a logograph, resembles its referent only in small part

M

markedness	relation whereby some members in a category or system, referred to as *marked*, are specific and thus not rep-

resentative of the entire category, while others, referred to as *unmarked*, are typical and thus representative of the category or system (In the indefinite article system of English, the form *a* is said to be *unmarked* because it is the general, or typical, form—*a boy, a girl, a man, a woman*, etc.; whereas *an* is the marked form because it is constrained to occurring before vowels—*an egg, an apple*, etc.).

mechanical transmission   transmission of messages through such means as radio, television, etc.

medium   the technical or physical means by which a message is transmitted

mental image   mental outline of something (a shape, a sound, etc.)

message   the meaning or concepts built into a signal or text

metalingual   the communicative function by which the code being used is identified

metaphor   the signifying process by which two signifying domains (*life, stage*) are connected (*Life is a stage*)

metonymy   the use of an entity to refer to another that is related to it (*There are a lot of faces in the audience* in which *face* stands for the entire person)

morpheme   smallest meaning-bearing unit or form in a language (the *un-mistake* and *-able* in *unmistakable* are all morphemes since they can not be segmented further into smaller "bits of meaning")

myth   any narrative that aims to explain the origin of something in metaphysical ways

mythology   the study of myths; the recycling of mythic themes in popular spectacles and representations

N

name   a sign that identifies a person, place, artifact (e.g. a brand name), and event (such as a hurricane)

narrative structure   the presence of universal elements of plot, character, and setting in story-telling

narrative   something told or written, such as an account, story, tale, etc. that has characters, situations, and identifiable plots.

narratology   the branch of semiotics that studies narratives

narrator   the teller of the narrative

narreme   a minimal unit of narrative structure

natural media   natural media of communication such as the voice (speech), the face (expressions), and the body (gesture, posture, etc.)

noise	anything that interferes with the reception of a message
novel	a fictional prose narrative of considerable length, typically having a plot that is unfolded by the actions, speech, and thoughts of the characters

O

object	what a sign refers to (also the *signified* or the *referent*)
onomastics	the study of names
onomatopoeia	coining of a word in imitation of the natural sound associated with the object or action to which it refers (*tinkle, buzz*, etc.)
open text	text with (in theory) an unlimited range of meanings (e.g. a poem by Baudelaire)
opposition	the process by which signs are differentiated through some minimal change or contrast (*good* vs. *evil*)
oxymoron	rhetorical technique by which two seemingly contradictory or incongruous words are combined (*thunderous silence*)

P

paradigm	a structural relation that keeps signs, texts, etc. distinct and therefore recognizable (a difference in shape, in sound, etc.)
paradigmaticity	a differentiation property of forms
paradox	statement that appears contradictory or inconsistent (*I am a liar; do I speak the truth?*)
parameter	term used in linguistics to designate the kinds of constraints imposed by culture on the universal principles of the speech faculty
parole	term used by Saussure to designate the actual use of language in speech
pathetic fallacy	attribution of human feelings and characteristics to inanimate things (*the angry sea*)
percept	a unit of perception (a stimulus that has been received and recognized) derived from sensation or feeling
persona	the Self that one presents in specific social situations
personal deixis	process of referring to the relations that exist among participants taking part in a situation
personification	rhetorical technique whereby inanimate objects or abstract ideas are portrayed as living beings (*Our cat speaks Italian*)

phatic function	the communicative function by which contact between addresser and addressee is established (*Hi, how's it going?*)
phenomenology	20th-century philosophical movement aiming to describe the forms and manifestations of experience as they present themselves to consciousness
phoneme	minimal unit of sound in a language that allows its users to differentiate word meanings
phonetics	description and classification of sounds in language
phonology	study of sound systems in language
phytosemiosis	semiosis in plants
phytosemiotics	the study of semiosis in plants
pictographic writing	type of writing system in which a character, known as a pictograph, bears pictorial resemblance to its referent
Platonic forms	Plato's (c. 428—347 BC) view that patterns of thought existed on two levels: one inhabited by invisible ideas or forms, and another by concrete familiar objects; the latter are imperfect copies of the ideas because they are always in a state of flux
plot	the plan of events or main story in a narrative or drama
poetic function	the communicative function based on poetic language
poetry	a piece of literature written in meter and verse
polysemy	process by which a sign bears multiple meanings: the word play is polysemous because it has distinct meanings: e.g. to occupy oneself in amusement, sport, or other recreation (*playing with toys*); to take part in a game (*No minors are eligible to play*); to act in jest or sport (*They're not serious about it, they're just playing*); a dramatic production (*That was a great play we saw the other night*); to perform on an instrument (*Can you play Beethoven's piano sonatas?*); to be received or accepted (*That was a speech that played poorly with the voters*); to unfold (*Let's see how it plays out*).
pop art	an artistic movement depicting objects or scenes from everyday life by employing techniques of commercial art and popular illustration
pop culture	form of culture, characteristic of twentieth-century technological societies, that emphasizes the trivial and the routine in its art and in various other forms of representation
postmodernism	contemporary state of mind which believes that all knowledge is relative and human-made, and that there is no purpose to life beyond the immediate and the present; movement in philosophy and the arts that crystallized in the latter part of the 20th century, utilizing

	mainly parody to unmask the hidden assumptions and ideologies in traditional verbal and art forms.
poststructuralism	movement in semiotics that denies any intrinsic meaning to referents in themselves, seeing them as human artifacts on their own with no connection to "reality;" central to this movement is the notion that in a text (a poem, a novel, etc.) there are layers of meaning that are constantly shifting and, therefore, that it is impossible to determine finally what a text means
proverb	short, traditional saying that expresses some obvious truth or familiar experience (*You've got too many fires burning*)
proxeme	a minimal unit of space between persons
proxemics	the branch of semiotics that studies the symbolic structure of the physical spaces maintained between people in social contexts

Q

qualisign	in Peircean theory, the type of sign that refers to a quality (a color, a shape, etc.)

R

receiver	the one who decodes a message; the target of an ad, ad campaign, commercial, etc.
referent	an object, event, feeling, idea, etc., that is represented by a form; what is referred to by a sign (any object, being, idea, or event)
referential domain	a class of objects, events, feelings, ideas, etc. represented by a form
referential function	the communicative function by which a straightforward idea is intended (*It is cold outside*)
regulator	gesticulant regulating the speech of an interlocutor (e.g. hand movements indicating *Keep going*, *Slow down*, etc.)
relativism	view that an individual's actions and behaviors are shaped primarily in relation to the culture in which s/he has been raised
representamen	Peirce's term for the sign itself as a physical entity
representation	process of ascribing a form to some referent; the process by which referents are designated by signs
rheme	in Peircean theory, the interpretant of a qualisign (i.e. what some sign representing a quality means and how it generates its meaning)

rhetoric	the study of the techniques used in all kinds of discourses, from common conversation to poetry
rhetorical question	rhetorical technique whereby a question is asked not to gain information, but to assert more emphatically the obvious answer to what is asked

S

secondness	in Peircean theory the second level of meaning that puts referents in relation to each other
semantics	the study of meaning in language
semasiology	study of relationships between signs and symbols and what they represent
semiology	alternative term for *semiotics*, but now largely restricted to meaning the study of verbal signs
semiosis	capacity of a species to produce and comprehend the specific types of forms (signs, signals, etc.) it requires for processing and codifying perceptual input in its own way
semiosphere	term referring to that level of human life governed by *semiosis*, rather than just by biology.
semiotic square	semiotician A. J. Greimas's (1917—1992), theory of signification whereby, given a unit of sense such as that encoded by the word *rich*, its meaning is gleaned only in terms of its relation with its contradictory (*not rich*), its contrary (*poor*), and its contradictory (*not poor*)
semiotics	the science or doctrine that studies signs and their uses in representation
sender	the transmitter of a message
setting	place and conditions in which a narrative takes place
sign	something that stands for something else in some way or capacity (a word, a gesture, etc.)
signal	any transmission of biological-based response to stimuli
signification	relation that holds between a form and its referent; the process of generating meaning through the use of signs
significs	Lady Victoria Welby's (1837—1912) term for the study of the nature of signification in all its forms and relations
signified	that part of a sign that is referred to (the referent, the object)
signifier	the part of a sign that does the referring (the form); the part of a sign that stands for something; the physical part of a sign
simile	rhetorical technique by which two ideas are compared explicitly with the word *like* or *as*

simulacrum	simulated form
sinsign	a sign that draws attention to, or singles out, a particular object in time-space
sound symbolism	the process by which referents are represented through some form of vocal simulation (imitation, repetition, etc.)
spatial deixis	process of referring to the spatial locations of referents (*here, there, up, down*, etc.)
structuralism	the approach that views signs as reflexes of intellectual and emotional structures; view that all human signifying systems, including culture, manifest regularity, systematicity, patterning, and predictability, keeping them differentiated
structure	any repeatable or predictable aspect of signs, codes, and texts
subtext	a text (message) hidden within a *text*; a concealed system of connotative meanings within an ad text
symbol	a sign that represents something through cultural convention; sign form that stands arbitrarily or conventionally for its referent (x to stand for unknown variable in algebra)
symbolicity	the process of representing referents with symbolic forms
symbolism	symbolic meaning in general
symptom	a bodily sign that stands for some ailment, physical condition, disease, etc.; natural sign designed to alert an organism to the presence of altered states in its body
synchronic	refers to the fact that forms are constructed at a given point in time for some particular purpose or function
synchronic analysis	the study of signs, codes, and texts at a specific point in time (usually the present)
syndrome	configuration of symptoms with a fixed *denotatum*
synecdoche	the signifying process by which a part stands for the whole (the *White House* for the American government)
synesthesia	the evocation of one sense modality (e.g. vision) by some other (e.g. hearing); the juxtaposition of sense modalities (*loud colors*)
synonymy	relation by which the meanings of different signs overlap (*hide-conceal, big-large*)
syntagmatic	the structural relation by which signs are combined in code-dependent ways; the structural relation that underlies how signs, texts, and codes are organized
syntagmaticity	combinatory property of forms
syntax	syntagmatic (organizational) structure of words in language undergirding sentences

T

temporal deixis	process of referring to the temporal relations that exist among things and events *(before, now, after, soon,* etc.)
tenor	the subject of a metaphor *(topic)*
text	something put together to represent complex (non-unitary) referents
text	the actual message with its particular form and contents; anything put together with signs to represent or communicate something—conversations, letters, speeches, poems, myths, novels, television programs, paintings, scientific theories, musical compositions, etc.
thirdness	in Peircean theory a third, highly abstract and culture-specific level of meaning based on symbolic processes
topic	the subject of a metaphor (the *life* in *Life is a stage)*
transmission	the sending and reception of messages
trope	figure of speech, figurative language generally

U

Umwelt	domain that a species is capable of modeling; the external world of experience to which a species has access
universal grammar	the notion that the brain has an innate set of design principles that undergird the development of specific languages

V

vehicle	the concrete part of a metaphor to which an abstract topic is connected (the *stage* in *Life is a stage).*

Z

zoosemiosis	semiosis in animals
zoosemiotics	the study of semiosis in animals

Appendix B

For Further Reading

In a volume such as this one, it is the customary practice to give the reader a comprehensive list of "suggested readings" for follow-up reading. We have decided to break somewhat with this tradition and, instead, to offer the reader a list of basic manuals, no more no less. We apologize for leaving out works that other experts in the field consider important. The instructor will note that such names as Derrida, McLuhan, Bakhtin, Jakobson, Metz, Todorov, Kristeva, Baudrillard, Lyotard, Merrell, Deely, to mention but a handful, are missing from the selection. We encourage the instructor using this volume as a textbook to fill-in the gaps left by our selection with his or her own supplementary list. This list is meant to help the student go just a "little deeper" into semiotic theory.

Dictionaries and Encyclopedias of Semiotics

Bouissac, Paul (1998). *Encyclopedia of Semiotics*. Oxford: Oxford University Press.

Colapietro, Vincent M. (1993). *Glossary of Semiotics*. New York: Paragon House.

Danesi, Marcel (2000). *Encyclopedic Dictionary of Semiotics, Media, and Communications*. Toronto: University of Toronto Press.

Sebeok, Thomas A. (1986), *Encyclopedic Dictionary of Semiotics*, 3 volumes. Berlin: Mouton de Gruyter.

Manuals in Semiotics

Chandler, Daniel (2002). *Semiotics: The Basics*. London: Routledge.

Cobley, Paul (2001). *Semiotics and Linguistics*. London: Routledge.

Cobley, Paul and Jansz, Litza (1997). *Semiotics for Beginners*. Cambridge: Icon Books.

Danesi, Marcel and Perron, Paul (1999). *Analyzing Cultures: A Handbook and Reference Manual*. Bloomington: Indiana University Press.

Danesi, Marcel (1999). *Of Cigarettes, High Heels, and Other Interesting Things: An Introduction to Semiotics*. New York: St. Martin's.

Eco, Umberto (1984). *A Theory of Semiotics*. Bloomington: Indiana University Press.

Nöth, W. (1990). *Handbook of Semiotics*. Bloomington: Indiana University Press.

Sebeok, Thomas A. (2001). *Signs: An Introduction to Semiotics*, 2nd ed. Toronto: University of Toronto Press.

Relevant Readings

Barthes, Roland (1957). *Mythologies*. Paris: Seuil.

Cobley, Paul (ed.) (1996). *The Communication Theory Reader*. London: Routledge.

Deely, John (2001). *Four Ages of Understanding: The First Postmodern Survey of Philosophy from Ancient Times to the Turn of the Twentieth Century.* Toronto: University of Toronto Press.

Lakoff, George and Johnson, Mark (1980). *Metaphors We Live By.* Chicago: Chicago University Press.

Lakoff, George and Johnson, Mark (1999). *Philosophy in the Flesh: The Embodied Mind and Its Challenge to Western Thought.* New York: Basic.

Langacker, Ronald W. (1999). *Grammar and Conceptualization.* Berlin: Mouton de Gruyter.

Petrilli, Susan and Ponzio, Augusto (2001). *Thomas Sebeok and the Signs of Life.* Duxford: Icon Books.

Posner, Roland, Robering, K., and Sebeok, Thomas A. (eds.) (1997—1998). *A Handbook on the Sign-Theoretic Foundations of Nature and Culture,* 2 vols. Berlin: Mouton de Gruyter.

Sebeok, Thomas A (2001b). *Global Semiotics.* Bloomington: Indiana University Press.

Sebeok, Thomas A. and Danesi, Marcel (2000). *The Forms of Meaning: Modeling Systems Theory and Semiotics.* Berlin: Mouton de Gruyter.

Vygotsky, L. S. (1962). *Thought and Language.* Cambridge, Mass.: MIT Press.

Printed in
September 2003
at Gauvin Press Ltd., Hull, Québec